CW00394327

The Cambridge Companion t

Don Quixote de la Mancha (1605) is one of the ‹
ture and the foundation of European fiction. Yet Cervantes himself remains an enigmatic figure. The Cambridge Companion to Cervantes offers a comprehensive treatment of Cervantes' life and work, including his lesser known writing. The essays, by some the most outstanding scholars in the field, cover the historical and political context of Cervantes' writing, his place in Renaissance culture, and the role of his masterpiece, *Don Quixote*, in the formation of the modern novel. They draw on contemporary critical perspectives to shed new light on Cervantes' work, including the *Exemplary Novels*, the plays and dramatic interludes, and the long romances, *Galatea* and *Persiles*. The volume provides useful supporting material for students: suggestions for further reading, a detailed chronology, a complete list of his published writings, an overview of translations and editions, and a guide to electronic resources.

THE CAMBRIDGE
COMPANION TO
CERVANTES

EDITED BY
ANTHONY J. CASCARDI

CAMBRIDGE
UNIVERSITY PRESS

PUBLISHED BY THE PRESS SYNDICATE OF THE UNIVERSITY OF CAMBRIDGE
The Pitt Building, Trumpington Street, Cambridge, United Kingdom

CAMBRIDGE UNIVERSITY PRESS
The Edinburgh Building, Cambridge CB2 2RU, UK
40 West 20th Street, New York, NY 10011-4211, USA
477 Williamstown Road, Port Melbourne, VIC 3207, Australia
Ruiz de Alarcón 13, 28014 Madrid, Spain
Dock House, The Waterfront, Cape Town 8001, South Africa

http://www.cambridge.org

© Cambridge University Press 2002

This book is in copyright. Subject to statutory exception
and to the provisions of relevant collective licensing agreements,
no reproduction of any part may take place without
the written permission of Cambridge University Press.

First published 2002

Printed in the United Kingdom at the University Press, Cambridge

Typeface Sabon 10/13 pt   *System* LATEX 2$_\varepsilon$ [TB]

A catalogue record for this book is available from the British Library

Library of Congress Cataloguing in Publication data

The Cambridge companion to Cervantes / edited by Anthony J. Cascardi.
p.   cm. – (Cambridge companions to literature)
Includes bibliographical references and index.
ISBN 0 521 66321 0 (hardback) – ISBN 0 521 66387 3 (paperback)
1. Cervantes Saavedra, Miguel de, 1547-1616 – Criticism and interpretation.
I. Cascardi, Anthony J., 1953–II. Series.
PQ6351.C27   2002
863'.3–dc21   2002017500

ISBN 0 521 66321 0 hardback
ISBN 0 521 66387 3 paperback

CONTENTS

ILLUSTRATIONS

CONTRIBUTORS

FREDERICK A. DE ARMAS is Andrew W. Mellon Professor in Humanities at the University of Chicago, where he teaches in the Department of Romance Languages. He has taught at Louisiana State University and Pennsylvania State University where he was Edwin Erle Sparks Professor in Spanish and Comparative Literature. He works mainly on the literature of the Spanish Golden Age. His books and edited collections include *The Invisible Mistress: Aspects of Feminism and Fantasy in the Golden Age*; *The Return of Astraea: An Astral-Imperial Myth in Calderón*; *The Prince in the Tower: Perspectives on La vida es sueño*; *Heavenly Bodies: The Realms of La estrella de Sevilla*; and *A Star-Crossed Golden Age: Myth and the Comedia*. His most recent book is *Cervantes, Raphael and the Classics* (Cambridge University Press, 1998).

ANTHONY J. CASCARDI is Professor of Comparative Literature, Spanish, and Rhetoric at the University of California, Berkeley, where he has also been the Richard and Rhoda Goldman Distinguished Professor in the Humanities. His works on the Spanish Golden Age include *The Limits of Illusion: A Critical Study of Calderón* and *Ideologies of History in the Spanish Golden Age*. In addition, Cascardi has written extensively on literature and philosophy and on aesthetic theory. His most recent book is *Consequences of Enlightenment: Aesthetics as Critique*.

ANNE J. CRUZ, Professor of Spanish at the University of Illinois, Chicago, received her AB, MA, and Ph.D. from Stanford University. She taught at the University of California, Irvine and, as Visiting Professor, at Stanford University. Her publications include: *Imitación y transformación: El petrarquismo en la poesía de Juan Boscán y Garcilaso de la Vega* (Purdue Monographs in the Romance Languages, 1988); *Discourses of Poverty: Social Reform and the Picaresque Novel in Early Modern Spain* (University of Toronto Press, 1999); and four co-edited anthologies, including (with

Carroll B. Johnson) *Cervantes and His Postmodern Constituencies* (University of Minnesota Press, 1999). She is currently finishing a study on female subjectivity in early modern Spain, for which she received a Mellon Postdoctoral Fellowship at the Newberry Library.

MARY MALCOLM GAYLORD is Professor of Romance Languages and Literatures at Harvard University. She is author of *The Historical Prose of Fernando de Herrera* and editor of *Frames for Reading: Cervantes Studies in Honor of Peter N. Dunn*, a special issue of the *Bulletin of the Cervantes Society of America*. She has written widely on medieval and early modern Hispanic literatures and historiography of Spain and America. In addition to essays on *Celestina*, Lope de Vega, Góngora, Ruiz de Alarcón, Calderón and others, she has published many studies of Cervantes' poetry, poetics, drama and prose fiction. Her current work, transatlantic in focus, considers New World shadows on Cervantes' experiments with genre in *Don Quixote* and on Renaissance and Baroque poetry.

B. W. IFE is Cervantes Professor of Spanish and Vice-Principal of King's College London. He works on the cultural history of early modern Spain and Spanish America, and on early modern Spanish music. Publications include *Reading and Fiction* (Cambridge University Press, 1985), *Christopher Columbus, the Journal of the First Voyage* (Aris and Phillips, 1990), *Miguel de Cervantes, Exemplary Novels* (Aris and Phillips, 1992), and *Letters from America, Columbus's First Accounts of the 1492 Voyage* (King's College London School of Humanities, 1992). He has published numerous articles on Cervantes and is working on a comprehensive study of the origins of the novel in Spain.

ADRIENNE L. MARTÍN is Associate Professor of Spanish Literature at the University of California, Davis. She has published numerous essays on all genres of Spanish Golden Age literature, including Cervantes, humor, sexualities, and eroticism. Her *Cervantes and the Burlesque Sonnet* (1991) is the first study to treat his humorous prose historically. She has recently completed a book on sexuality and transgression in early modern Spanish literature.

MELVEENA McKENDRICK is Professor of Spanish Literature, Culture and Society at the University of Cambridge, and author of *A Concise History of Spain*, *Woman and Society in the Spanish Drama of the Golden Age*, *Cervantes*, *Theatre in Spain 1490–1700*, a composite edition of Calderón's *El mágico prodigioso* (with A. A. Parker), and *Playing the King: Lope de*

Vega and the Limits of Conformity, as well as many articles on the early modern Spanish theatre with particular emphasis on social, political and ideological issues.

ALEXANDER WELSH is Emily Sanford Professor of English at Yale University and the author of numerous books on English literature, including studies of Charles Dickens, Sir Walter Scott, George Eliot, and Thackeray. His most recent book is *Hamlet in his Modern Guises* (2001). Welsh's study of the "quixotic hero" in literature, *Reflections on the Hero as "Quixote"*, was published by Princeton University Press in 1981.

DIANA DE ARMAS WILSON is Professor Emerita of English and Renaissance Studies at the University of Denver. She has published *Allegories of Love: Cervantes's "Persiles and Sigismunda"* (Princeton University Press, 1991); *Quixotic Desire: Psychoanalytic Perspectives on Cervantes*, co-edited with the late Ruth El Saffar (Cornell University Press, 1993); a Norton Critical Edition of *Don Quijote* (Norton, 1999); and *Cervantes, the Novel, and the New World* (Oxford University Press, 2000).

1547   Miguel de Cervantes Saavedra born in Alcalá de Henares, son
        of Rodrigo de Cervantes, a surgeon, and Leonor de Cortinas,
        his wife. No birth record exists, but it is possible that he was
        born on the feast of St Michael (San Miguel), September 29.
        Church records indicate that Cervantes was baptized on
        October 9. The first Index of Prohibited Books is issued, as
        are the first Statutes of Purity of Blood.

1554   Publication of the *Lazarillo de Tormes* (anon.), the first
        picaresque novel.

1559   Publication of *La Diana*, a pastoral novel, by Jorge de
        Montemayor.
        Philip II of Spain marries Isabel of Valois.

1556   Charles V abdicates the throne.
        Philip II crowned in Valladolid.

1561   Madrid becomes the official capital of Spain.
        Publication of the anonymous "Moorish" novella, *Historia
        del Abencerraje y de la hermosa Jarifa* (*Story of the
        Abencerraje and the Beautiful Jarifa*).

1563   Birth of Lope de Vega. Conclusion of the Council of Trent
        (1545–63).
        Construction of the grand monastery "El Escorial" begins
        outside Madrid.

1564   During this time, Cervantes is likely enrolled in a Jesuit high
        school (*colegio*).
        Birth of Shakespeare.

1566–67 Cervantes begins writing poetry and publishes his first sonnet
        (1567) in celebration of the birth of Princess Catalina
        Michaela, second daughter of Philip II and Isabel of Valois.

1568–69 Cervantes studies with the humanist-oriented Juan López de
        Hoyos, head of the "Estudio de la Villa," who charges him to

write four poems on the occasion of the death of Isabel of Valois.

Uprising of the Christian subjects of Moorish ethnicity (*moriscos*) in Granada.

1569   Cervantes travels to Rome, in the service of Cardinal Giulio Acquaviva.

1570   Cervantes embarks on a military career, which takes him to Naples.

1571   The Christian fleet defeats the Turks at Lepanto. Cervantes loses the use of his left hand in this battle.

1575   Cervantes continues his military service, and spends additional time in Italy. En route to Spain Cervantes and his brother are captured by Muslim pirates, taken to Algiers and held for ransom.

1576–79   During this period Cervantes makes four attempts to escape.

1580   Cervantes is ransomed by Trinitarian friars and returns to Spain.

1581   Cervantes attempts a career as a dramatist in Madrid, without much success. He writes the plays *The Siege of Numancia* and *The Ways of Algiers* during this time.

1585   Publication of Cervantes' first book, a pastoral romance entitled *La Galatea*.

1587   Cervantes becomes a commissary requisitioning provisions for the "Invincible" Armada and travels to Andalucía.

1588   Defeat of the Armada by the English.

1590   Cervantes petitions the President of the Council of the Indies for one of several vacant official posts, but is denied.

The story of Zoraida and the Captive incorporated in *Don Quixote* (I, 39–41) dates from this time.

1593   Some of the stories later published in the *Exemplary Novels* ("Rinconete and Cortadillo," "The Jealous Man from Extremadura") may date from this time.

1597   Cervantes is employed as a tax collector in Andalusia and is jailed in Seville for irregularities in his accounts.

1598   Death of Philip II. Accession of Philip III, who allows his "favorite," the Duke of Lerma, to govern.

1599   Publication of the picaresque novel *Guzmán de Alfarache*, I, by Mateo Alemán.

1601   The Royal court moves to Valladolid.

1603   Francisco de Quevedo writes *El buscón* (*The Swindler*).

1604   Mateo Alemán publishes *Guzmán de Alfarache*, II.

1605	Cervantes publishes *Don Quixote*, I, printed by Juan de la Cuesta in Madrid, with immediate success.
1609	Cervantes becomes a lay brother in the Congregation of the Slaves of the Most Holy Sacrament. Philip III decrees the expulsion of all *moriscos* from Spain.
1613	Cervantes publishes the *Exemplary Novels* (twelve stories), dedicated to the Count of Lemos and printed by Juan de la Cuesta in Madrid. Cervantes becomes an acolyte (one of the "minor orders") in the Franciscan Order of the Roman Catholic priesthood.
1614	Cervantes publishes a mock-heroic literary allegory in verse, the *Voyage to Parnassus*. Someone writing under the pseudonym Alonso Fernández de Avellaneda publishes a continuation of *Don Quixote*.
1615	Cervantes publishes *Don Quixote*, II, and *Eight Plays and Interludes, New and Never Performed*, the latter dedicated to the Count of Lemos.
1616	Cervantes takes permanent vows in the Third Franciscan Order. Cervantes dies in Madrid on April 22. Death of Shakespeare approximately one week earlier.
1617	Posthumous publication of Cervantes' last work, *The Trials of Persiles and Sigismunda*, a Byzantine romance inspired by Heliodorus, dedicated to the Count of Lemos.

As the preceding remarks may well suggest, the body of texts that comprise Cervantes' complete works is of considerable size (a full listing of titles is given below). But unlike his near contemporary Lope de Vega, of whom we have more autograph manuscripts than all of Shakespeare's published plays, Cervantes scholarship is limited by the fact that it must work largely without the benefit of autograph texts. Textual critics take the first published editions as their point of departure. Facsimile versions of the first editions of the complete works were published in Spain by the *Revista de Archivos, Bibliotecas y Museos* between 1917 and 1923, and this edition was subsequently reprinted by the Real Academia Española (*Facsímil de las primeras ediciones*, Madrid, 1976–90). The six volumes of this facsimile edition contain *Don Quixote, I* (1976), *Don Quixote, II* (1976), *Novelas ejemplares* (1981), *Ocho comedias y entremeses* (1984), *La Galatea* (1985) and *Los trabajos de Persiles y Sigismunda* and the *Viaje del Parnaso* (1990). A monumental nineteenth-century critical edition of Cervantes' complete works was prepared by J. E. Hartzenbusch and C. Rosell, published in twelve volumes between 1863 and 1864: *Obras completas de Cervantes* (Madrid: Rivadeneyra, 1863–64). Among important nineteenth-century critical editions of *Don Quixote* is the one in six volumes edited by Diego Clemencín (Madrid: D. E. Aguado, 1833–39). Among twentieth-century editions the most notable are the *Obras completas de Miguel de Cervantes Saavedra*, ed. R. Schevill and A. Bonilla (Madrid, Imprenta de Bernardo Rodríguez, Gráficas Reunidas, 1914–41) in eighteen volumes, and the *Obras completas*, ed. A. Valbuena Prat (Madrid: Aguilar, 1943). The fourth edition of the "Clásicos Castellanos" version of *Don Quixote* prepared by Francisco Rodríguez Marín likewise occupies an important place in the history of critical editions of the work in Spanish (Madrid: Tipografía de la Revista de Archivos, Bibliotecas y Museos, 1947–49). Among more recent editions of *Don Quixote* in Spanish, two are especially useful: *Don Quixote*, 2 vols., ed. John Jay Allen (Madrid: Cátedra, 1976) provides an informative introduction and helpful notes. The three volume edition prepared by Luis Andrés Murillo (*Don Quixote de la Mancha* [Madrid: Castalia, 1978]), includes a separate, indexed, bibliography and a judicious system of notes. Those wishing to tackle Cervantes in Spanish will find invaluable assistance in the various lexicographies that are listed in volume III of the Murillo edition as well as from the more recent *Don Quixote Dictionary* compiled by Tom Lathrop (Newark, DE: Juan de la Cuesta Hispanic Monographs, 1999). Richard Predmore's *Cervantes* (New York: Dodd, Mead, 1973), provides a traditionally conceived historical introduction along with handsome illustrations.

Not surprisingly, *Don Quixote* has been the most widely translated of Cervantes' works. It was first translated into English by Thomas Shelton (1612, 1620), into French by César Oudin (Part I, 1614) and F. de Rousset (Part II, 1618), and into Italian by Lorenzo Franciosini (1622, 1625). The first German translation, in 1648, appeared under the pseudonym of Pahsh Bastel von der Sohle (possibly Sahle). The first Russian translation, by Nicolai Osipov, did not appear until 1769. There are numerous modern English translations of *Don Quixote*; among them are those by J. M. Cohen (Harmondsworth: Penguin, 1950), Walter Starkie (London: Macmillan, 1964), Burton Raffel (New York: Norton, 1999), and John Rutherford (Harmondsworth: Penguin, 2001). The farces are available in an English translation by Edwin Honig: *Interludes* (New York: Signet, 1964). But there is no currently available English translation of all of Cervantes' works. The project for a twelve-volume English translation of the complete works, begun in 1901–02 under the editorship of James Fitzmaurice-Kelly, was suspended at seven volumes, which contain *Galatea*, *Don Quixote* and the *Exemplary Novels*.

CERVANTES' WORKS

An indispensable point of departure for any further engagement with Cervantes is a list of his works:

Poetry

Poesías sueltas (*Collected Poems*)
Viaje del Parnaso (*Voyage to Parnassus*)

Theatre

El cerco de Numancia (*The Siege of Numantia*)
Los tratos de Argel (*The Traffic of Algiers*)
Ocho comedias y ocho entremeses nuevos, nunca representados (*Eight Plays and Eight Interludes, New and Never Performed*)
  Comedies (*Comedias*)
    El gallardo español (*The Gallant Spaniard*)
    La casa de los celos y selvas de Ardenia (*The House of Jealousy and Woods of Ardenia*)
    Los baños de Argel (*The Bagnios of Algiers*)
    El rufián dichoso (*The Fortunate Ruffian*)
    La gran sultana (*The Grand Sultana*)
    El laberinto de amor (*The Labyrinth of Love*)
    La entretenida (*The Comedy of Entertainment*)
    Pedro de Urdemalas (*Peter Mischief-Maker*)
  Comic interludes (*Entremeses*)
    El juez de los divorcios (*The Divorce-Court Judge*)
    El rufián viudo llamado Trampagos (*Trampagos the Widower Pimp*)
    La elección de los alcaldes de Daganzo (*Electing the Magistrates in Daganzo*)
    La guarda cuidadosa (*The Watchful Guard*)

El vizcaíno fingido (*The Sham Biscayan*)
El retablo de las maravillas (*The Miracle Show*)
La cueva de Salamanca (*The Cave of Salamanca*)
El viejo celoso (*The Jealous Old Man*)

Novels

Primera Parte de "La Galatea," dividida en seis libros (*First Part of "Galatea," Divided in Six Books*)
El Ingenioso Hidalgo don Quixote de la Mancha (*The Ingenious Gentleman Don Quixote of La Mancha*)
Segunda parte del ingenioso caballero don Quixote de la Mancha (*Second Part of the Ingenious Knight Don Quixote of La Mancha*)
Exemplary Novels (*Novelas ejemplares*):[1]
   "La gitanilla" ("The Little Gypsy Girl")
   "El amante liberal" ("The Generous Lover")
   "Rinconete y Cortadillo" ("Rinconete and Cortadillo")
   "La española inglesa" ("The English Spanish Lady")
   "El licenciado Vidriera" ("The Glass Graduate")
   "La fuerza de la sangre" ("The Force of Blood")
   "El celoso extremeño" ("The Jealous Man from Extremadura")
   "La ilustre fregona" ("The Illustrious Kitchenmaid")
   "Las dos doncellas" ("The Two Damsels")
   "La señora Cornelia" ("Lady Cornelia")
   "El casamiento engañoso" ("The Deceitful Marriage")
   "El coloquio de los perros" ("The Colloquy of the Dogs")
Los trabajos de Persiles y Sigismunda: Historia septentrional (*The Trials of Persiles and Sigismunda: A Northern Story*)

---

[1] There is speculation that a thirteenth novel, "La Tía fingida" ("The False Aunt") may also belong to Cervantes. The piece remained in obscurity until 1814, when it was published by Agustín García Arrieta in a volume entitled *El Espíritu de Miguel de Cervantes Saavedra.*

I

ANTHONY J. CASCARDI

Introduction

A colleague once remarked, half in jest, that prevailing impressions of Spanish culture in the English-speaking world are dominated by two images: Don Quixote and the Spanish Inquisition. The image of the Inquisition has been reinforced from many angles, not least among which is a Monty Python comedy routine wherein absurdly garbed Inquisitorial figures issue strings of mock-harsh injunctions but manage only to stumble over their own commands.[1] The matter of *Don Quixote* is, to say the least, more challenging. It is the case of a wonderfully complex and beguiling text that has become reduced in the popular mind to the pencil-thin profile of its principal character, an errant knight of La Mancha seen tilting at windmills or towering precariously over his paunchy squire. As for Cervantes, we are faced with an author whose identity has become similarly reduced, either to this single text or, less frequently, to a sole physical mark – the hand that was maimed by gunfire in the battle of Lepanto. Miguel de Cervantes Saavedra, "The Man Maimed at Lepanto" ("El Manco de Lepanto"), author of *Don Quixote*. Whether in spite of or because of these reductive encapsulations, images of Don Quixote the character, Cervantes the author, and *Don Quixote* the text have spawned a range of successors that are nearly impossible to characterize, from Flaubert's "female Quixote," Madame Bovary, to the pop idealism of the 1965 Broadway musical, *Man of La Mancha*, and from the richly orchestrated tone-poem by Richard Strauss, *Don Quixote*, to the infinitely subtle variations of Borges' most famous text, now also massively consumed, "Pierre Menard, Author of the 'Quixote.'" *Don Quixote* is itself a text that has reached mass audiences, but it is unjustly treated when reduced to a few scenes from Part I – the tilting at windmills, the mistaking of an inn for a castle. Although Cervantes was, by his own description, the "stepfather" of *Don Quixote* (he attributes fatherhood to a fictional Arabic historian), he was substantially more than this. His great ambition in the early stages of his career was to be a successful poet and dramatist, and his considered view at the end of his life was that the long and intricate Byzantine novel that remained unpublished at the time of his death – the *Trials of Persiles and Sigismunda* (*Los trabajos de Persiles y Sigismunda*) – was by far his most important work. *Don Quixote* was a *succès de scandale*, and Cervantes was justly gratified by its popularity, but his literary ambitions and career amount to considerably more than this. The overwhelming importance of *Don Quixote* has secured Cervantes an unquestioned place in the history of literature, but it presents challenges for readers who may know Cervantes from *Don Quixote* alone. Moreover, *Don Quixote* is itself an uncommonly difficult text, and readers may feel at a loss when faced with its extraordinary range of literary and historical references, its internal narrative complexities, and its disarming combination of earthy humor and philosophical depth.

The present volume is a "companion" to Cervantes. Without slighting *Don Quixote* in the least, it aims to provide an accompaniment to the broad range of Cervantes' work – in prose fiction, in drama, and in verse. The essays assembled here, all written with this purpose in mind, strive to situate his work historically, to place it within the wider context of early modern (Renaissance) literature, and to give an account of its importance for the subsequent development of the major literary genres. Among these, the novel has pride of place. Rather than look at Cervantes' works as literary creations situated in the distant past of a relatively unfamiliar culture, these essays show how scholars and critics in the present day have come to engage Cervantes's works. Historical interpretation is of course well represented among those modes of engagement, since it represents an unavoidable way of thinking about the relationships not just between a work and its originating context but between that context and our own. But in keeping with the "perspectivism" that has so often been identified as the hallmark of Cervantes' own writing in *Don Quixote*, and in opposition to any narrow historicism, the essays in this volume draw on the multiple perspectives of modern literary criticism as a way to approach a body of writing that is itself enormously diverse. If Cervantes' works invite complex critical perspectives – psychoanalytical, genre-based, gender-inflected, myth-critical, philosophical, political, and more – this is because the works themselves have important things to say about the core issues that these different approaches raise. The matter is not so much that of a revisionist reading of Cervantes' texts, as it is a discovery of the ways in which Cervantes anticipates, challenges, and in some cases outstrips the insights that contemporary literary criticism brings to them. Reading Cervantes can be a sobering experience, for in doing so one discovers that literary criticism is only now giving systematic formulation to many of the things that he knew intuitively to be true. Rather than striving quixotically to retrieve the past, we as readers of Cervantes are more often in the position of trying to catch up with an author whose thinking frequently runs far ahead of our own. A basic Cervantes chronology, a list of his works, recommendations for further reading, and indications of contemporary research tools provide the reader of this volume with a set of scholarly resources that complement the essays' interpretive work. Without presupposing any prior knowledge of Cervantes' writings or the ability to read them in Spanish, these essays provide critical direction for readers who might well have expertise in allied fields, but who may require some orientation to Cervantes' works.

But in introducing Cervantes it is difficult to resist the temptation to allow Cervantes to introduce himself, as he sometimes does in his writings. The temptation is all the greater because of the indirections involved of his self-presentations, which allow us to glimpse their author not just in a primary, visual way but from oblique and ironic angles. These self-presentations typify his writing at its most cagy and complex. In the prologue to the *Exemplary Novels* (*Novelas ejemplares*, 1613), for instance, Cervantes muses that a well-known artist, his friend Juan de Jáuregui, has painted a portrait of him that might well adorn the collected *Novels*, thereby saving its author the trouble of writing the prologue in question. This would be all the more welcome, Cervantes remarks, since he did not fare very well with the prologue to his earlier *Don Quixote* (Part 1, 1605). But it seems that the publisher of the *Novels* did not in the end include the Jáuregui portrait. A prologue must be written after all, but it turns out to include a verbal description of the picture that might have appeared in its place. This bit of ecphrasis is as acute as the portrait is compellingly direct. The result is inimitably Cervantine:

He whom you here behold with aquiline visage, with chestnut hair, smooth and unruffled brow, with sparkling eyes, and a nose arched, although well proportioned, a silver beard, although not twenty years ago it was golden, large moustache, small mouth, teeth not important, for he has but six of them and those in ill condition and worse placed because they do not correspond the one with the other, the body between two extremes, neither large nor small, the complexion bright, rather white than brown, somewhat heavy-shouldered, and not very nimble on his feet; this, I say, is the portrait of the author of the *Galatea* and of *Don Quixote of La Mancha*, and of him who wrote the *Voyage to Parnassus* in imitation of César Caporal of Perugia, and other works which wander up and down, astray, and perchance without the name of the writer. He is commonly called Miguel de Cervantes Saavedra. He was a soldier for many years, and for five and a half a captive, where he learned to be patient in adversity. He lost in the naval battle of Lepanto his left hand from a shot from a harquebus, – a wound which, although it appears ugly, he holds for lovely, because he received it on the most memorable and lofty occasion that past centuries have beheld, – nor do these to come hope to see the like, – when serving beneath the victorious banners of the son of the thunderbolt of war, Charles the Fifth, of happy memory.[2]

The image described in this 1613 text is that of a proud, old man, one to whom recognition arrived late in life. Cervantes began his literary career at an early age, but he only achieved fame when the first part of *Don Quixote* was published in 1605. Certain facts about his personal and professional life may help explain why success was so late in coming. Cervantes was born outside Madrid, in the town of Alcalá de Henares, in 1547. He was the fourth son of a surgeon, Rodrigo de Cervantes, and of Leonor de Cortinas. While the family may have had some claim to nobility they often found themselves in financial straits. Moreover, they were almost certainly of *converso* origin, that is, converts to Catholicism of Jewish ancestry. In the Spain of Cervantes' day this meant living under clouds of official suspicion and social mistrust, with far more limited opportunities than were enjoyed by members of the "Old Christian" caste. Indeed, the very year of Cervantes' birth coincides with the issuance of the first of a series of statutes concerning the racial relations among Christians, Moors, and Jews – the so-called statutes of "purity of blood" (*estatutos de limpieza de sangre*).[3]

While very little is known about Cervantes' earliest years, a more or less continuous trail of events can be picked up beginning in 1566 when his family moved to Madrid and Cervantes began to compose his first poems. In 1568 he attended classes given by the humanist teacher López de Hoyos at the Estudio de la Villa, an academy in Madrid financed by the city. Under the auspices of López de Hoyos, Cervantes wrote a sonnet and three miscellaneous poems that appeared in a 1569 volume on the occasion of the death of Queen Isabel of Valois.[4] In that same year Cervantes moved to Rome, where he entered the service of Cardinal Giulio Acquaviva. The reasons for the move have never been ascertained, but there is speculation that he may have been fleeing prosecution for having assaulted a man by the name of Antonio de Sigura. Cervantes' works are filled with memories of Italy, and, as Frederick de Armas makes abundantly clear in his contribution to this volume, the influence of Italian culture, combined with Cervantes' humanist education, placed him at the height of contemporary literary and intellectual currents. Ever since the Spanish critic Américo Castro published *El pensamiento de Cervantes* (*Cervantes' Thought*) in 1925, the idea that Cervantes was a kind of "lay genius" has given way to the image of a writer who knew the art and literature of the Italian Renaissance, as well as many of its classical antecedents, first-hand.

The following year, 1570, finds Cervantes in Naples, and in 1571 he and his brother Rodrigo joined the company of Diego de Urbina, a division of the regiment under the command of Don Miguel de Moncada. It was in this capacity that Cervantes fought aboard the galleon *Marquesa* in the battle of Lepanto where the Turkish forces were routed by the combined Papal, Venetian, and Spanish fleet (October 7, 1571). It was here that he lost the use of his left hand, "for the greater glory of the right." (As for his right hand, he says in the "Prologue" to the *Exemplary Novels* that he would sacrifice it too if the stories should offend against virtuous ideals.[5]) Looking back on the occasion of Lepanto from the vantage point of the 1613 Prologue to the *Exemplary Novels*, Cervantes describes it with overbrimming pride as "the most memorable and lofty occasion that past centuries have beheld, or that future centuries may hope to see" ("la más alta ocasión que vieron los siglos pasados, los presentes, ni esperan ver los venideros").[6] These terms of praise were repeated nearly verbatim in the Prologue to *Don Quixote*, Part II. By way of indirect response to Alonso Fernández de Avellaneda, the author of a spurious sequel to *Don Quixote*, Part I, Cervantes remarks that

> it hurts, of course, that he [Avellaneda] calls me "old," and "one-handed," as if I could have stopped Time and kept it from affecting me, or I'd lost my hand in some tavern brawl, rather than the noblest battle ever seen by any past ages, or this age, or any age still to come. My wounds may not glow when you look at them, but they're worthy enough, at least, to those who know where I got them; the soldier looks a lot better killed in action than alive because he ran away – and this means so much to me that, if anyone were right this minute to suggest and even make possible that which is impossible, I'd rather have been at that wonderful battle than, here and now, be cured of my wounds but never before have been there. The marks you can find on a soldier's face, and on his body, are stars, guiding other men to that Heaven which is Honor, and to a longing for well-deserved praise.[7]

The pride remains untarnished, even after thirty-four years.

After recovering from his injury Cervantes returned to military service (1572), this time in the company of Manuel Ponce de León, regiment of Don Lope de Figueroa. In 1575 he began his return to Spain with his brother, but the ship aboard which they were traveling, the *Sol*, was boarded en route by a band of Turkish pirates led by Arnaute Mamí. Cervantes was taken to Algiers, where he spent five years in captivity. The experience of captivity filters into several of his works, including the Captain's story in *Don Quixote*, Part I. It was the time when Cervantes learned what he describes as the ability to have "patience in adversity."[8] Following several unsuccessful escape attempts, Cervantes' freedom was won on September 19, 1580, when he was ransomed by Trinitarian friars, principal among them Juan Gil. Cervantes returned to Spain on October 24, 1580.

The 1580s mark the beginning of Cervantes' serious literary production, as well as the point where the details of his personal biography cede to his increasingly important literary career. His first novel, a pastoral work entitled *Galatea*, was published in 1585. Two early plays, *The Siege of Numantia* (*El cerco de Numancia*) and *The Ways of Algiers* (*Los tratos de Argel*) also date from this period (1583–85). Neither of these plays shows the influence of Cervantes' chief dramatic rival, the creator of the Spanish "new comedy" (*comedia nueva*), Lope de Vega; Cervantes' are four-act works in the tragic vein, whereas Lope's works were comedies written in three acts. In part because Lope achieved such extraordinary popular success with the invention of the "new comedy" Cervantes did not flourish as a dramatist and suffered financially as a result. Possibly for this reason he accepted a commission as Commissary of the Royal Galleons in Seville (1587), where he was charged with securing wheat and oil for what was to be the ill-fated "Invincible" Armada, then preparing for battle against England. In 1590 his application to the Council of Indies to fill a vacancy in the New World was denied, possibly because of his family's *converso* status. He subsequently took work as a tax collector and was jailed for irregularities in his accounts. His suggestion in the Prologue to *Don Quixote*, Part I, that the book was engendered in prison, bears at least this degree of plausibility.

These years of misfortune no doubt contributed to an ideological shift that in turn opened new avenues in Cervantes' mature literary works. Though one can identify moments of nationalistic pride as late as the 1613 Prologue to the *Exemplary Novels* there is no doubt that his works reflect a growing disillusionment with Spain, the colonial-imperial project, and the domestic politics of an absolutist regime bent on achieving the greatest degree of racial, ethnic, religious, and linguistic homogeneity possible. Beginning in this period Cervantes' poetry begins to take notably parodic turns, anticipating the mock-heroic attitude which turned out to be his strongest literary suit. For example, a burlesque sonnet written to the catafalque of Philip II in 1598 stages a Spanish soldier gasping in awe at the monument, and in doing so turns praise on its head: "¡Voto a Dios que me espanta esta grandeza!" (By God, all this grandeur frightens me!). *Don Quixote*, several of the *Exemplary Novels*, and all of the comic interludes or farces (*entremeses*) involve some degree of parody or exaggeration, but the most interesting of these take as their target the historical fictions that were being promulgated in the popular theatre. Among the farces is a piece entitled *The Wonder Show* (*El retablo de las maravillas*) in which the widely held Spanish social ideal of "purity of blood" is exposed as a grandiose social illusion. (Cervantes' farces were published in 1615 along with a group of his later plays [*comedias*] in a collection entitled *Eight Plays and Eight Interludes, New and Never Performed* [*Ocho comedias y ocho entremeses nuevos, nunca representados*].) But certain core elements of the *Quixote* engage the process by which dramatists like Lope de Vega had appropriated the popular ballads in order to fashion glossy, heroic images of the Spanish past and to idealize the national character. Indeed, the Spanish philologist Ramón Menéndez-Pidal speculated in 1940 that the initial episodes of the *Quixote* may in fact have been inspired by an anonymous farce that was directed against the popular ballads, the so-called *Farce of the Ballads* (*Entremés de los romances*).[9] After all, in the early chapters of the novel Don Quixote is as likely to cite the ballads as he is the romances of chivalry.

But it would be wrong to think that the shift in Cervantes' attitude from a youthful idealism inspired by Renaissance Humanism to the kinds of critique that works best by parody was coupled with insurmountable pessimism or despair. Humanism encompassed diverse cultural tendencies sympathetic to new kinds of learning, the values of human judgment, and the products of the creative and critical intellect, and some of the central texts of the movement, such as Erasmus' *Praise of Folly* no doubt had a profound influence on Cervantes early in his career.[10] But Cervantes' mature works continue to show strains of genuine good will within their critical vision. Whether the topic is the absurdities of a foolish gentleman who imagines himself to be a knight errant, or of a man who thinks he is made of glass ("The Glass Graduate" ["El licenciado Vidriera"]), or of two dogs whose conversation is overheard by someone just recovering from syphilis ("The Colloquy of the Dogs" ["El Coloquio de los perros"]), there is a lightness in Cervantes' comic works that undercuts the potentially devastating effects of his otherwise critical stance. The perspectivism for which he is justly famous represents a further development of the great patience with which he learned to face adversity while a captive in Algiers. It affords the possibility of a critical stance that allows Cervantes to blunt the force of authoritarian views, but it produces a hopeful irony that keeps cynicism at bay by refusing to take itself too seriously. The importance of Cervantine humor becomes all the more apparent when one contrasts the first part of *Don Quixote* with the spurious continuation of Part I published by Avellaneda in 1614. Avellaneda's *Quixote* is relatively flat and one-dimensional, and Cervantes was among the first to label it as such.[11] Cervantes seems to have learned of Avellaneda's *Quixote* after he was well into the writing of Part II (his first mention of Avellaneda's book is in chapter 52 of *Don Quixote*, Part II), and in the 1615 Prologue Cervantes does not miss the opportunity to address his tactless rival in a manner that manages to be just barely oblique:

Oh Lord, distinguished (or even plebeian) reader, how you must be eagerly awaiting this prologue, expecting to watch me take revenge on, laugh at, and spit in the face of whoever wrote the second *Don Quixote*, the one they say was conceived in Tordesillas and born in Tarragona! But the fact is, I'm not planning to give you any such satisfaction: it's true, insults may make even the humblest hearts thirst for vengeance, but the rule will have to let me be an exception. You want me to call him an ass, tell him he's a liar, an imprudent, but the idea has never so much as occurred to me: his own sin can punish him, he can eat it with his bread, and that's that.[12]

Debates about the differences between the two parts of *Don Quixote* have long transcended efforts to characterize the one as "Renaissance" and the other as "Baroque," or to chart Cervantes' diminishing optimism as the years advance. There are major differences between the two parts of the *Quixote*, indeed, but foremost among them is the fact that there are characters in Part II who have read Part I. These characters are able to "rig" the world, sometimes mechanistically, so that it appears to coincide with, and to defeat, Don Quixote's expectations. As we enter Part II, we move from the quixotic mishaps of Part I to a world of planned pranks, some of them so cruel as to drive Vladimir Nabokov to declare them downright offensive.[13] Nabokov's view may seem extreme, and may fail to account for the fact that violence in Cervantes' day may have been tolerated at different levels than in our own. Still, Nabokov's reaction to the *Quixote*'s violence is notable:

there is something about the ethics of our book that casts a livid laboratory light on the proud flesh of some of its purpler passages. We are going to speak of cruelty. The author seems to plan it thus: Come with me, ungentle reader, who enjoys seeing a live dog inflated and kicked around like a soccer football, who likes, of a Sunday morning, on his way to or from church, to poke his stick or direct his spittle at a poor rogue in the stocks; come, ungentle reader, with me and consider into what ingenious and cruel hands I shall place my ridiculously vulnerable hero. And I hope you will be amused at what I have to offer.[14]

But it would be mistaken to think that Cervantes' "mature" writing consists of works all resembling the *Quixote*, however gentle or violent one may in the end assess its humor to be. Indeed, one of the great puzzles of Cervantes scholarship is the fact that Cervantes must have been busy at work composing an elaborate, Byzantine romance, the *Trials of Persiles and Sigismunda: A Northern Story* (*Los trabajos de Persiles y Sigismunda: Historia septentrional*), written in imitation of Heliodorus' *Ethiopian History*, just as he was finishing *Don Quixote*, Part II. The *Persiles* seems to run counter to *Don Quixote* in many important respects: in its treatment of character development, in its narratological structure, and in its moral vision.[15] The *Persiles* is a romance, albeit one that Cervantes worked to purge of the "defects" he thought common in other romances – a lack of verisimilitude, an illegitimate use of marvelous elements, a disregard for the classical unities, etc. – by adherence to a mix of neo-Aristotelian and Horatian literary principles.[16] The issue of Cervantes' simultaneous engagement with and critique of romance is important to bear in mind because it also affects the *Exemplary Novels* (1613), which were published in between the two parts of the *Quixote*. There are numerous works in the *Exemplary Novels* that have a certain affinity with the more "novelistic" aspects of *Don Quixote*, whereas others are far more *Persiles*-like in their allegiance to the project of literary romance.[17] Cervantes seems always to have stood in a contradictory relationship to the genre of romance, either in the form of the critical parody we see in *Don Quixote* or, in the case of the *Persiles* and the romance-like *Novels*, in the form of an attempt at some kind of "purification" of the romance. When Cervantes reached the very end of his life (1616), the *Persiles* remained unpublished. (It would appear posthumously the following year.) The work he thought of as his greatest achievement has only recently begun to attract the level of critical attention it merits.[18] But this is through no fault of Cervantes. The fact of the matter is that academic literary criticism has followed "high" literary history, which has gone the way of *Don Quixote*. It has consistently stressed the role of the *Quixote* in the formation of the novel as a genre and has expanded its own critical idiom in order to embrace the philosophical insights that one finds in the writings of Miguel de Unamuno, Georg Lukács, and José Ortega y Gasset.[19] But one would be remiss not to see the genre of romance as having survived at least as well as the novel, if in a different register. Romance is the form of every film of the *Indiana Jones* sort, and every hero of romance revived in a later age represents an exercise in quixotism. And as many theorists have pointed out, the novel as we know it would be impossible to conceive outside of its tense and contradictory relationship with romance.[20]

NOTES

1 I owe this reference to Mary Gossy (Rutgers University), Modern Language Association annual meeting, December, 2000. The Monty Python skit is available on line at http://www.ai.mit.edu/people/paulfitz/spanish/script.html. The Inquisition has of course been the subject of much serious recent study. See, for example, Henry Kamen, *The Spanish Inquisition: A Historical Revision* (London: Weidenfeld & Nicolson, 1997). See also Américo Castro, "Cervantes y la Inquisición," in *Hacia cervantes*, 3rd edn. (Madrid: Taurus, 1967), pp. 213–21.

2 *The Complete Works of Cervantes*, trans. N. MacColl, ed. James Fitzmaurice Kelly, (Cowans Gray: Glasgow, 1902), vol. III, p. 5.

3 See Albert Sicroff, *Les Controverses des Statuts de "pureté de sang" en Espagne du XVe au XVIe siècle* (Paris: Didier, 1960).

4 Cervantes' very first work was a poem published in the previous year to celebrate the birth of Princess Catalina, the second daughter of Philip II and Isabel of Valois.

5 "Si por algún modo alcanzara que la lección destas *Novelas* pudiera inducir a quien las leyera a algún mal deseo o pensamiento, antes me cortara la mano con que las escribí, que sacarlas en público."

6 I follow the MacColl translation, ed. Fitzmaurice Kelly, p. 5.

7 *Don Quijote*, trans. Burton Raffel (New York: Norton, 1999), p. 360.

8 Cervantes, Prologue to the *Exemplary Novels*. Essential contemporary information can be obtained from Diego de Haedo, *Topographía e historia general de Argel (Topography and General History of Algiers)* (1612).

9 See Ramón Menéndez-Pidal, "The Genesis of 'Don Quijote,'" in M. J. Bernardete and Angel Flores, eds., *Cervantes Across the Centuries* (New York: Dryden Press, 1948).

10 See Walter Kaiser, *Praisers of Folly* (Cambridge, MA: Harvard University Press, 1963).

11 See Stephen Gilman, *Cervantes y Avellaneda, Estudio de una imitación* (Guanajuato: El Colegio de México, 1951).

12 *Don Quijote*, trans. Raffel, p. 360.

13 Vladimir Nabokov, *Lectures on Don Quixote* (San Diego: Harcourt Brace Jovanovich, 1983).

14 Ibid., pp. 51–52.

15 See Américo Castro, "La Ejemplaridad de las 'Novelas Ejemplares,'" in *Hacia Cervantes*, pp. 451–74.

16 See Alban Forcione, *Cervantes, Aristotle, and the "Persiles"* (Princeton: Princeton University Press, 1970); E. C. Riley, *Cervantes's Theory of the Novel* (Oxford: Clarendon Press, 1962); and Stephen Gilman, "Los Inquisidores Literarios de Cervantes," *Actas del tercer Congreso Internacional de Hispanistas* (Mexico City: El Colegio de México, 1970), pp. 3–25.

17 See Ruth El Saffar, *Novel to Romance: A Study of Cervantes' Novelas ejemplares* (Baltimore: The Johns Hopkins University Press, 1974).

18 Notable exceptions are Forcione, *Cervantes, Aristotle, and the "Persiles"*, and Diana de Armas Wilson, *Allegories of Love: Cervantes's "Persiles and Sigismunda"* (Princeton: Princeton University Press, 1991).

19 José Ortega y Gasset, *Meditations on Quijote*, trans. Evelyn Rugg and Diego Marín (New York: Norton, 1961); Miguel de Unamuno, *Our Lord Don Quixote: The Life of Don Quixote and Sancho with Related Essays*, trans. Anthony Kerrigan (Princeton: Princeton University Press, 1976); Georg Lukács, *The Theory of the Novel*, trans. Anna Bostock (Cambridge, MA: MIT Press, 1971); Anthony J. Cascardi, *The Bounds of Reason: Cervantes, Dostoevsky, Flaubert* (New York: Columbia University Press, 1986); Félix Martínez-Bonati, *Don Quixote and the Poetics of the Novel*, trans. Dian Fox in collaboration with the author (Ithaca: Cornell University Press, 1992).

20 See Michael McKeon, *Origins of the English Novel, 1600–1740* (Baltimore: The Johns Hopkins University Press, 1987).

2

B. W. IFE

The historical and social context

At a critical point in his short story "La española inglesa" ("The English Spanish Lady") Cervantes has to repatriate the heroine Isabela from London to Seville. Writers of romance conventionally handled journeys of this kind by supernatural means or by an authorial stroke of the pen. But Isabela would be taking with her a dowry of 10,000 *escudos*, and England and Spain were at war: how was she going to get home with the fortune intact? Interested readers can consult the text to see exactly how it was done, but the solution is a masterpiece of early modern capitalism involving a network of French merchant bankers acting on commission: one in London to take care of the cash and arrange the transfer; another to issue the documents in Paris to throw the authorities off the scent; and another to cash the cheque once Isabela arrives back in Seville.

This mixture of high romance and precise documentary detail is a trademark of Cervantes, and one of the reasons why it is important to try to understand, four centuries later, the relationship between his work and the world in which he lived. Reputation has transformed the historical Cervantes into a universal genius, independent of time or place; yet the very work which made his name, *Don Quixote*, is not only profoundly steeped in the social and economic reality of Habsburg Spain, but has anachronism as its central theme. So we have two leaps of the historical imagination to make if we want to place Cervantes in context: back to the sixteenth and early seventeenth centuries, to the reigns of Philip II and Philip III; and then beyond that to the late medieval world of knight errantry which Don Quixote was so keen to revive. *Don Quixote* telescopes together nearly 150 years of Spanish history, and unless we adjust our sights accordingly, we are likely to misread the complex relationships between past and present which are a central theme of Cervantes' fiction.

When Don Quixote first rode out onto the plains of La Mancha, the rural landscape he encountered would have seemed reassuringly familiar. The windmills, the flocks of sheep and the fulling mills testified to the long-standing importance of agriculture in general and the wool industry in particular in the Spanish economy and way of life. The country roads and wayside inns which populate the novel, and the drovers and the goatherds that frequent them, would hardly have struck the contemporary reader as worthy of comment. Yet this was a world which was experiencing profound social, political and economic change; change to which Don Quixote was largely oblivious, but from which he could not remain unscathed. La Mancha lay at the heart of one of the greatest empires the world has ever seen. In a little over a hundred years Spain had undergone an astonishing transformation from a collection of intermittently warring kingdoms to become an emerging nation state, and had then rapidly gone on to acquire a world-wide empire. It is vital to understand the outlines of this process because the long-term consequences for Spaniards at all levels of society were both profound and far-reaching, and because it is important to dispel some myths about Spain and empire, particularly those which detect in, or read back into, the events of the long sixteenth century a conscious strategy for world domination by a unified political machine. Throughout the early modern period, what we think of as (and for convenience will continue to call) "Spain" had very little constitutional basis: both as "nation" and "empire," Spain was never more than a composite monarchy, an association of autonomous realms united only by what they had in common: a single monarch. At its most extensive, this global *monarquía* had as many as seventeen constituent parts, and like all federal or quasi-federal structures (such as the United States of America, the European Union, or Spain since Franco) it was as diverse as it was homogeneous. Time and again in the development of Spain and empire we see the laws of serendipity and unintended outcomes prevailing over those of historical inevitability.

The emergence of Spain as a world power in the sixteenth century can be understood in terms of two major cycles of growth and development characterized by a small number of recurring issues: how to balance political unity with cultural diversity; assert crown authority while working constructively with powerful elites; maintain and defend the growing number of territories within the monarchy; discharge responsibilities for defending the Catholic faith; and meet the growing costs of operating on an international stage.

The first of these two cycles begins with the so-called "union of the crowns," initiated by the marriage of Isabel, step-sister of Henry IV of Castile, to Ferdinand, son of John II of Aragon, in 1469. Although this marriage created the potential to unite two of the major powers in the Iberian peninsula, the potential was not realized without several years of struggle, in which Isabel's determination and Ferdinand's strategic and diplomatic skills were forged into an outstanding partnership. On the Castilian side, Isabel's claim to succeed her half-brother Henry would not normally have taken precedence over that of his daughter, Joanna. But it was widely rumored that Henry was impotent and Joanna was illegitimate. Henry's sudden death in 1474 precipitated a succession crisis and civil war which was resolved in Isabel's favor in 1479. It was during the struggles of the 1470s that Isabel laid the unassailable foundations of the power base on which she and her successors would build. On the Aragonese side, the political landscape was dominated by a long-term dispute with France and civil war in Catalonia. Ferdinand's marriage to a Castilian had therefore been seen as an effective alliance against the French.

The first ten years of their marriage were a testing time for both Ferdinand and Isabel, but when Ferdinand succeeded his father in 1479, two of the four major power blocks of the Iberian peninsula had begun to forge a stable alliance bordering on union. But this "union" was both provisional and conditional. The two crowns were united only by virtue of the marriage and only for its duration: the terms of the marriage contract preserved the independence of both parties and their respective territories. This provision was designed to ensure that the property of the partner who died first could not be alienated by the surviving spouse. Similar provisions are found in the contracts of other dynastic marriages, such as that of Mary Tudor and Prince Philip, later Philip II of Spain; and they are increasingly used in modern pre-nuptial agreements.

Furthermore, Castile and Aragon were unequal partners: Castile was much the larger territory in geographical terms, and enjoyed numerically superior human and economic resources. The constituent kingdoms had been moulded into a much more unitary state than Aragon, and a more absolutist style of monarchy had been developed. Aragon was physically and economically less powerful, but had possessions in the Mediterranean (Majorca, Minorca, Ibiza, Sardinia, Sicily and, from 1504, Naples), and was still a federation of distinct kingdoms or principalities (Aragon, Catalonia and Valencia) under a single monarch who governed by consent rather than by absolute right. The kingdoms in the Aragonese federation were all fiercely loyal to different systems of local government and different sets of rights and privileges, all of which the monarch was required to respect as a condition of allegiance.

Once the foundations of the union had been laid, the second phase of the reign, to the early 1490s, was concerned with consolidation and development. One of the most frequently debated questions about the reign of Ferdinand and Isabel concerns unification: did they set out to unify the peninsula, and if they did, were they successful? There is no evidence that they pursued a conscious policy of unification, but it might be argued that, if they had, their principal policies would have been much the same. The territories over which they had only recently consolidated control were diverse in every conceivable way, and Ferdinand and Isabel had none of the structures and resources – army, exchequer, administration – which would normally be considered necessary for unitary rule; the Council of the Inquisition was the only body with a unified responsibility for an aspect of the affairs of both kingdoms.

It is hardly surprising that the monarchs made no effort to harmonize the varied patchwork of local government, taxation, currency, or internal trade conventions across the peninsula: over a century later, when the protagonists of "Rinconete y Cortadillo" ("Rinconete and Cortadillo") arrive in Seville, the party they are traveling with is stopped at the Custom-house Gate (La Puerta de la Aduana) for payment of import duty on the goods they are carrying. Instead, the monarchs appear to have concentrated on a few major, interrelated themes: enforcing law and order; restructuring relations between the crown and the local elites; reinforcing the power of the church; securing the territorial integrity of the peninsula; and developing the structures and systems needed to deliver these. It was an ambitious agenda designed to assert the authority of the crown, secure popularity with the people, promote a common ideology and harness the military power of the nobility by giving them something useful to do.

The re-establishment of law and order was long overdue. The peninsula had been dominated by military conflict for several centuries, the frontier culture was a violent one, and internal security had rarely been strong. Powerful local elites were able to capitalize on the general feeling of insecurity both in the towns and the countryside. The civil wars of the 1470s had not helped this situation. It was therefore essential that Ferdinand and Isabel act quickly to restore the confidence of the common people in a system of security and justice which clearly had support at the very top. By reorganizing the local militias or *hermandades* into larger units responsible to the crown, by increasing the number of crown officials (*corregidores*) charged with maintaining a watching brief over local government, and by reforming the administration of justice, Isabel was able to gain popular support and curb the power of the municipalities and the nobles. The fruits of this stability are apparent in the pages of *Don Quixote*. Don Quixote sets out to rescue damsels and right wrongs, but whenever there is a fight it is Quixote who starts it; the criminals he encounters have been lawfully convicted and are being transported to serve their sentence; and the only example of banditry comes late in Part II and in the neighbourhood of Barcelona. Law officers and crown officials (the *alcalde* and the *corregidor*) are ever-present in the pages of Spanish Golden Age literature, and when a dead man falls at Periandro's feet in *Persiles y Sigismunda* (Book III, chapter 4) the Santa Hermandad are at the scene of the crime within seconds. The sex and violence which feature in the more urban context of the *Novelas ejemplares* (*Exemplary Novels*) undoubtedly reflect, if not always literally, the more dangerous world of the larger towns and cities, although it is important to remember that there was a long-standing literary prejudice against the sophistication of town-dwellers and in favor of the supposedly superior moral values of country folk.

In terms of stability, the nobles were a particular problem. The feudal model of allegiance had never been strong in Spain, and the military and political power of the aristocracy was considerable. The image of the medieval baron living in a fortified castle on a huge estate, running a private army and living off tributes and taxes extorted from terrified peasants may be a caricature, but it is one which came close to reality in parts of late fifteenth-century Spain. Although Isabel had found the nobles useful while they were supporting her claim to the throne, once she had secured it, their habit of fighting amongst themselves, and their potential to act as focal points for sedition and rebellion, had to be addressed. The solution to this and to many other problems was one favored by governments throughout the ages: war. Governments find wars useful because they distract the populace from more immediate problems, encourage people to sink their differences in the face of a common enemy, and if they end in victory, wars invariably make governments popular.

The war against Granada, which was successfully concluded in January 1492, fulfilled all of these objectives, and more. The capture of the last remaining Muslim territory in the peninsula brought to an end a long period of invasion and reconquest which began in 711. Muslim domination once extended almost as far north as the Pyrenees, but from the early thirteenth century the Christian territories had begun to fight back. A relatively peaceful coexistence (*convivencia*) had been achieved between the Christian kingdoms and the Emirate, and had lasted for over two centuries. Political coexistence, however, had not always been matched by religious and racial tolerance. Whereas the advancing Muslims had been generally tolerant of Christianity, and had encouraged Jews to settle and practice their religion in the peninsula, the reconquering Christians pressed for conversion of the Jews and the Muslims living under Christian rule, or their expulsion. Only in Valencia and Aragon were the civil and religious customs of Muslims respected to any great extent. The capture of Granada gave Isabel the excuse she needed to impose a single religion in Castile. In 1492 all Jews were required to be baptized or be expelled, and within ten years the same requirement was made of the Muslims.

Had this happened today, NATO planes would undoubtedly have been in action over southern Spain; but ethnic cleansing of the kind which took place in the former Yugoslavia in the 1990s was not to become policy in Spain until 1609, when Philip III decreed the expulsion of all descendants of former Muslims (*moriscos*). What Isabel was trying to achieve in Granada was the logical consequence of a series of measures which she and Ferdinand had already taken to strengthen the power of the Church. Isabel had been concerned that not only were there obvious signs of laxity in several areas of public life, such as public security, the administration of justice, and the collection of taxes, but the Church itself was clearly corrupt and in need of reform. Many years before these issues surfaced in northern Europe at the time of the Reformation, Isabel perceived widespread ignorance, venality, absenteeism and peculation among all levels of clergy; and superstitious, unorthodox and near heretical beliefs among the lay people. She and Ferdinand set about reforming the secular clergy and the religious orders, gained control of ecclesiastical appointments, and introduced the Holy Office of the Inquisition in Castile (1478) and Aragon (1487).

But the war had to be paid for, and Ferdinand and Isabel could not meet the costs themselves. They relied on a tax granted by the Pope (the *cruzada* or "crusade") and on troops and supplies from the nobles. Isabel and Ferdinand thereby created a powerful alliance of religious and aristocratic interests around a crusading ideal which helped them to achieve several military, religious, and political objectives. First, they significantly extended their territories by annexing the third great power block of the peninsula (the fourth, Portugal, would have to wait until 1580). Secondly, by giving the nobles a bigger stake in the crown's own success, Ferdinand and Isabel began to build a stronger alliance with them. They rewarded service not by payment in cash but by various kinds of patronage, including grants of land in the conquered territories, and exemption from direct taxation, one of the most important traditional privileges granted in exchange for personal service. The disadvantage to the crown was the opportunity cost involved: no money changed hands, but the crown "bought" the services it could not afford to pay for by forgoing future income from the land, and from direct taxation. The arrangement also transferred large stretches of land into private ownership, and the prosperity which resulted for a number of noble families began to change the long-term relationship between the nobles and the crown. Don Quixote strikes a similar bargain with Sancho. Quixote cannot afford to pay him a wage, so in exchange for Sancho's help and support in achieving his objectives, Quixote promises to reward him with the governorship of an island.

Sancho is therefore bound to stick with Quixote throughout the novel: if he leaves his service at any time, he gives up any chance of ever getting a reward.

Thirdly, and most significantly, the completion of the reconquest enabled Isabel to implement a policy of forced conversion or expulsion. The ending of religious pluralism strengthened the position of the Church and imposed a militant, white, Christian ideology to which every local political and cultural interest in the peninsula was subordinate. This ideology was increasingly underwritten by the growing supremacy of Castilian as the preferred language for government and education, recognized by the publication of the first grammar of Spanish (indeed, of any European vernacular language) by the scholar Antonio de Nebrija in 1492. Ferdinand and Isabel gave a high priority to education at all levels, and this enabled them to develop an administrative cadre of *letrados* (educated people) selected and trained on a meritocratic basis, to support the crown in managing the complexities of early modern statecraft.

Many of the achievements outlined above were to have very significant, and unforeseen, long-term disadvantages: the imposition of a single religion entailed the loss of a significant body of creative and entrepreneurial talent among the religious minorities who chose exile, and created two disaffected and marginalized ethnic minorities from among the *moriscos* and *conversos* who remained; and the concentration of land ownership in a small number of powerful families brought about long-term structural inequalities in the distribution of wealth. But there were also many benefits, including the priority given to education: some twenty universities were created in the peninsula by the end of the sixteenth century, and Spain became one of the most cultured and literate societies in early modern Europe. Without that readership, the work of Cervantes and his contemporaries would have been inconceivable.

Within months of the conclusion of the reconquest of Granada, Isabel and Ferdinand's reign entered its third phase prompted by an event which could not have been planned, but which was also the logical consequence of royal policies: the "discovery" by Christopher Columbus of islands in the Atlantic at approximately the longitude at which China and Japan were thought to be located. Isabel had agreed to permit, and partly to fund, a speculative voyage to investigate the feasibility of a westerly, transatlantic route to the Far East. As Columbus made clear in the prologue to the account he presented to the monarchs in 1493, there were four principal objectives to the voyage: scientific, economic, diplomatic, and religious. As far as Columbus was concerned, the 1492 voyage was designed to strengthen Christian alliances against Islam, facilitate the recapture of Jerusalem, and generate sufficient income for the enterprise to pay its own way.

From the moment that Columbus claimed the first small island in the Bahamas, Castile began to acquire extensive transatlantic possessions and Spain graduated almost overnight from embryonic nation state to emergent world empire. The crown and its advisers quickly assessed the true significance of Columbus's discoveries and staked an early territorial claim against the rival Portuguese. The resulting treaty of Tordesillas (1494) paved the way for future Spanish domination of the Caribbean, Mexico and the greater part of the South American continent, and by 1503 the Casa de Contratación had been established in Seville to regulate trade with the New World, which was soon being run as a full-fledged offshore company. Seville would grow rapidly throughout the sixteenth century, fueled by the trading opportunities offered by the New World. There were rich pickings to be had, and one fifth of all income went to the crown.

The discovery of large native populations who appeared to have no religion of their own gave plenty of scope for the salvation of souls. Spain had been granted sovereignty over the new territories by Pope Alexander VI in 1493, but this "donation" was not without conditions. Ferdinand and Isabel were expected to use their sovereignty to advance the cause of Christianity, and in 1496, Alexander gave them the title "Reyes Católicos" (Catholic Monarchs) in recognition of their support for the Church in Granada and the New World. When Isabel died in 1504 she could look back on a productive reign with a clear conscience that she had fulfilled the duties of a Christian monarch. But the burdens of empire were to become much greater with the passage of time, and the acquisition of an overseas empire was to prove a mixed blessing.

The reign of the Catholic Monarchs began with a succession crisis and ended with one. On Isabel's death, Ferdinand remained King of Aragon, but not of Castile, to which the succession was problematic. Isabel and Ferdinand had arranged marriages for each of their four children to strengthen alliances with Portugal, England, and Burgundy. But their efforts to secure the future of the union were frustrated when their only son John died in 1497, his sister Isabella died the following year, and the nominated successor Joanna ("Juana la Loca") was judged mentally unstable and unfit to rule. When Joanna's husband, Philip of Burgundy, also died unexpectedly in 1506, Ferdinand became regent of Castile on behalf of Joanna and her infant son Charles of Ghent (born in 1500). When Ferdinand died in 1516, Charles acquired a three-fold inheritance: in his person the two crowns of Castile and Aragon were finally united, together with the reconquered territories in the peninsula, the Atlantic, the New World, the Mediterranean (including Naples, recaptured by Ferdinand from the French in 1504), and North Africa; and to these territories he also added the Burgundian inheritance of the Netherlands, Luxembourg, and Franche-Comté. When he was elected Holy Roman Emperor in 1519, the same year in which the first Spaniards reached Mexico, a fourth group of territories were added to the monarchy: the Habsburg lands in Germany, Poland, Austria, and Hungary. Within a three-year period, King Charles I of Spain – the Emperor Charles V – became the most powerful man the world had ever seen.

Charles's accession established the Habsburg dynasty in Spain and ushered in the second great cycle of development for Spain and the empire. In many ways, this second cycle replays on a grander scale the central themes of the first. Like the Catholic Monarchs, the Habsburg kings of Spain had to grapple with problems of imposing and maintaining their authority on a politically diverse and geographically widespread collection of territories; they had to defend the territorial integrity of the empire; they took very seriously their responsibilities as defenders of the Christian faith; and they needed to raise large sums of money to do so. Charles adopted many of the solutions devised by the Catholic Monarchs – he became a skillful diplomat, traveled a great deal, led from the front and imposed his authority through the power of his personality while keeping the powerful elites on his side. But initially he had a number of disadvantages: he was a foreigner, a French-speaking Fleming, and he got off to a bad start by sidelining native Spaniards and appointing Burgundians to senior positions, while giving the impression that he intended to strip the assets of Castile and Aragon to fund his imperial ambitions.

The early years of Charles's reign were marked by suspicion and resentment which boiled over in a series of revolts by the *comuneros* and the *germanía* (1520–21). In Castile, a number of towns experienced serious disturbances fueled by resentment at the conspicuous presence of Burgundians in influential positions, the King's hasty departure from Spain on imperial business, and various long-standing complaints about the privileges of the aristocracy. In Valencia, the grievances were against the Muslims as well as the nobles. Both revolts had the effect of rallying the nobles in support of the royal cause, and were quickly suppressed. The rebels had made their point, nevertheless, and Charles spent most of the 1520s making amends for his high-handedness and for having taken the Spaniards and the regional parliaments (*Cortes*) for granted. The years 1522–29 were the longest continuous period he ever spent in Spain; he made sure he learned the language and understood the local customs, and in 1526 he contracted a popular marriage with Isabella of Portugal, who gave him an heir, the future Philip II, the following year. Charles had put down roots in Spain and won the hearts of Spaniards, and, more important, their political and financial support in defending the faith and the territories outside the peninsula.

Charles was at pains to make clear that he had no intention of extending the empire in Europe by conquest. But, equally, he would not contemplate surrendering territory on any front. There were three main troublespots: in the south and the east there was the old enmity with Islam, and the need to maintain naval power across the long and difficult frontier in the Mediterranean and North Africa, and along the Danube. Across the centre of the empire, and effectively dividing it in two, lay France. In the north, the greatest threat of all came from the rise of Protestantism. What began as a religious movement quickly took a political turn as secular leaders throughout northern Europe turned the mood of rebellion to their own advantage. Charles accepted that there was corruption and abuse among the clergy and the religious orders which needed to be dealt with, and encouraged a Catholic Counter-Reformation in response. But as the secular guardian of the Church, the Emperor became increasingly alarmed at the political threat of the German princes, and the way in which perfectly justified calls for moral reform were causing widespread civil unrest and rebellion against the authority of the Pope. It was Charles's confrontation with Luther in 1521 which led him to pledge his "kingdoms, dominions and friends, body and blood, soul and life" in defence of Christendom. With that pledge he committed Spain and the Spaniards to more than a century of conflict throughout Europe and the Mediterranean, and with it vast amounts of resource, both human and financial.

Charles was in a better position than Ferdinand and Isabel had been to afford a religious war on such a scale, but the cost to Castile in particular was high. Imperial armies depended on Spanish manpower and military expertise, but they had to be paid and the Emperor had increasing recourse to the *cruzada*, to general taxation, and to international sources of capital. The nobles were exempt from direct taxation, and constant recourse to grants and taxes to meet imperial commitments made the tax system more and more regressive as the burden fell increasingly on those least able to pay. Charles's greatest asset, however, was the ability to raise loans. By the early 1530s, when imports of silver bullion began to flow in large quantities, it was becoming clear that the economic potential of America was enormous. But the impact on Spain proved much less favorable than it might have been, and on balance was sharply negative.

Charles could raise large loans from German and Italian bankers to fight his wars in Europe because he could use imported silver from Peru as collateral. As a result, income was mortgaged for years in advance, and when the loans could not be paid, the crown was regularly bankrupt. Far from being a benefit to Spain, America proved a triumph for international venture capitalism: for the Genoese who underwrote much of the cost of the discoveries and then cashed in on the trading opportunities, and for the Italian and German bankers who saw Charles, and later Philip, struggling to hold back an unstoppable tide of social change by throwing huge sums of money at it, and were happy to feed their habit because Spain had good credit. Vast quantities of money flowed into the royal exchequer from America, but it did not benefit Spain, and Spaniards became net contributors to the cost of sustaining the empire.

The struggle to maintain control over such a large and turbulent empire eventually began to take its toll. Quite apart from the effort of securing the empire on several fronts in Europe, Charles also had to contend with a range of other important issues. The bad press which Spain was receiving about the conquests in South America and the abuse of the native populations by the conquerors and settlers led to a high-profile inquiry into the legitimacy of conquest and brought about changes in the law governing the rights of Indians and the responsibilities of settlers. The growing pressure for reform of the church from within the Catholic sector, coupled with the increasing incidence of heretical belief, was met by higher levels of activity from the Inquisition, tougher censorship, and the final suppression of Islam in Aragon in 1526. And the need to ensure that adequate systems of government were in place in Spain during his frequent absences abroad brought about an extension of the system of councils – early examples of modern government departments – and placed more power in the hands of the civil servants. By the 1550s Charles had concluded that his vast multinational conglomerate was too large to be manageable and he planned a phased abdication and demerger: he split the empire into two parts, handed on the original Holy Roman Empire inherited from the Austrian Habsburgs to his brother Ferdinand, and left the Castilian, Aragonese, and Burgundian inheritances to his son Philip. Charles himself retired to a monastery at Yuste, in Extremadura.

The accession of Philip II in 1556 brought about a change of style but not of substance. Philip had been groomed to be king from an early age, and he regarded being king as a job to be taken seriously. He learned the lessons of his father's reign and was determined that he would not spend his life traveling from one city to another. He established a capital in Madrid, built a headquarters at the Escorial and ran the empire from a tiny office with the help of a small group of trusted advisers. Where his father had been a general, he preferred the role of chief executive. On the domestic front, Philip remained unswervingly loyal to the Catholic cause, and cracked down even more strictly on the merest suspicion of unorthodoxy, using a range of repressive measures – the Inquisition and the *auto de fe*, the index of prohibited books and a ban on Spaniards studying abroad – to reinforce the prevailing orthodoxy. In the 1560s he decided that he needed to intensify the assimilation of the *moriscos* and reduce the security threat posed by a substantial ethnic minority in the east and south of the peninsula. In the face of a series of prohibitions against speaking Arabic, reading Arabic literature, and wearing traditional dress, the *moriscos* rebelled in 1568 and after a savage two-year conflict, the rebellion was crushed and the *moriscos* were forcibly dispersed throughout the peninsula.

Philip's regime was more centralist, more absolutist and more repressive than his father's, but the major foreign policy issues remained unchanged, and there was no let-up in the associated cost. Charles's division of the empire no doubt made good sense, but it left Philip two principal hot-spots to deal with: the on-going Islamic threat in the Mediterranean and the political and religious conflict in the Netherlands. Fighting on both these fronts continued to be ruinously expensive, and proved impossible to direct from an office in central Castile. Even a defensive policy in the Mediterranean needed a large, well-equipped navy. The Spanish fleet scored a number of successes in the 1560s in defence of Oran and Malta, and in the 1570s as part of the Holy League with Italy in defence of Cyprus. In 1571, at Lepanto, off the coast of Greece, the combined Christian fleet under the command of Philip's half-brother, Don John of Austria, inflicted a decisive defeat on the Turkish fleet, the battle in which Cervantes took part and in which he took such pride. But Philip's efforts to defend Spanish possessions in North Africa and in the Mediterranean were compromised by the need to deal simultaneously with a serious revolt in the Netherlands.

Unrest in the Netherlands was brought about by a cocktail of interrelated factors: resentment that the political centre of gravity of the empire had shifted to Spain; the virulence of the local brand of Protestant religious thought (Calvinism); separatist movements in the northern provinces led by William of Orange; and Spanish heavy-handedness, including a conspicuous military presence and unsubtle attempts to gain control of local affairs. Had Philip spent more time in the area he might have been able to respond more sensitively to the changing mood. But after Calvinists rioted and desecrated Catholic churches in 1566, Philip sent the Duke of Alba to investigate. Alba sentenced more than a thousand people to death and imposed a draconian tax to pay for the army. By the early 1570s, virtually the whole of the Netherlands was in revolt, supported by Protestant allies in Germany, France and England.

In 1585, England signed a treaty agreeing to aid the rebels, and Philip decided that, unless he could stop English involvement, he would never recapture the United Provinces. The result was the attempted attack on London by the 'Invincible Armada' in 1588. The invasion was doomed to failure by lack of surprise, poor communication between the navy in the English Channel and the army in Flanders, bad weather, and the fact that the commander-in-chief was directing operations from Madrid. The failure of the Armada cost hundreds of lives, was a massive waste of money, and caused a serious loss of confidence among Spaniards. Philip's reputation never fully recovered. The debacle was widely interpreted as a punishment for overweening pride. In fact it was a classic case of over-commitment on too many fronts, but there is no evidence that the lessons were learned in Philip's lifetime. He went on taxing and borrowing, and when he died in 1598, the crown was in debt for eight times its annual revenue.

The Netherlands were an insoluble problem, but Philip's decisive annexation of Portugal in 1580 finally brought the whole peninsula within a single monarchy, and added another overseas empire (Brazil, parts of Africa, India and the far east) to the growing extent of Spain's possessions in the New World. Philip III succeeded his father in 1598, and the turn of the century brought mixed fortunes; Spanish influence on the world stage had never been greater, but the mood at home was more somber. A serious outbreak of plague weakened an already overstretched populace and a bout of national introspection gave rise to a wide-ranging review of international strategy. The new regime moved quickly to address the balance of payments crisis by concluding treaties and cease-fire agreements with England and the United Provinces, and by trying to control the import of manufactured luxury goods such as textiles.

Philip III has often been perceived as a weak king, largely because he delegated much of his executive authority to a "favorite" or first minister, the Duke of Lerma, and dedicated himself to more regal pursuits such as hunting and collecting works of art. Lerma was undoubtedly the wrong choice in the long term: his most serious error of judgment came with the expulsion of the *moriscos* in 1609 – a policy which was heavily criticized by Cervantes in the Ricote episode in *Don Quixote*, Part II, chapter 54 – and over time he allowed power to corrupt him absolutely. But Philip's decision to share the burdens of office with a first minister was sensible, and Lerma's initial assessment of the problem was undoubtedly correct: Spain was over-committed and under-resourced for the role it was attempting to play, and a period of retrenchment was essential if the structural weaknesses in the Spanish economy were ever to be corrected.

All forms of historical narrative are misleading, and in the case of Spain and the empire the risks are particularly great. A narrative of growth, overreach and exhaustion can easily become, as it did for the Spaniards of Cervantes' time, a providentialist account in which pride goes before a fall. Yet the process by which the empire, particularly the empire in Europe, grew by leaps and bounds with each successive generation, was as much the result of accident as of design. The union of the crowns of Castile and Aragon was only one of a number of possible outcomes from the turbulence of the 1470s, and Charles's succession in 1516 was an endgame which few could have foreseen when Isabel died over a decade earlier. Even Charles's attempt to downsize the unruly empire in the 1550s was thwarted by Philip's decisive assertion of his claim to the throne of Portugal in 1580. And all the while, the astonishing extent of the discoveries in the New World regularly added thousands upon thousands of square kilometers to the sum of Spanish possessions – and of Spanish responsibilities – overseas. But it would be foolish to ignore the recurring themes which dominate the successive cycles of growth and development, and which help to explain the social complexity of Spain at the turn of the seventeenth century: the gradual but inexorable emergence of an absolutist monarchy and a normative culture; the changing dynamic between the crown and the other power bases within society, particularly the nobility, the Church, and the urban elites; the importance of religion as an ideological driver; and the role of America in sustaining imperial ambitions abroad and widening the wealth gap at home.

Although in many ways Spain at the end of the sixteenth century was more cohesive, both in concept and reality, than it had been a century earlier, the Spaniards then, as now, defined themselves in terms of a range of distinctions: differences of region, class, wealth, ethnicity, religion, culture, language, and sex. Distinctions of these kinds are inherent in all societies, but what makes them particularly important in early modern Spain was the shifting nature of certain established correlations, especially changes in the distribution of wealth, the relationship between wealth and rank, and the balance of religion, ethnicity, and culture.

Wealth is the key to understanding these changes and divisions. Taken as a whole, Spain was an extremely prosperous country in the early modern period, but the gap between the rich and the poor grew steadily wider throughout the sixteenth century. At the same time, the traditional correlation between social class and economic circumstances came under significant strain. New routes to wealth were open to all classes and ethnic groups, and no class was immune from poverty. The result was to reverse the polarity between wealth and status: where once membership of the ruling class would almost inevitably bring prosperity, in the changing circumstances, wealth was increasingly used to buy rank. There were three major factors driving these changes: demographic stability and growth, major shifts in land use and tenure, and the new commercial opportunities offered by the New World.

With very few exceptions (the revolts of the *comuneros* and the *germanía* in the early 1520s, and the rebellion of the *moriscos* in the 1560s) Spaniards enjoyed over a century of peace and stability within the peninsula itself. By exporting military conflict to America and other parts of Europe, the conditions were created for sustained net growth of the population until well into the 1580s. This growth was not uniform, however, and some significant changes took place in its shape and distribution. Emigration caused by forced expulsions, the demands of conquest and colonization in America, and wars in Europe was balanced by the immigration of Catholic refugees from the religious wars and merchants attracted by the investment potential of New World trade. The outflow of able-bodied men opened the way for women of all classes to take a more active role in society, a significant social change which is reflected in the prominence given to women in Cervantes' fiction and on the contemporary stage. At the same time, there was a pronounced shift in the economic center of gravity of the peninsula from north to south, and from the countryside to the towns. Both trends account for the emergence of Seville as a major commercial and cultural center during the sixteenth century, a role reflected in several of Cervantes' *Exemplary Novels*, such as "Rinconete and Cortadillo," "The English Spanish Lady," "The Jealous Man from Extremadura," and "The Illustrious Kitchenmaid."

The Spanish economy depended on agriculture, and the political stability and population growth of the sixteenth century favored both livestock and farming. Sheep farming was particularly successful. The mountainous terrain of much of the country made sheep and goats the only viable industry, the fine wool of the merino sheep fetched good prices among weavers in northern Europe, keeping sheep was not labor- or capital-intensive, and it was compatible with the long-standing aversion of the upper classes to anything having to do with manual labor. Sheep farming was also extremely well organized by a powerful guild, the Mesta, which enjoyed political support from the crown. Despite growing competition from silk and cotton, wool continued to be a major industry throughout the sixteenth century, and would undoubtedly have made a greater contribution to the economy had the domestic textile industry been developed in parallel. As it was, the export of wool did not cover the cost of importing finished cloth, of which Spain was a net importer.

Farming also flourished in response to stability and growth, and large amounts of additional land were brought into cultivation. The reluctance of emigrants to the New World to adjust to local conditions and diet created a strong export market for foodstuffs, wine and olive oil, as well as manufactured goods, and Spain remained a net importer of food. With favorable political and economic conditions and a wealth of natural resources, Spain could have done a good deal better had more American silver been used for investment and less for conspicuous consumption. Nevertheless, it was possible to make a good living from farming and many people did. We have only to look beyond the surface rural poverty of *Don Quixote* to see how many prosperous gentlemen farmers there are in the subtext. As examples, note the precision with which Cervantes fills in the family background of Grisóstomo and Marcela, the two protagonists of the pastoral episode in Part I, chapters 11–14, both of whom have inherited wealth from parents who worked hard and did well from farming; or consider the case of Don Diego de Miranda (Part II, chapter 18), another gentleman farmer, whose only major worry seems to be that his son writes poetry in Castilian rather than Latin or Greek; or Camacho, the "labrador rico" whose wedding is spoiled by the theft of his bride in Part II, chapters 20–22, but who has the consolation of knowing that his wealth will soon attract another girl.

But the real beneficiaries of a strong agricultural economy were the large landowners – corporate bodies, including the Church and the orders of chivalry, as well as private individuals. Land is a finite resource, and a primary source and repository of wealth. We have already seen how the Catholic Monarchs bought political and military service from the nobles by making grants of land and associated income in conquered territories, and this process continued in different forms under the Habsburg kings, with large areas of crown lands being granted to a rapidly growing aristocracy, or sold into private ownership to raise capital for military expenditure. Many of these disposals were of *baldíos*, crown lands in common use, and the privatization of ownership often brought severe hardship to common people whose traditional rights of access and use were denied. As more land was granted or purchased, large estates were accumulated by families who made sure that they would be transferred intact to subsequent generations by using a legal device called *mayorazgo*, which provided for succession to the eldest son (primogeniture) as opposed to the more traditional model of equal inheritance by all children, male or female. The "land grab" by the Spanish nobility in the sixteenth century undoubtedly helps to explain the growing obsession with lineage, the association of identity with place, and the importance given to legitimate, patrilineal, succession and the sexual integrity of women: rich, powerful men do not want their carefully accumulated assets accidentally transferred to another man's son.

The benefits of land ownership were also open to members of other classes, including those on both sides of the Atlantic who got rich from trade: Carrizales, the protagonist of "The Jealous Man from Extremadura," is a prime example of the *indiano*, the emigrant who makes his fortune in the New World and returns home to Spain, in this case to find a wife to give him an heir. There was no monopoly of class or ethnic group, and the aristocracy, the urban middle classes, and the *conversos* were all represented among the successful merchant class. Large fortunes were made from American bullion: for every 20 percent that went to the crown, 80 percent went into private pockets and ultimately had to be banked, invested, or traded for another asset. Many of the "new rich" preferred to invest in status rather than trade or industry. A crown which was desperate for cash was more than willing to sell patents of nobility, with the associated tax-exempt status, in exchange for large, up-front contributions to the imperial revenue account. The emergence of a "new rich" concentrated in the southern half of the peninsula and including descendants of religious minorities caused considerable concern among the nobility and gentry of Old Castile, many of whom had missed out on the prosperity brought by reconquest at home and conquest abroad. In the face of influential new money, the old Christian ruling classes closed ranks and hit back with the one thing money cannot buy: blood.

Long-standing discrimination against *conversos* became institutionalized in Toledo during the 1540s, and took the form of statutes of *limpieza de sangre*, which restricted access to a wide range of ecclesiastical and secular posts and privileges to those who could demonstrate that their blood was of pure Christian origin. Philip II ratified this practice in 1556 and it came into common use. Purity of blood was a social and economic issue as much as a religious one. In practice, and over time, the importance attached to purity of blood also reinforced the claims of low-born old Christians to enhanced social status: a humble, "blue-blooded" peasant might have a greater claim to be considered honorable than a social superior of less immaculate racial origin. The blood factor added a further dimension of confusion to a social order which had already been rendered fluid by money. No one could be certain which was the true indicator of status: inherited wealth, new money, or Christian blood.

These conflicting views of status – the *hidalgo* versus the self-made man (*hijo de sus obras*) – recur throughout Cervantes' work. They intersect, for example, in Don Quixote's discussion of Dulcinea's lineage (Part I, chapter 8) where the emphasis on lineage in chivalric literature conflicts with Dulcinea's *parvenue* status: her lineage is in the future rather than the past. Grisóstomo and Marcela are carefully distinguished in terms of social and economic rank: he is the son of a rich farmer, but described as an "hijodalgo rico" and heir to a sizeable estate; she is the daughter of "William the wealthy man . . . a worker somewhat wealthier than Grisóstomo." He appears to have greater rank (he is an *hidalgo*), but her father is richer, even though he is a peasant. Note also the family circumstances of the prospective husband and the lover of Feliciana de la Voz in *Persiles and Sigismunda*, Book III, chapter 3: her parents are "nobles rather than wealthy people"; her lover is the son of a "very rich *hidalgo*...a gentleman in the opinion of the public" and he is described as heir to an "infinitely large estate"; the prospective husband's family is, like her parents, more noble than rich and lives in the "honorable middle class" ("honrada medianía"). She falls for the rich one and has his baby, which no doubt helps her father and brother eventually to come to terms with the dishonor.

But the wealth of the few was gained at the expense of the majority. For every farmer or merchant who made good there were many more who barely lived above subsistence level. Over and above the daily vicissitudes of early modern rural life – low life expectancy, malnourishment, disease, infant and early male mortality – the Spanish peasantry had to contend with two devastating consequences of imperial ambition: inflation caused by American bullion and the resulting excess liquidity in the European economy, and high taxation needed to meet the costs of religious wars abroad. Ground down by these two millstones, many agricultural workers deserted the countryside, flocked to the towns and joined the ranks of the urban poor. The lucky ones were able to scrape a hand-to-mouth existence from casual labor in manufacturing or service; many had recourse to begging, prostitution, or organized crime. The urban underclass which grew up in the shadow of the conspicuous prosperity of early modern Spain is featured in Cervantes' short fiction, in the picaresque novels of the early seventeenth century, and in the visual art of painters like Velázquez and Murillo.

Cervantes was a shrewd observer of the world around him, but the literary realism which is such a feature of his fiction is not primarily documentary in nature. The world he depicts is clearly recognizable as his own, but he does not write simply to record the fact. Cervantes' world was complex and full of conflict, and writers of fiction need conflict to generate plot and character. His genius consists in allowing the circumstantial evidence of his own society to act as testimony to a much wider range of issues. This may be why readers and critics of Cervantes have found it difficult to detect what he really thinks about his material. Very occasionally, as in the Ricote episode of *Don Quixote* where he is outspoken about the expulsion of the *moriscos*, we can detect genuine anguish in the writing. More often, he comes across as a wryly detached, non-committal ironist who can see both sides of the question. Does he really think that Quixote is a fool, or does he secretly admire his misplaced idealism?

Cervantes is much more an analyst and observer than a policy-maker, but he clearly had strong views about many of the political and social issues which preoccupied his age. He took a close interest in the complexities of class, wealth, and status and developed many permutations of these themes in his work. His religious views appear to be orthodox, notwithstanding the occasional touch of anticlerical satire; divine providence is a frequent driving force behind the construction of plots in which vicissitudes turn out for the best and hidden truths must be revealed; and the overtly Catholic agenda of his prose romance *Persiles y Sigismunda* is only conceivably open to question on the grounds that it protests too much. Cervantes is often discreetly critical of divisiveness and intolerance in his own society by indirect reference to societies outside Spain: "The English Spanish Lady" and "El amante liberal" ("The Generous Lover") are both set in worlds – one Protestant, the other Islamic – where religious and cultural diversity is shown to be rather more tolerantly managed than it was within the peninsula. He was a brilliant observer of regional and linguistic diversity, urban life and manners, and he clearly had strong views about the sexual basis of the honor code.

Spanish society in Cervantes' time was a complex weave of many potentially contradictory strands. Traditional structures were under strain: the ruling class was becoming increasingly segmented; the grandees were growing in number and wealth but had been effectively emasculated by prosperity; many of the gentry had fallen on hard times, while the "new rich" were rising up to take their place. Alonso Quijano was clearly dysfunctional in this context. While all around him the land-owning classes were enlarging their estates and begetting heirs, he was allowing his estate to decline, selling off land to buy books which encapsulated an outworn ideology, living with his niece and housekeeper, unmarried and childless. And when he reinvents himself as Don Quixote in a desperate attempt to put the clock back to the frontier society of the fifteenth century, he rides out into a world in which rich farmers put their sons through university and dukes and duchesses have transformed their castles into chateaux where they pass the time playing effete masquerades. The old ethos of service has disappeared, along with the respect due to the chivalric ideal; everyone now wants to be paid – innkeepers, his squire Sancho, even his lady-love Dulcinea tries to touch him for the loan of six *reales*.

Although Spain remained largely free of political and military conflict for most of Cervantes' lifetime, the internal boundaries between regions, languages, classes, and castes were all too apparent. The towns and cities, Seville above all, were a potent melting pot in which rich and poor, criminals and polite society, Old Christians and new, lived side by side. Rinconete and Cortadillo experience both the permeability of these boundaries and the way in which large parts of Spanish society moved to the margins. The world of organized crime centered on Monipodio's headquarters mimics the self-deluding order of conventional respectability, but Cervantes does not treat the criminal underworld and polite society as worlds apart. Cervantes' characters are continually crossing geographical, political, cultural, and religious boundaries, negotiating and testing the sometimes artificial distinctions between the different spheres. Preciosa ("The Little Gypsy Girl"), Isabela ("The English Spanish Lady"), Costanza ("The Illustrious Kitchenmaid") are all exiled into other worlds, to be redeemed by the power of integrity, truth, and love. It is difficult not to look for the origins of this recurrent narrative structure in Cervantes' own experience of captivity and redemption in Algiers during the late 1570s.

Each of these three female characters is rescued from some form of internal or external exile back into her rightful place within the ruling class, but Cervantes is not foolish enough to believe that virtue and nobility are linked: he is merely using conventional measures of distinction associated with literary romance – youth, beauty, ability, breeding, blonde hair, and a pretty dress – to indicate other more significant forms of distinctiveness and value. But there is one manifestation of exile which Cervantes treats more literally: the untouchable status of the violated woman. Cervantes clearly had no problem with female sexuality: his works are full of feisty women who are prepared to make the first move as well as those who allow themselves to be seduced and live to regret it. But rape is another matter, and a novel like "La fuerza de la sangre" plays out the vivid drama of violent sex and retributive marriage which dominated the Spanish stage for over fifty years. Amid all the fluidity of Spanish society, Cervantes seems to argue, there are some things that never change. The violated woman has no value in the sexual economy of the time, and she can only be redeemed by marriage to the rapist, however implausibly this is brought about. Once her virginity is lost, or her faithfulness compromised, she cannot provide that essential guarantee that a man's children are his own, or that his property will pass to his heir. In a society obsessed with lineage and with an abhorrence of miscegenation, honor and status are reduced to a simple biological fact: blood is the most powerful delineator of all.

FURTHER READING

Casey, James. *Early Modern Spain: A Social History*. London and New York: Routledge, 1999.

Defourneaux, Marcelin. *Daily Life in Spain in the Golden Age*. Trans. Newton Branch. Stanford, California: Stanford University Press, 1970.

Edwards, John. *The Spain of the Catholic Monarchs 1474–1520*. Oxford and Malden, MA: Blackwell, 2000.

Elliott, J. H. *Imperial Spain 1469–1716*. London: Arnold, 1963.
  Spain and its World, 1500–1700. New Haven and London: Yale University Press, 1989.
Johnson, Carroll B. *Cervantes and the Material World*. Urbana and Chicago: University of Illinois Press, 2000.
Kamen, Henry. *Spain 1469–1714: Society of Conflict*. London and New York: Longman, 1983.
Lynch, John. *Spain 1516–1598: From National State to World Empire*. Oxford and Cambridge, MA: Blackwell, 1991.
  The Hispanic World in Crisis and Change 1598–1700. Oxford and Cambridge, MA: Blackwell, 1992.

3

FREDERICK A. DE ARMAS

Cervantes and the Italian Renaissance

During the last months of 1569, the twenty-two year-old Cervantes travels to Italy and enters the service of the soon-to-be Cardinal Giulio Acquaviva in Rome. Italian sojourns were almost *de rigueur* for Spanish poets, writers of prose fiction, and humanists during the early modern period. Cervantes' voyage, then, resembled the ones of Acuña, Aldana, the brothers Argensola, Cetina, Figueroa, Garcilaso, Hurtado de Mendoza, Medrano, Santillana, and Villamediana. Such voyages were facilitated by the fact that the kingdom of Naples was part of the Spanish empire, while other regions of the peninsula were under Habsburg influence. Cervantes came to Italy after studying in Madrid with the Spanish humanist Juan López de Hoyos and after writing his first verse compositions, which imitated Garcilaso, using his metrical forms, adjectives, and themes. Cervantes' brief humanistic training, and his interest in Garcilaso, who was deeply influenced by the Italian Renaissance, prepares him for an Italian sojourn. While it is said that López de Hoyos taught Cervantes an Erasmism that was no longer tolerated in Spain, Rome would reveal to him the ecclesiastic pomp, ritual, and luxuriant majesty that the humanist from Rotterdam often criticized. It was also a Rome teeming with ruins, which impelled humanists and artists of the Renaissance to turn to archeological pursuits, to focus their attention on rediscovering antiquity, finding in the ancients "a powerful impetus to revive the contemporary world in light of its accomplishments."[1]

But Cervantes had come to Rome too late. The sack of Rome of 1527 by troops of Charles V had emptied the city of many of its great treasures; and the last Renaissance pope, Paul III, had died in 1549. Now, the Counter-Reformation, a reform movement within the Catholic Church in response to the Protestant Reformation, was in full swing. Its proponents viewed Rome and the other humanistic centers of Italy as locations "infected" with paganism, and sought to cleanse them. Cervantes, as chamberlain to a cardinal, was able to view the work of Michelangelo in the Sistine Chapel. But he would have seen it covered, censored, by Daniele da Volterra. Only five years earlier, in 1564, the Council of Trent, a meeting of Church officials that laid down the rules for the Counter-Reformation, had decreed the correction of the parts of the *Last Judgment* thought to be indecent. Volterra, although an admirer of Michelangelo, was assigned to place draperies over a number of nude figures in the fresco. Walking through the Vatican, Cervantes would have been aware of the contrast between a Counter-Reformation ideology that labeled the Sistine Chapel "a bathroom full of nudes,"[2] and the remnants of a brilliant Renaissance that evoked the ancients while respecting Christian theology. A number of Cervantes' conceptual and imagistic elements could derive from this frisson between ancient, Renaissance and Counter-Reformation cultures. By obscuring a past that had so recently been rediscovered, the Vatican may not have always achieved its aim to make visitors/pilgrims more religiously minded. Instead, thinkers like Cervantes may have sought to discover what the Church was hiding – the alluring forms of an ancient culture. Of course, Cervantes did not have to go to Italy to discover the end of an age of significant spiritual freedom and moral autonomy. In Spain, the strictures of the Counter-Reformation, under Philip II, were already undoing the more open era of Charles V. In the years before his departure for Italy, Cervantes would witness the two defining moments of this new Spain: the 1559 prohibition that students attend foreign universities and the 1564 decree that made into law the edicts of the Council of Trent.[3] With these two laws Philip II sought to limit outside influences and to return Spain to a stricter observance of Catholic doctrine.

Although the Italian states also assimilated elements of the Counter-Reformation, its impact was nowhere as noticeable as in Spain. Thus, Cervantes' continuing desire for Italy, as revealed in his works, is in part a desire for a return of the Renaissance. This notion of return is parodied in *Don Quixote* through the notion of the return of the mythical Golden Age. The desire for Italy can be located biographically in Cervantes' repeated appeals to his patrons for a return to the peninsula. In the dedication to Ascanio Colonna at the beginning of his pastoral romance *La Galatea* (*Galatea*, 1585), written only five years after his release from captivity in Algiers, he already asks for such a return. Thus, the Algerian world had not erased Italian memories, although it certainly enriched his experiential knowledge. Although some critics today argue that Algiers is Cervantes' primal scene, elements from this period cannot simply be labeled as the matter of Algiers, since they are intermingled with Italian figures. As a captive, Cervantes encountered Italian humanists in Algiers and befriended them. Indeed, he dedicates a sonnet to the Sicilian humanist and captive Antonio Veneziano. And he discovers that some of the highest authorities in Algiers are of Italian background. The pasha, for example, was a Venetian renegade now named

Hassan. Of course, the Italian elements of the Algerian captivity must be juxtaposed with an even more ancient Islamic humanism.[4] Cervantes was thus a part of this circulation of humanistic ideas from the east and the west.

In later years, Cervantes' desire to return to Italy did not diminish. When the Count of Lemos, his patron, was named Viceroy of Naples in 1610, Cervantes once again hoped to return to Italy. Cervantes dedicates to him many of his most important works: the *Novelas ejemplares* (*Exemplary Novels*, 1613), *Ocho comedias y ocho entremeses* (*Eight Plays and Eight Interludes*, 1615), Part II of *Don Quixote* (1615) and even the posthumously published *Persiles y Sigismunda* (*Persiles and Sigismunda*, 1617). He was never invited. The inabilty to fulfill this desire found a place in his works, where the very nature of desire is forever questioned. The Spanish novelist often locates Italy at the very surface of his texts through the many references to its cities (Bologna, Florence, Genoa, Lucca, Milan, Naples, Rome, Venice), their culture, and their architecture. In his novella "El licenciado Vidriera" ("The Glass Graduate") Cervantes chronicles a trip to Italy that biographers believe follows Cervantes' own journey. Indeed, his posthumously published *Persiles* narrates a pilgrimage that ends in Rome.

This desire for Renaissance Italy leads to more subtle recollections through the constant and consistent rivalry and imitation of its literature (Ariosto, Boiardo, Boccaccio, Caporali, Castiglione, Dante, Folengo, Leone Ebreo, Petrarch, Tasso) and art (Michelangelo, Raphael, Titian). On yet another level, this desire carried with it the Renaissance's impetus for a necromantic revival, conversation, and competition with the ancients (Apuleius, Aristotle, Cicero, Lucan, Plato, Virgil). Cervantes' interest in the ancients is not an erudite and philological one. Although Cervantes points to Greek literature, he does not read it in the original language but constructs his perception of its meanings through translations, summaries, and adaptations. Even when dealing with some of the Latin writers, mediation is utilized. His interest in the ancients has much to do with visuality and culture. After all, Cervantes' first real confrontation with the ancient past was a visual one – when he came face to face with the art and architecture of Genoa, Rome, and Naples. Indeed, the sonnet on Rome in the *Persiles* is enunciated as a group of pilgrims view the city from Monte Mario. The text tells us that before entering Rome they passed through the gardens of the Villa Madama – a villa designed by Raphael, one of the artists Cervantes would recall in many of his works.[5]

The very textuality of his works, the constant reference to classical and Italian Renaissance authors, is often conjoined with the visual, since there seems to be both an acceptance of poetry and painting as sister arts and a desire to surpass the visual through the written word. Whether using models from literature or art, Cervantes makes a point of distinguishing imitation from literary thievery, a point he makes both in *Don Quixote* and in the *Adjunta al Parnaso* (*Postcript to Parnassus*, 1614), where Cacus, the Virgilian thief, represents the bad and thieving poets. Although the "friend" in the Prologue to *Don Quixote* suggests that the author use thieving devices to authorize his work, the novel flaunts its originality while exhibiting a textual and pictorial cornucopia that ranges from ancient epics to the romances of chivalry and the frescoes of the Renaissance. While the practice of imitation "served as a stabilizing response to the problems generated by the increasing preoccupation with authority and desire in history," the proliferation of models in Cervantes points to a desire which cannot be contained or even localized.[6] Italy, then, mediates other and more hidden desires, which Cervantes explores and censors. Although the Renaissance concept of *imitatio* included "the need to do so in a way which is neither servile nor too visible,"[7] many Cervantine works would take such concealment to an extreme. For example, the Spanish author often uses the technique of the double truth: "Cervantes was obliged to practice the 'heroic hypocrisy' characteristic of some of the Renaissance's most enlightened men, and tacitly to espouse Pomponazzi's principle of 'double-truth,' which legitimized the simultaneous endorsement of religious dogmas and of philosophical opinions contrary to them."[8] He also conflates texts and paintings in ways that disorient the reader. These practices at times mimic Counter-Reformation censorship. Even the process of censorship is at times replicated in Cervantes' works, as in *Don Quixote* I, 6, where the priest and the barber hold an "Inquisition" over the knight's books, and order most of them to be burned.

This constant Cervantine confrontation with the Renaissance and the classics does not mean that Cervantes' thought formed a coherent system which had as its grand Renaissance theme the conflicted dialogue between poetic universals and historical particulars, as Américo Castro has proposed (*El pensamiento de Cervantes*, pp. 40–41). Cervantes often dialogues with neo-Aristotelian treatises, works that offer commentaries on the *Poetics* and *Rhetoric*. He examines their views on the division of styles, on whether an epic could be written in prose, and on topics such as invention, imitation, and poetic universals. Although these elements may underlie his aesthetics, the repeated change of perspectives, the Socratic questioning, found in Cervantes' works undermines the formation of a model which consistently illuminates all of Cervantes' works. As Anthony Close warns, Américo Castro's comprehensive view fails to take into account, among others, "considerations about artistic form and the aims proper to it" (*The Romantic Approach to "Don Quixote"*, p. 197).

One way to organize Cervantes' works and assess their relations to the Italian Renaissance is through artistic form. This essay will thus move through the genres utilized by the Spanish author. Upon his return to Spain from his Algerian captivity, Cervantes turns to the theatre. His experiments here are much less successful when compared to his prose fiction. Indeed, late in life he published eight plays and eight interludes which had never been performed. Cervantes ascribes his failures here to Lope de Vega's new art, which had displaced his own theatrical works. Lope de Vega became the most successful Spanish playwright of the period, composing hundreds of dramas. In his *Arte nuevo de hacer comedias* (*New Art of Writing Plays*, 1613) Lope contrasts his new theatre to the old precepts of Aristotle. Emphasizing the imitation of nature, he advocates the joining of the comic and the tragic, of commoners and nobles. Although Lope's theories were indeed new, Cervantes' early popularity as a playwright, together with recent critical reassessments of his theatre, show that his dramatic work is startlingly different from that of his Spanish contemporaries. A number of his ten extant plays show clear links to the Italian Renaissance. Two will be used as examples.

Critics have consistently labeled *La casa de los celos* (*The Abode of Jealousy*, 1615) as the weakest and most episodic of his theatrical works. It deals with the rivalry between Roland and Reinaldos for the amorous attentions of Angelica. The open-endedness of the conclusion, which does not resolve the rivalry between Roland and Reinaldos, goes against Lope's theatrical precepts, which require resolution. However, this open-endedness also brings to the fore the complex nature of desire. Desires and rivalries are also textual, as Cervantes seeks Italian, classical, and Spanish models and attempts to emulate them. Although in *Don Quixote* Cervantes will turn to Ariosto's *Orlando furioso* (*Mad Orlando*, 1516), here Ariosto's impact is much less prominent since Cervantes mainly imitates Ariosto's predecessor, Boiardo. Even though Boiardo's *Orlando innamorato* (*Orlando in Love*, 1495) lacks some of Ariosto's wit, style, and irony, Cervantes adds a lighter tone, including comic interludes. He also ironizes some of the Boiardian situations. The excessive interweaving of episodes in both Boiardo and Ariosto, the way in which they interrupt an episode to go to a second and break with this one to move to a third, only then returning to the original action, provides Cervantes with an appropriate model for ridiculing the excesses of chivalry. The work also includes the Spanish legendary warrior who defeats the French, Bernardo del Carpio. In addition, the play features the allegorical motif of the *Abode of Jealousy*, which can be traced back to Spanish ballads on the subject and even to Ovid's *Abode of Envy*, a gruesome place that houses this horrid allegorical figure. All this is presented with considerable spectacle, probably derived from the scenic splendor of Italian Renaissance theatre. The commingling of genres and tones in *The Abode of Jealousy* can be considered as an early experiment, which will eventually succeed when new Italian models (Ariosto's romance and Tasso's epic) impose themselves; when a comic style replete with paradoxes is used; when the romance elements are relegated to the imagination of the protagonist; and when a new form (prose fiction) more suitable to the notion of variety is utilized. This experiment which "glorifies fictional reality and the reality of fiction,"[9] will eventually lead to *Don Quixote*, but only after the proliferation of models are not represented as a cornucopia of authoritative desires, but instead are shown as "lost or eclipsed... broken loose from the organizing structure that history once provided" (Cascardi, *Ideologies of History*, p. 198).

While many see *The Abode of Jealousy* as a failed experiment, another play by Cervantes, *The Siege of Numantia*, has been called the greatest Spanish tragedy of all times. Its topic is the establishment of a myth of origins for the Spanish empire. Cervantes fashions his play out of the ruins of an ancient Celtiberian city destroyed by the Romans (Numantia). The work's archeological impetus leads to the establishment of parallels between the fall of Troy and the rise of the Roman empire and the fall of Numantia and the rise of Spanish rule. For the history of Numantia, Cervantes turns to the humanist Ambrosio de Morales' history of Spain. This text parallels Cervantes' archeological interest since Morales turns to inscriptions on Spanish stones and information on ancient coins in order to reconstruct the past. Morales also is very careful to scrutinize ancient histories looking for the "true" events. Both Cervantes' and Morales' archeological interests derive from the Renaissance's fascination with the past. One of Raphael's last projects, for example, was the creation of accurate architectural drawings of ancient Rome. Cervantes revels in the complex architecture of his play, drawing not only from Morales, but from a number of classical writers and even from the frescoes of Raphael at the Vatican (De Armas, *Cervantes, Raphael and the Classics*, pp. 16–61).

The Siege of Numantia (1580s) clearly surpasses other tragedies being written at the time, since Cervantes "creates a thematic structure which unifies motifs through an internal point of reference rather than incidents and characters in an external framework" (Friedman, *The Unifying Concept*, p. 42). This play not only unifies diverse motifs, but also brings together a number of models into a cohesive whole. It does so by placing each in a different *locus*. Contained within each act, each of the four key models of Cervantes' action will battle each other. *La Numancia* points to a quaternity of authorities from the past: Virgil (Act I), Lucan (Act II), Homer (Act III) and Cicero/Macrobius (Act IV). Virgil's *Aeneid* provides the trappings for empire and the notion that this empire is predestined to flourish. Lucan's *Pharsalia* is used to question and even subvert some of the notions ascribed to the canonical epics. Here, divine prophecy is in the hands of a witch; and the heroic mode is subverted by Fortune and the horror of bodily mutilations. The Homeric epics prepare the reader/audience for a debate as to who is the perfect hero: the Numantians or the Roman general Scipio (cf. Achilles or Odysseus). Although the play seems to be constructed as a tragedy in the manner of Aeschylus' *Persians*, its epic models provide ample material for notions of conquest and imperial dominion.

At the end of the play, the figure of Fame appears to provide the work with a happy ending. Although Numantia has been destroyed, its example will live on and help establish a Spanish empire in the sixteenth century. The triumphant Fame in the play may derive from Petrarch's *Triumphs*. But Cervantes' text also turns to classical literature and particularly to Macrobius. This author, who flourished at the end of the fourth and beginning of the fifth century, wrote a Commentary on the last book of Cicero's *Republic*, a work that discusses the ideal state with reference to Rome. This last section of the *Republic* is known as the *Dream of Scipio*. The Spanish humanist Juan Luis Vives included in his works a version of Cicero's *Dream of Scipio* along with his own commentary. These texts problematize the final triumph. In *Numantia* Fame favors the inhabitants of the city, but in Cicero, Macrobius, and Vives she sides with Scipio. Cervantes' own desire for fame, as depicted at the end of *Numantia*, is tied to his desire for Italy. After all, it was Petrarch who discovered and popularized Cicero's speech "Pro Archia" ("For Archias"), where poets are praised for rendering service to the state "by conferring immortality on its heroes."[10] This, in turn, brings glory to the poets. It is the fame of the ancients, acquired through textual feats, that emboldens Cervantes to create in *La Numancia* a myth of empire to rival and problematize the fictions of Virgil, singer of Rome.

The Siege of Numantia may have led Cervantes to consider yet another great Virgilian myth, that of the origins of a great poet. The *Rota Virgilii* (Virgilian Wheel), which became a commonplace in medieval rhetoric, distinguishes three styles (humble, middle, and high), to which correspond three occupations (shepherd, farmer, warrior). These are based upon Virgil's *Bucolics*, *Georgics*, and the *Aeneid* respectively. Utilizing what were once considered to be the first four lines of the *Aeneid*,[11] the three styles also became the three stages that the poet must master in his literary career. The poet must begin with pastoral, move to the farming fields of the *Georgics*, and end in the martial fields of epic. Throughout the Renaissance, European poets sought to emulate the career patterns of the ancients, particularly Virgil's: while Petrarch's Latin verses includes a pastoral poem and the *Africa*, an epic on the Punic War, Spenser's output ranges from *The Shepheardes Calender* (pastoral) to *The Faerie Queene* (epic). Cervantes uses this myth of the poet in his own literary career, but he chooses prose fiction instead of poetry as its medium.

Cervantes' first attempt at prose fiction came in 1585 with the publication of his pastoral novel, *Galatea* (1585). This work connects very clearly with Cervantes' Italian sojourn. Here he tells the reader that he served Cardinal Acquaviva in Rome. This pastoral also contains a clear announcement of Cervantes' projected career, thus connecting his vision of Rome to the discovery of an ancient career pattern.[12] The prologue to *Galatea* is perhaps the most succinct statement of his intention to follow the Virgilian literary career. Here, Cervantes advocates, first of all, the use of Latin to enrich the vernacular. It has been argued that the real linguistic revolution of the Renaissance was not the restoration of classical Latin, "but the national vernacular writers' invention of neoclassical styles in the modern European languages."[13] The prologue to *La Galatea* argues for this new language and style, following Cicero and Virgil, who invented a classical Latin; and Boscán and Garcilaso, who "invented" classical written Spanish. The enrichment proposed by Cervantes is not only of language, but also of culture and ideas. In addition to its many latinisms, *Galatea* contains numerous borrowings from Italian Neoplatonists such as Leone Ebreo and Castiglione, passages that develop notions of love, nature, and beauty. Although their ideas enrich the novel, Cervantes' application is often unorthodox and original, as the concepts are humanized and made to fit characters who at times even invalidate Neoplatonist precepts through their actions.[14]

More importantly, Cervantes argues that this enrichment must start with the lower poetic forms and proceed to the higher ones. In Virgilian fashion, then, Cervantes is telling his reader that eclogue is but an apprenticeship for the higher forms – mainly the epic. Eclogue is typified by its low style and subject matter (the concerns of shepherds), while epic sings in high style of the deeds of great warlike heroes and supports the ideals of empire. But eclogue or pastoral can hide the higher genres and ideals within it. For this reason, eclogues and georgics may seem audacious. Cervantes follows suit and says that in his publication of the *Galatea* he has given hints of his audaciousness. As in Virgil, audaciousness is found in the promise of future works which take on graver questions such as those of war and empire. In addition, Cervantes takes pastoral eclogue to the very edge, to the point where Mars begins to sing and Venus (or in this case the allegedly chaster Galatea) loses ground to the epic impetus.

The sixth and last book of *Galatea* includes both the most visible example of the classical style and the fusion of eclogue and epic. The funeral of a great shepherd-poet Meliso (representing the Renaissance courtier and poet Diego

Hurtado de Mendoza) takes place in a classical landscape that resembles the natural world of Garcilaso's eclogues. Cervantes' pantheistic description calls for a Platonic return to nature and evokes a harmonious universe. The Tagus river is compared to the Tiber, the Po, and the Sebeto, recalling Cervantes' trip to Italy and his appreciation of the natural beauty of the peninsula, an appreciation of nature that was very much a part of Renaissance sensibilities. But this imitation of nature is coupled with an imitation of Renaissance texts and paintings. Allusion to the Sebeto points to the literary description of this river in Jacopo Sannazaro's *Arcadia* (1501), an Italian romance of un-requited love written in prose and verse, and set in a pastoral environment.

There are also epic intrusions. The funeral rites described by Cervantes derive from Virgil's rites for Misenus in the sixth book of the *Aeneid*. It is no coincidence that the centerpiece of the funeral rites and of the last book of this pastoral is the appearance of Calliope to the shepherds. This Muse, cen-tral to Raphael's fresco of *Parnassus* in the Vatican, clearly identifies herself in Cervantes as the ruler of epic. She surrounds herself with ancient exponents of this genre: Homer, Virgil, and Ennius – three poets that are also present in Raphael's painting. In addition, Cervantes uses Raphael's *Triumph of Galatea* (Plate 1) to fashion the eponymous heroine of his pastoral romance. Both the painting and the pastoral partake of a Neoplatonic aesthetics, which discards Venus's lascivious voluptuousness in favor of Galatea's chastity. In both works, the nymph, although surrounded by eroticism, is able to stand apart from it, thus representing a New Humanism "which celebrated both a chaste love and the idea of an aesthetically inspiring redemptive concept of beauty... It was these specific qualities which invalidated the image of Venus, who had enjoyed her own vogue during the reign of courtly love, as an image of sensuality unsuitable for the new aesthetic ideals of the sixteen century."[15] But just as Cervantes' *Galatea* contains both pastoral and epic elements, it also represents a battle between two goddesses and two pictorial traditions. There are also in the work two partial ecphrases of Botticelli's *Primavera*, exhibiting Venus, goddess of desire.[16] From the very beginnings of his career, then, Cervantes constantly juxtaposes rival classical epics, Re-naissance paintings, and career-forming genres in order to exhibit the past and problematize its cultures and their relation to both the Renaissance and Cervantes' own times.

While up to this point, Cervantes' texts have given evidence of their mod-els, his next work, the 1605 *Don Quixote*, published twenty years after *Galatea*, begins with a prologue that seems to critique such imitation. Here, a friend advises the "author" on how to adorn his book and make it seem erudite. Actually, the prologue serves as commentary on *Don Quixote*, foregrounding the question of what constitutes true or appropriate uses of

Plate 1   Raphael, *Triumph of Galatea* (Palazzo della Farnesina, Rome)

learning. Two types of knowledge are exhibited, each leading to a very different disorder: Don Quixote's brings on madness while the friend's advice on
the uses of erudition denotes vanity and pretentiousness. Don Quixote knows
almost too much but is unable to transform the books of chivalry into a
social reality, while the "author's" friend knows so little that he boasts of
his erudition. This contrastive approach, so typical of Cervantes, lends an
ethical dimension to the uses of learning. Does erudite adornment serve
to create a fictional representation of an author as authoritative? Are the
writers of chivalric fiction guilty of poisoning Don Quixote's mind? Is Don
Quixote's madness contagious? Does it lead him to heroism or foolishness?
Don Quixote's learning, derived from the reading of literature, also foregrounds Plato's critique of the poet. Plato was concerned with the ability of

a text to convince in the face of its fictionality. Don Quixote is thus poisoned by literature since he is convinced of its reality. Cervantes' novel includes antidotes to this poison: it warns that the rapture of fiction can bring madness; and it uses numerous devices to "protect" the reader, to break the illusion.[17] Some of these devices are in themselves Platonic. The questioning of authority is typical of the method used by Socrates in Plato's dialogues; while notions of a double truth used by Neoplatonists underlines the importance of multiple perspectives.

This concern with the role of literature is certainly part of Cervantes' preoccupation with the development of his literary career. After all, an author must understand literature's role in his own society if he is to follow the Virgilian call to epic as a genre that reflects the myth and the realities of empire. The prologue to *Don Quixote* shows that Cervantes has not ignored the classicist position regarding literature. The author's friend states that the work aims to overthrow the ill-based fabric of the books of chivalry. Although this intention seems to simplify the many contexts of the work, it characterizes what many Renaissance humanists sought to accomplish. Indeed, some of these humanists would point to Heliodorus' *Aethiopica* as a prose epic, fostering imitation of this work in opposition to the romances. Cervantes' public would have to wait until 1617 to read his imitation of Heliodorus, his epic in prose, *The Trials of Persiles and Sigismunda*. After all, epic was meant to crown a poet's career, and the *Persiles* was Cervantes' last work.

Don Quixote may have been conceived as an apprenticeship in the epic genre. After all, Torquato Tasso, the author of a widely read epic, the *Gerusalemme liberata* (*Jerusalem Delivered*, 1581), and a neo-Aristotelian theorist, "was unorthodox enough to maintain that the classic epic could be revitalized only if it were to incorporate such features of the romances of chivalry as had made them so appealing to the modern audience – variety, marvelous subject matter and the relative contemporaneity in the events and customs they depict."[18] *Don Quixote* would include all three features, but would be guided by Tasso's new and cautionary interpretations. Tasso argues that excessive variety was known to lead to confusion, and that the use of the marvelous should be carefully restricted. Cervantes centers his episodes around Don Quixote's adventures so as to avoid confusion and locates the marvelous in the mad visions of the knight. Indeed, the novel includes a dialogue between the Canon of Toledo and the priest (I, 47–48) and later between the Canon and Don Quixote (I, 49–50) which in many ways reflects this tension between romance and the classicist view of poetry. Even though the Canon takes up the classicist view, he finds positive elements in the romances, particularly their imaginative freedom. *Don Quixote* is far from being the ideal novel envisioned by the Canon. This ideal may be reflected in the *Persiles and Sigismunda*. But while *Persiles* is less read today precisely for imitating too closely a particular model and mode of fiction, *Don Quixote* is forever the cause of new interpretations through its greater scope and inclusiveness. The protean nature of Cervantes' work is thus amply evinced in the parody of both romance and classicist positions.

Since Don Quixote, against the Canon, espouses the glory of romance, much of the action of the work is derived from it. Not only are Spanish romances of chivalry key to the text, but also Ariosto's *Orlando furioso*, a work to which Cervantes refers at least twenty times in *Don Quixote*.[19] Cervantes's novel, very much like Ariosto's poem, starts with the ancient romances, but attempts to transform them into something new. Mockery thus coexists with understanding. This contest between the old and the new Italian romance is clearly inscribed in Cervantes' text. For example, when the knight decides to do penance in the Sierra Morena, he wonders whether to imitate the melancholy penance portrayed in Montalvo's *Amadís de Gaula* (*Amadís of Gaul*, 1508) or the choleric madness found in *Orlando furioso*. In the end, Don Quixote decides to follow Amadís more closely. This decision says much as to Cervantes' imitation of his Italian model. It is an imitation that foregrounds radical differences. The serene self-confidence of Ariosto's characters contrast with Cervantes' blustery and unstable knight who draws his confidence from books. The Manchegan knight does not live in the magical and aristocratic world of Ariosto's romance, where the power of the upper nobility is reflected in the magic of the work. As a mere *hidalgo*, a nobleman of the lowest possible rank, Don Quixote lacks social and economic position. His separation from the aristocratic and courtly world is foregrounded by geography. While Ariosto's knights travel the world and even go to the Moon, Don Quixote searches for adventure in the dry and prosaic plains of La Mancha. His one celestial voyage is a hoax and Clavileño a purposely wooden imitation of Ariosto's hippogryph. As opposed to Ariosto's knights, Don Quixote is forever unable to fulfill his chivalric dreams, a situation that has been said to reflect the growing incapacities of the Spanish empire. It is his tenacity in the face of constant defeat and ridicule that slowly provides him with heroic stature and forever divorces him from Ariosto's romance.

Don Quixote's heroism, although based on defeat, can be related to the epic. While constantly imagining chivalric occurrences, the knight is often unaware that, in many cases, these have a basis in the epic tradition. But there are times when Don Quixote actually points to the epic. Readying himself to do penance at the Sierra Morena, the knight asserts that only the most perfect originals should be imitated. In addition to Orlando and Amadís,

Don Quixote points to two epic figures, Ulysses and Aeneas (1, 5). The knight's speech serves as foreshadowing for the debate between Don Quixote and the Canon of Toledo, thus compounding the perspectivism and ambiguity of the novel. For in the later debate, it is the Canon who invokes these and other figures to show how the ideal hero should combine the best qualities of the most exemplary heroes. The Canon's words derive from Tasso's discourses on poetry. Thus, Don Quixote's speech serves to problematize the debate between the proponents of romance and the neo-Aristotelians. Between the two are Tasso's discourses, which relax some of the more stringent Aristotelian strictures.

While the knight is content to do penance imitating Amadís and Orlando, his classicist opponents, the priest and the barber, look for ways to return him to sanity. This they try to do through the agency of Dorotea, who disguises herself as Princess Micomicona. Beyond the comical and grotesque onomastics of the disguise, the reader can detect in Dorotea's actions glimpses of Boiardo's Angelica as she appears at Charlemagne's court (an episode already borrowed by Cervantes for *The Abode of Jealousy*), and even of Ariosto's recollection of it. But what is particularly fitting here is that Dorotea is much more like Armida, the malefic enchantress of Tasso's *Gerusalemme*. Like Armida, who, in an attempt to distract a famous captain from the conquest of Jerusalem, prostrates herself in front of him and requests that he help her save her kingdom from a usurper, Dorotea kneels in front of Don Quixote and asks the same boon as Armida.[20] The knight is thus taken away from his romance pursuits through actions that imitate the more classical Tasso. This constant move from one genre to its opposite, from romance to Tasso's modern epic, and even to the epic, creates an instability that is fertile ground for the birth of a new genre, the novel.

Even though the novel's tone, techniques, and style seem to have little to do with the epic, Cervantes' conception of the work developed from discussions on how to write epic anew. A study on the ideology of figure in the epic includes Cervantes' masterpiece along with Homer's *Iliad*, Virgil's *Aeneid*, Milton's *Paradise Lost*, and Spenser's *The Fairie Queene*. It even labels *Don Quixote* as an epic in prose, while noting differences in narrative technique. Cervantes' narrator "uses no epic similes, avoids invocations...resists personifying the landscape or the settings of his poem; his principal figure, one might say, is Don Quixote himself, a walking (or riding) machine of figuration."[21] Beneath the chivalric surface, a deeper subtext can be perceived: "The parody of the novels of chivalry was in reality only a smoke screen intended to mask Cervantes' primary intention in *Don Quixote*, which was to imitate and improve upon Virgil's *Aeneid*."[22] *Don Quixote*'s playfulness is a way of approaching the unapproachable, of turning to epic without being engulfed in its monumentality. Revising and rethinking classical motifs, Cervantes is preparing himself for *Persiles and Sigismunda*. The irony, of course, is that in playing with the ancients, Cervantes can display his own sense of authority, his own originality, whereas in *Persiles y Sigismunda*, his desire to surpass Heliodorus derails the contradictions of desire.

Cervantes inscribes the need for creating this apprenticeship to epic in the pastoral episode of Marcela and Grisóstomo (I, 11–14). When Marcela fails to respond to Grisóstomo's passion and his verse, he lets himself die, and orders that his poetry be destroyed. But Vivaldo counters this desire using as an example Augustus Caesar's decree disallowing the clause in Virgil's will where he ordered that his *Aeneid* be burned. Some of Grisóstomo's poems are then rescued from the blaze. His poetic works consist of some sacred poems and plays written earlier in life and his amorous poems composed while disguised as shepherd, the act of disguise linking these poems with the Virgilian eclogue. These two Virgilian gestures, the writing of amorous poetry by shepherds and the order that his poetry be destroyed, alert us to the possibility of a literary career. It may be argued that, since Grisóstomo's life was cut short, the text may be challenging the notion of an ideal career. After all, how can a poet plan to fulfill his literary career when the length of life is uncertain? By writing an apprenticeship to epic, Cervantes shows the direction in which his career is leading, even if time does not allow him to complete his work. And, within the pastoral tale, he shows how Grisóstomo had also pointed to epic. When Grisóstomo's last poem is saved from the fire, as Virgil's *Aeneid* was saved by Varius and Augustus, the work turns out to be contaminated by epic, evincing Grisóstomo's slow but inexorable move from low to high style.

Grisóstomo's "Canción desesperada" focuses on the lament for a lost love. The poem is indeed a "denaturing complaint that serves principally to reinforce the idea of nature as a site of irreducible strife" (Cascardi, *Ideologies of History*, p. 232). But the complaint is recuperated into the civilizing functions of poetry through its epic models. The vision of the underworld in the poem rivals Aeneas' travels to Hades in the sixth book of the *Aeneid*, from where Cervantes had already borrowed the funeral rites for Grisóstomo. In a contrastive shift typical of Cervantes' style, the epic images of Grisóstomo's last poem also imitate Lucan's *Pharsalia,* a work that "counters" many of Virgil's ideals, structure, and style. In Lucan's sixth book, the witch Erichto, in order to perform a necromantic resurrection, screams at a dead body with sounds compared to the fiercest and deadliest animals. In Grisóstomo's "Canción desesperada" (Song of Despair) it is the poet-lover himself who uses these witching sounds in order to express the disharmony created in his heart by Marcela's alleged cruelty. Grisóstomo makes use of Lucan's necromancy in a metaphoric sense. First of all, Grisóstomo's poem contains a voice that will be heard after death – it represents his own lament emerging from the grave. He is revivifying not only his own voice, but also that of the ancient epic poets. He not only wishes to bring back to life Virgil's epic body, but he seeks to combine it with that of Lucan, Virgil's rival.

Don Quixote, then, serves as another step in the progression of Cervantes' literary career. The possibility of such a career is inscribed in the novel through the tale of Marcela and Grisóstomo. What is ironic, of course, is that this step led to modernity, to the novel or to what has been called a post-epic. In this type of literature "the concept of an archaic, heroic world as providing an immediate and undifferentiated groud of desire is shown to be self-limiting insofar as it relies on the naive conception of an 'original' context of desire and the possibility of establishing an unmediated relationship to the past" (Cascardi, *Ideologies of History*, p. 196). What must also be recognized is that *Don Quixote*'s roots can also be encountered in the counter-epic. This genre, foregrounded by Grisóstomo's poem, impinges upon Don Quixote's portrayal since the imitated *Pharsalia* became a model of "epics of the defeated" during the Renaissance.[23] Although Don Quixote's vision of a Golden Age refers back to the *Aeneid*, the failure of his quest points to the *Pharsalia*. Don Quixote, then, has a vision of a return to the past, a return not only to the mythical first age of humankind (which includes the Renaissance's recuperation of the myth), but also to the rule of Emperor Charles V, which was viewed as an imperial Golden Age akin to the Augustan epoch evoked by Virgil. Ariosto's *Orlando furioso* includes a prophecy of this perfect age with Charles V as ruler. But this imperial age where knights can show their valor, skewing modern inventions such as gunpowder, and where Spain's power is unrivaled, gives way in Cervantes' novel to the representation of defeat and impotence. This defeat goes hand in hand with repression. Inquisitional controls, evoked by the burning of Don Quixote's books, interfere with the knight's quest. It is a quest dominated by the vision of Dulcinea, a Petrarchan lady who some have seen as either inspirer of the imperial project or an embodiment of empire.[24]

The image of the perfect knight and emperor dashing to battle and defeating the enemy in the fashion of the romances of chivalry is portrayed by Titian in his *Charles V at Mühlberg* (Plate 2). This emperor, whose deformed jaw is transformed by Titian into a jaw of determination, is parodied by Cervantes in the figure of Don Quixote, who is first given the name of Quijada, which means jaw. The decorum and triumphal grandeur of Titian's painting are turned into the transgressive and comic-melancholic defeats of Cervantes' novel. Instead of upholding a utopian vision of empire, the novel presents

Plate 2   Titian, *Charles V at Mühlberg* (Museo del Prado, Madrid)

"a powerful antidote to the extensive and intellect-stifling utopianism in sixteenth-century Spain."[25]

It is out of the conflict between utopianism, imperialism, and inadequacy, and out of the debates on how to turn away from romance and construct a prose epic, that the tale of *Don Quixote* and the creation of the modern novel has its origin. But this creation arises out of parody. Here, the Italian Renaissance also provides its models. Teofilo Folengo's *Baldus* is a parody of humanistic learning that includes elements not only from the romances but also from both the modern epic and the *Aeneid*. It could well have served Cervantes as point of departure for his parodic apprenticeship in the writing of romance/epic.[26] And the Italian Renaissance could have provided still other comic models for Cervantes. The Italian comics Giovanni or Zan Ganassa and Stefanello Bottarga lent their names to the two opposing characters in a carnivalesque battle. While Ganassa's leanness made him an embodiment of Lent, Bottarga's corpulence and enjoyment of food and drink led him to become Carnival itself. These figures, which could well serve as sketches for Don Quixote and Sancho,[27] may have been part of Cervantes' experience during his trip to Italy.

Cervantes' next published work, the *Novelas ejemplares* (*Exemplary Novels*, 1613), contains several tales which celebrate Italy and describe journeys that biographers often equate with Cervantes' own Italian sojourn. Perhaps the most noted evocation of Italy derives from "El licenciado Vidriera" ("The Glass Graduate"), where a student from Salamanca travels to Italy, and describes its major cities, showing that both study and the experience of Italian culture are necessary elements in a well-rounded education. The very title of the collection evokes Italy, as the *novella* was an Italian form which Cervantes appropriates. The Italian *novelle* were short works of prose fiction included in a collection that usually tied them together through a frame narrative. Cervantes asserts that he is the first to write this type of fiction in Spain. As early as the *Galatea* Cervantes imitates Boccaccio (his third interpolated tale derives from the *Decameron* 10.9), but totally transforms his brief tales. In the *Exemplary Novels* Cervantes reworks the novella genre, making the tales less anecdotal, less concentrated on rapid action and denouement. Cervantes' title adds the adjective exemplary to the term *novela*, thus creating an oxymoron. The *novelle* of Boccaccio and his followers were often considered bawdy and licentious, mirroring a more permissive age and locale. As the Counter-Reformation becomes more and more constrictive in Spain, Cervantes chooses a title that incorporates both the openness of the past and the strict moral rules of the present. In his title, Cervantes also mirrors the reception of the *Decameron*. Boccaccio's work suffered severe censoring as several revised or "chastised" editions were published after the original was placed in the Inquisitional Index of 1559. These editions expurgated the bawdy and anti-clerical elements, while adding a moral tone to the work.[28] Cervantes' *Exemplary Novels* includes its own censoring mechanism derived from the revised Boccaccio, one that foregrounds exemplariness while at the same time provoking individual responses to difficult issues through extreme situations and perspectivism. Cervantes' mechanism also brings to the fore the question of censorship and the opposition between Renaissance and Counter-Reformation ideals. The use of a play of opposites in the title is not surprising. Cervantes in his works often inscribes opposite aesthetics and ethics (classicism vs. romance; imperial epic vs. counter-epic; Christianity vs. paganism; Galatea's chaste humanism vs. Venus' celebration of desire, etc.), calling forth the reader's participation and thus the active development of a personal viewpoint. Indeed, by imbuing a Renaissance genre with Counter-Reformation morals, Cervantes may have been tilting the title to the past, since "The interaction of contraries is one of the major issues of Renaissance thought," as exemplified in the writings of Castiglioni and Paracelsus.[29]

The presence of Italy can be most clearly detected in what critics have often called the "idealized" novellas. "La señora Cornelia" ("Lady Cornelia"), for example, deals with two Spaniards who visit Italy and decide to study at the University of Bologna. There, they are embroiled in an affair of love and honor in which both the Duke of Ferrara and the prominent Bentivoglio family of Bologna are involved. Two important issues are developed in the novella: education and the perceptions of Spaniards in Italy. In 1559, Philip II had decreed that Spaniards could not study at a university outside of Spain. This law, which was in place until the mid nineteenth century, served to isolate Spain from European currents of thought. The only exception to this law was the University of Bologna. By locating the action here, and showing the mutual admiration between the Spanish and the Italians, the novella broadens the desire for Italy to include the desire to learn at their many universities. By presenting an idealized portrait of two Spaniards in Italy, the novella also counters the negative view which Italians often had of the Spanish, who were seen as uncultured boasters and were ridiculed for their insistence on pompous dress, courtesy, gestures, and ceremony.[30] While the Spanish in the novella vindicate their country through ideal behavior, they also point to the separation of Spain from the rest of Europe. Although they are allowed to study in Bologna, they cannot take back with them the Italian wives whom they are promised. By stating that they must marry within their country, these students may be also saying that they must conform to Spanish ideals and not take home the ideals and values of Italy.

The desire for Italy can also be found in the most famous and perhaps the darkest of Cervantes' tales, "El celoso extremeño" ("The Jealous Man from Extremadura"). Its narrative economy and the sharp focus on the central action, which leads swiftly to climax and denouement, link it to Boccaccian narrative and its many descendants. The plot of the useless precaution also places the work in the tradition of the Italian novella. The complexity of the novella's oppositions – inside/outside, fate/free will, confinement/freedom – points in the direction of Erasmus, who believed in the gift of liberty, in the autonomous personality.[31] But this belief in the dignity of the human being is also central to the Italian Renaissance, and Pico della Mirandola, in his famous *Oration on the Dignity of Man*, argues that a human being is neither celestial nor terrestrial but may become mortal or immortal through the exercise of his free will. It is this gift of liberty which Cervantes emphasizes, one that may have roots in Erasmus, but also stems from the Italian Neoplatonists.

Two literary events of 1614 focused squarely on Cervantes' fame as writer. The first was the publication of his lengthy poem *Viaje del Parnaso* (*Voyage to Parnassus*), where he travels to Parnassus in search of Apollo's blessings. More than a satire on the glut of unskilled poets in his time, the work is an attempted revindication of Cervantes' literary career in the face of marginalization. This burlesque epic, which includes a witty description of Mercury's boat constructed of verse forms, a battle between good and bad poets, a portrayal of poetry, fame, and vainglory, and an encomiastic and ironic catalogue of close to 130 poets, contains numerous Renaissance motifs and models. Cervantes singles out for imitation Cesare Caporali's *Viaggio in Parnaso* (*Voyage to Parnassus*, 1582), an Italian poem by an author who, like Cervantes, had served the Acquaviva family. He had also emulated Teofilo Folengo's wit. Folengo is but one of the many models of a "multigeneric" text whose "kaleidoscopic heterogeneity" can only be comprehended if studied under the mode of satire.[32] The poem, then, points to Cervantes' learning, to his uses of Horace and Lucan, thus contradicting the description of himself as an uncultured poet. It attempts to evaluate his contributions, his fame, in a literary culture that seems to thrive in ignorance and mediocrity. Much of the satire is masked, using blame by praise and other techniques of concealment, methods Cervantes had already learned in his voyage to Italy, while viewing the censored frescoes by Michelangelo and reading a chastised Boccaccio. By clothing his satire in the garb of laudatory language and humble presence, he is able to create a devastating panorama of the Spanish Parnassus, one which questions his place in the literary canon. At the same time, the poem inscribes again a desire for Italy, as Cervantes evokes the Gulf of Genoa, the Tiber, and the Bay of Naples. In a dream, the Spanish poet joins the court of the Count of Lemos in Naples, only to wake up back in Madrid.

The second event of 1614 which impinged upon the literary fame of Cervantes was the publication of a work by Avellaneda that continued the adventures of Don Quixote. Although Part 1 had ended with a verse by Ariosto which called for another poet to continue the adventures of Angelica, Cervantes was stung by Avellaneda's lack of respect for his model. Thus, Cervantes publishes his own second part in 1615. Having imitated Ariosto in the 1605 *Quixote*, Cervantes knew very well that "the *Orlando furioso* was itself a continuation of Boiardo's *Orlando innamorato*, and that Ariosto had decidedly overgone his predecessor poet."[33] Anxious to derail the authority of Avellaneda's continuation, Cervantes changes the plan of the novel, including a refusal on the part of Don Quixote to go to Zaragoza. Cervantes thus recognizes the complex nature of originality: "The originality of the

Renaissance artist was thus to be measured not only against the past but also the future…The authentic originality of the *Quixote* lies not merely in its invention but in its *inimitability*, and that can only emerge from the test of history, from a perspective unavailable to its author" (Quint, *Origin and Originality*, p. 4). One way to ensure this inimitability is by making the predecessor indispensable. Thus, Cervantes, in Part II, replaces the focus on the romances of chivalry with a focus on Part I of his own novel. His fictional hero now knows of his real-life fame. Furthermore, in order to give a melancholic grandeur to his comic character, Cervantes no longer has Don Quixote envision a chivalric reality drawn from his imagination. Instead, his fictions are now the domain of the public, as many (fictional) characters are said to have enjoyed reading *Don Quixote* and now seek to ridicule the knight, creating illusions for him.

This new focus not only reflects Cervantes' concern with (in)imitability, but also his continued use of the epic tradition. The scene in the *Aeneid* "where Aeneas comes upon a series of paintings in the temple of Juno at Carthage which represent episodes in the Trojan war," provides Cervantes with "the ingenious idea of making the 1605 *Don Quixote* an important literary element in the 1615 novel – as in the case of Odysseus and Aeneas, Don Quixote's fame will precede him, causing the characters to compare the 'real' Don Quixote with his literary representation" (McGaha, "Cervantes and Virgil," p. 38). There is even a parodic imitation of the scene from the *Aeneid* in *Don Quixote* (II, 71), where the knight comes upon some crude leather hangings depicting the abduction of Helen and the story of Dido at an inn. Virgil's paintings on the Trojan war were a challenge to Homer's depiction of the siege. Cervantes' novel includes a Homeric and a Virgilian painting to represent the novel's rustic and comic continuation of the epic. In this second part, Don Quixote has awakened to his epic role, boasting that if he had lived in ancient times, Troy would not have been burned nor Carthage destroyed. But his new illusions are balanced by his more frequent inability to envision chivalric illusions.

One of the very first adventures in the novel, and the one that will control the action of Part II, has to do with Don Quixote's inability to imagine the fictional creations handed to him by others. When Sancho Panza points to three peasant women riding donkeys and tells Don Quixote that he is in the presence of Dulcinea and her ladies, the knight can only see the reality of the scene. The shock of seeing his princess as a peasant who speaks in an earthy manner could have had drastic consequences. Instead, the knight "finds a solution which prevents him both from falling into despair and from recovering his sanity: Dulcinea is enchanted."[34] The drive to disenchant Dulcinea will then become the main motivation of Part II. This key episode is very

Plate 3   Sandro Botticelli, *La Primavera* (Uffizi, Florence)

carefully crafted. It includes a speech by Don Quixote that shows his mastery of rhetoric, of the elevated style and all its devices. More importantly, this scene where Don Quixote cannot see the beauty and enchantment of the picture drawn to him by Sancho is in all its major details an ecphrasis of one of the most mysterious and enchanting paintings of the Renaissance, Botticelli's *Primavera* (Plate 3). In this double vision where narrative recalls and redraws a painting upon a rustic landscape, Sancho appears as Mercury the messenger, Dulcinea as Primavera/Venus herself, the three peasant women as the three Graces, the west wind as Zephyr seeking Chloris, and the flowers of springtime as Flora.[35]

Since this second part will slowly turn away from enchantment, it recalls the enchantments of Italy only to move toward a desire for Counter-Reformation purification. It has been argued that the 1615 *Quixote* is a salvation epic where Don Quixote and Sancho are purified in a purgatory of this world. Its most anguished section is found in the knight and squire's visit to the Duke and the Duchess. As opposed to Ariosto, who provides a delightful courtly ambience which shines with the illusion of power, Cervantes' second part darkens the atmosphere. His text shows an almost shocking degree of "out-and-out cruelty" while the knight and the squire "are subjected to the entourage of the Duke and Duchess."[36] For these are the punishments they receive in this purgatory that begins with the episode of the Cave of Montesinos. Although the cave represents a journey to the underworld in the classical and Virgilian sense, it is also the entrance to purgatory. For his conception of this place, Cervantes had to turn to a very different Renaissance model, Dante's *Purgatorio* (Sullivan, *Grotesque Purgatory*, p. 103).

The final transformation of Don Quixote into Alonso Quijano the Good is not only a reflection of Counter-Reformation emphasis on purgatorial purification. It also evokes classical models, thus continuing, albeit in a more muted manner, the Renaissance's impetus to imitate the classics. Both Aeneas' and Don Quixote's descent into the underworld serve to purify and transform these figures. While Aeneas enhances his piety through his encounter with his father in the underworld, Don Quixote abandons chivalry for Christian goodness (McGaha, "Cervantes and Virgil," p. 36). An even more dramatic example of transformation in antiquity is found in the character of Lucius in Apuleius' *The Golden Ass*. This ancient romance contributed to the structure and motifs of Part I of Cervantes' novel and particularly to the composition and interpolation of "El curioso impertinente" ("The Tale of Foolish Curiosity").[37] Key to Part II of Cervantes' novel is the trajectory of Apuleius' protagonist. Lucius, who is transformed into an ass owing to his excessive curiosity (his desire to learn the secrets of witchcraft), goes through many comic adventures until a vision of the Egyptian deity Isis leads him back to human form, at which time he chooses to become a priest of the goddess. Don Quixote, who is transformed into a knight because of his excessive reading and curiosity concerning chivalry, regains his sanity at the end of Part II, paralleling Lucius' transformation. Indeed, the fact that Sansón Carrasco, disguised as the Knight of Mirrors and the Knight of the Moon, is the one who defeats him, points to the importance of lunar imagery in the text, which in turn reflects the main attribute of Isis as moon goddess. Since Apuleius' text was thought to reflect the wisdom of Hermes Trismegistus, it may be useful to study *Don Quixote* in terms of the hermetic tradition so valued by Florentine Neoplatonists.

While *Don Quixote* moves from madness to Christian conversion, Cervantes' last work, the posthumously published *Persiles and Sigismunda*, moves from the demonic locales of the northern adventures to Rome, the culmination of a pilgrimage which brings together in marriage the two main characters. Cervantes had high hopes for this prose epic, the culmination of his literary career, written in imitation of Heliodorus' *Aethiopica*. Many of the concerns found in *Don Quixote* are revisited here such as Apuleius' myths,[38] neo-Aristotelian principles, and Tasso's revisionist poetics. But it is the relentless movement south that attracts the reader – the closer to Italy, the sharper and more alluring the narrative becomes. The final book of the *Persiles* contains a vision of Rome, which, although praising ancient and Renaissance achievements, foregrounds Christian motifs. The great works of the ancients and of the Renaissance, such as paintings by Polignotus, Raphael, and Michelangelo, located in Hipólita's *loggia*, are associated with demonic, non-Christian forces and with a false paradise (Forcione, *Cervantes' Christian Romance*, p. 102). In contrast, the Church of St. Paul casts its providential shadow across the ending, serving as background for the marriage of Persiles and Sigismunda. Although this is one of the seven principal churches of Rome, the fact that the ending takes place here rather than at St. Peter's may point to a "conciliatory attitude toward Protestantism," and may show that "the impact of Erasmus on Cervantes' religious development survives in his final and most orthodox work" (Forcione, *Cervantes' Christian Romance*, p. 103). Thus, even at the very end of his life and works, Cervantes continues to experiment with perspectivism and the double truth. While apparently praising the Counter-Reformation church, the text turns away from the power of the papacy (St. Peter's) to foreground the more personal Christianity espoused by Paul. The church of St. Paul, which featured traditional pictorial cycles from the lives of St. Peter and St. Paul, triggered Raphael to compose tapestries on the subject which were placed under Michelangelo's frescoes in the Sistine Chapel. Although the subject matter is Christian, it is now re-thought and represented in the light of the ancients. Like Raphael's tapestries, Cervantes' last novel often represents the Christian in light of the ancients, and mediated by his desire for Renaissance Italy.

The brilliance of the past sheds light on Counter-Reformation control in Cervantes' texts. At times, when this desire for Renaissance Italy is subjected to agonic defeats and Socratic questioning, it reveals its fragmented models, its unattainability. Otherwise, Italy seems a *locus* for imitation and originality, bawdiness and Neoplatonic rapture, clerical excesses and reform, hermeticism and carnival, a place where the ruins of the ancients called forth the need for a new civilization that would exalt the dignity of man, the desire for fame, the glories of nature, the divinity of painting and poetry, and the enchantments of the ancient gods.

NOTES

1 Charles L. Stinger, *The Renaissance in Rome* (Bloomington: Indiana University Press), 1985, p. 2.
2 George L. Hersey, *High Renaissance Art in St. Peter's and the Vatican* (Chicago: University of Chicago Press, 1993), p. 25.
3 Juan Bautista Avalle-Arce, "Cervantes and the Renaissance," in Michael D. McGaha, ed., *Cervantes and the Renaissance* (Newark, DE: Juan de la Cuesta, 1980), p. 5.
4 Edward Said, "Presidential Address 1999: Humanism and Heroism," *PMLA* 115 (2000): 285.

5 Frederick A. De Armas, *Cervantes, Raphael and the Classics* (Cambridge: Cambridge University Press, 1998), pp. 18–19.

6 Anthony Cascardi, *Ideologies of History in the Spanish Golden Age* (University Park: Pennsylvania State University Press, 1997), pp. 198, 201.

7 Nicholas Mann, "The Origins of Humanism," in Jill Kraye, ed., *The Cambridge Companion to Renaissance Humanism* (Cambridge: Cambridge University Press, 1996), p. 13.

8 Anthony Close, *The Romantic Approach to "Don Quixote"* (Cambridge: Cambridge University Press, 1978), p. 204. See also Américo Castro, *El pensamiento de Cervantes* (Madrid: Noguer, 1972), p. 55.

9 Edward H. Friedman, *The Unifying Concept: Approaches to the Structure of Cervantes' Comedias* (York, SC: Spanish Literature Publications, 1981), p. 127.

10 Michael D. Reeve, "Classical Scholarship," in Kraye, ed., *The Cambridge Companion to Renaissance Humanism*, p. 20.

11 "I am he who once tuned my song on a slender reed, then, leaving the woodland, constrained the neighbouring fields to serve the husbandmen, however grasping – a work welcome to farmers: but now of Mars bristling." Virgil, *Eclogues, Georgics, Aeneid*, trans. H. R. Fairclough (Cambridge, MA: Harvard University Press, 1978), vol. I, p. 241.

12 For a discussion of different career patterns from the classical to the early modern periods see Patrick Cheney and Frederick A. de Armas, eds., *European Literary Careers: The Author from Antiquity to the Renaissance* (Toronto: University of Toronto Press, 2002).

13 Elias L. Rivers, "Cervantes and the Question of Language," in McGaha, ed., *Cervantes and the Renaissance*, p. 25.

14 Juan Bautista Avalle-Arce, *La novela pastoril española* (Madrid: Istmo, 1974), pp. 240–41.

15 Edward Dudley, "Goddess on the Edge: The Galatea Agenda in Raphael, Garcilaso and Cervantes," *Calíope* 1 (1995): 32.

16 George Camamis, "The Concept of Venus-*Humanitas* in Cervantes and Botticelli," *Cervantes* 8 (1988): 182–223.

17 B. W. Ife, *Reading and Fiction in Golden-Age Spain: A Platonist Critique and Some Picaresque Replies* (Cambridge: Cambridge University Press, 1985), p. 84.

18 Alban K. Forcione, *Cervantes' Christian Romance: A Study of "Persiles y Sigismunda"* (Princeton: Princeton University Press, 1972), p. 7.

19 Thomas R. Hart, *Cervantes and Ariosto. Renewing Fiction* (Princeton: Princeton University Press, 1989), p. 3.

20 Pedro Ruiz Pérez, "La hipóstasis de Armida: Dorotea y Micomicona," *Cervantes* 15 (1995): 147–63.

21 Susanne Lidgren Wofford, *The Choice of Achilles: The Ideology of Figure in the Epic* (Stanford: Stanford University Press, 1992), p. 398.

22 Michael McGaha, "Cervantes and Virgil," in McGaha, ed., *Cervantes and the Renaissance*, p. 34. See also Arturo Marasso, *Cervantes: La invención del "Quijote"* (Buenos Aires: Hachette, 1954).

23 David Quint, *Epic and Empire* (Princeton: Princeton University Press, 1993), pp. 131ff.

24 Lisa Rabin, "The Reluctant Companion of Empire: Petrarch and Dulcinea in *Don Quijote de la Mancha*," *Cervantes* 14 (1994): 84.

25 José Antonio Maravall, *Utopia and Counterutopia in the "Quixote"*, trans. Robert W. Felkel (Detroit: Wayne State University Press, 1991), pp. 17–18.

26 Francisco Márquez-Villanueva, *Fuentes literarias cervantinas* (Madrid: Gredos, 1973), pp. 258–358.

27 Agustin Redondo, *Otra manera de leer el "Quijote"* (Madrid: Castalia, 1998), pp. 209–13.

28 Victor F. Dixon, "Lope de Vega no conocía el *Decameron* de Boccaccio," in J. M. Ruano de la Haza, ed., *El mundo del teatro español en su Siglo de Oro. Ensayos dedicados a John E. Varey* (Ottawa: Dovehouse Editions, 1989), pp. 185–96.

29 Robert Grudin, *Mighty Opposites: Shakespeare and Renaissance Contrariety* (Berkeley: University of California Press, 1979), p. 14.

30 Joseph V. Ricapito, *Cervantes's "Novelas Ejemplares": Between History and Creativity* (West Lafayette, IN: Purdue University Press, 1996), pp. 126–27.

31 Alban K. Forcione, *Cervantes and the Humanist Vision* (Princeton: Princeton University Press, 1982).

32 Ellen D. Lokos, *The Solitary Journey: Cervantes' "Voyage to Parnassus"*, Studies on Cervantes and His Times, vol. I (New York: Peter Lang, 1991), p. 59.

33 David Quint, *Origin and Originality in Renaissance Literature* (New Haven and London: Yale University Press, 1983), p. 4.

34 Erich Auerbach, *Mimesis: The Representation of Reality in Western Literature*, trans. Willard R. Trask (Princeton: Princeton University Press, 1953), p. 340.

35 Frederick A. de Armas, "The Eloquence of Mercury and the Enchantments of Venus: *Humanitas* in Cervantes' *Don Quixote*, II. 10," *Laberinto: An Electronic Journal of Early Modern Hispanic Literatures* 2 (1998): n.p.; reprinted in William S. Haney, ed., *Humanism and the Humanities in the 21st Century* (Lewisburg: Bucknell University Press, 2001), pp. 118–36.

36 Henry W. Sullivan, *Grotesque Purgatory: A Study of Cervantes's "Don Quixote,"* Part II (University Park: Pennsylvania State University Press, 1996), p. 1.

37 A. Scobie, "*El curioso impertinente* and Apuleius," *Romanische Forschungen* 88 (1976): 75–76; Frederick A. de Armas, "Interpolation and Invisibility: From Herodotus to *Don Quixote*," *Journal of the Fantastic in the Arts* 4 (1992): 8–28.

38 Diana de Armas Wilson, "Homage to Apuleius: Cervantes' Avenging Psyche," in James Tatum, ed., *The Search for the Ancient Novel* (Baltimore and London: The Johns Hopkins University Press, 1994, pp. 88–100).

FURTHER READING

Cascardi, Anthony J. *Ideologies of History in the Spanish Golden Age.* University Park: Pennsylvania State University Press, 1998.

Castro, Américo. *El pensamiento de Cervantes.* Ed. Julio Rodríguez-Puértolas. Barcelona: Noguer, 1972.

Cheney, Patrick and Frederick A. De Armas. *Western Literary Careers. Ancient, Medieval, Renaissance.* Toronto: Toronto University Press. In press.

Close, Anthony. *The Romantic Approach to "Don Quixote."* Cambridge: Cambridge University Press, 1977.

De Armas, Frederick A. *Cervantes, Raphael and the Classics.* Cambridge: Cambridge University Press, 1998.

Dudley, Edward. "Goddess on the Edge: The Galatea Agenda in Raphael, Garcilaso and Cervantes." *Calíope* 1 (1995): 27–45.

Forcione, Alban K. *Cervantes, Aristotle and the "Persiles"*. Princeton: Princeton University Press, 1970.

Cervantes and the Humanist Vision. Princeton: Princeton University Press, 1982.

Hart, Thomas R. *Cervantes and Ariosto: Renewing Fiction*. Princeton: Princeton University Press, 1989.

Higuera, Henry. *Eros and Empire. Politics and Christianity in "Don Quixote"*. Lanham, MD and London: Rowman & Littlefield, 1995.

Maravall, José Antonio. *Utopia and Counterutopia in the "Quixote"*. Trans. Robert W. Felkel. Detroit: Wayne State University Press, 1991.

McGaha, Michael D., ed. *Cervantes and the Renaissance*. Newark, DE: Juan de la Cuesta, 1980. pp. 1–10.

Rabin, Lisa. "The Reluctant Companion of Empire: Petrarch and Dulcinea in *Don Quijote de la Mancha*." *Cervantes* 14 (1994): 81–92.

4

ANTHONY J. CASCARDI

Don Quixote and the invention of the novel

When seen from the perspective of *Don Quixote*, the origins of the novel can appear unfathomable. Looking backwards from where we stand, it can seem as if *Don Quixote* always existed, or as if *Don Quixote* somehow had to exist. Such has been the force of its impact on literary history. Before *Don Quixote*, we can identify a variety of fictional genres, not without interest in themselves, but of relatively minor importance when compared with what the *Quixote* spawned. In the European tradition these forms include the chivalric romances such as *Amadís of Gaul*, to which Cervantes makes direct and repeated references, as well as fictional autobiographies of rogues such as the *Lazarillo de Tormes*, pastoral tales like *La Diana* of Jorge de Montemayor and *L'Arcadia* of Jacopo Sannazaro, and a number of Italian Renaissance epics, of which Ludovico Ariosto's *Orlando furioso* is arguably the most important. In the still more distant literary past stand the archaic adventure romances, such as Heliodorus' *Ethiopian History* and the anonymous *Apollonius of Tyre* and, before these, the towering tradition of ancient epics written in verse. Some of these pre-novelistic genres were strong enough to exert a continuing pressure on literary history in spite of the novel's rise to a position of near complete dominance; as for others, the novel became their unforeseeable and incongruous continuation. But no matter which way the picture is turned the *Quixote* remains a watershed work in the history of literature. Before it, things seem relatively remote; after it, we are in a far more familiar universe. During the four centuries since the publication of *Don Quixote* there has been no doubt that to write a major work of fiction was to write a novel. And while Cervantes could not possibly have known that in writing *Don Quixote* he was about to initiate the most important literary genre of the modern age, it can retrospectively be said that, among novels, *Don Quixote* was the first.

How did this happen? What sort of literary transformation did *Don Quixote* bring about, and what, toward the beginning of the seventeenth century, were the various prose forms that the *Quixote* seemed to displace?

These questions are particularly challenging when considered in light of the peculiar nature of the novel as a genre. Indeed, one has only to recall Henry James's description of the novel as a "loose, baggy monster" to realize that what Cervantes invented was something without any fixed form. James was hinting at the novel's ability to incorporate a seemingly limitless number of components and to assume an unpredictable variety of shapes. Think of the differences between Dostoevsky's *Crime and Punishment* and Virginia Woolf's *To The Lighthouse*, or between Stendhal's *The Red and the Black* and Gabriel García Márquez's *One Hundred Years of Solitude*. All of these clearly count as novels, but they are novels of very different, even incompatible sorts. If one looks to find a "family resemblance" among them, one is bound to be disappointed, for the family they comprise is simply too varied and inconsistent to be reduced to any single "look." The novel is a polymorphous genre, with a capaciousness that seems to have been built in from the very start. The German Romantics speculated that it was a form of writing in which different discourses were hybridized or mixed.[1] But what the Romantics saw as a property of the novel's form was in fact a principle of its composition: the "invention" of the novel resulted from the re-fashioning of literary genres already in place, and *Don Quixote* stands in relation to the origins of the novel not as the invention of something radically new, but as the uncovering of new possibilities for the combination of elements that preexisted it. On the threshold of the modern age, what Cervantes "discovered" was that new forms originate from the transformation of the old ones. It is this kind of discovery about the nature of literary invention, which philosopher-critic Mikhail Bakhtin linked to the process of "novelization," that best explains Cervantes' role in the formation of the novel.[2]

In the rest of this chapter I shall have something more to say about the preexisting genres that the *Quixote* incorporated, eclipsed, and transformed. And I shall likewise say more about some competing views of the novel's invention: for example, that it is a continuation of the tradition of epic literature in a post-heroic age, that it begins with the realistic rendering in prose of "ordinary life," and that it grows out of an interest in legitimizing the "fictions" of romance in the face of the truth-claims of history writing. But I take my bearings by Bakhtin's ideas about the "novelization" of preexisting discourses because those ideas can in fact encompass the others just proposed, transforming their perspectives in a way that allows us to link an understanding of the novel's origins to equally powerful views about *Don Quixote*'s influence over the history of a genre. Some important questions of detail, such as the differences between the first and second parts of *Don Quixote* (1605, 1615), can likewise be addressed within this framework.

Bakhtin's view was that the novel was fashioned from a diversity of "social speech types," sometimes from a variety of national languages, and always from a plurality of voices. The result was a genre "multiform in style and variform in speech and voice."[3] Without naming Cervantes in this particular instance, but having the example of Cervantes nonetheless prominently in mind, Bakhtin helps explain important facts about the way in which *Don Quixote* was shaped. His view of the novel as formed from many different discourses suggests how, for example, Cervantes brings the peasant speech of Sancho Panza into contact with the language of educated men and women, such as the Canon of Toledo, the Knight of the Green Greatcoat, and the Duke and Duchess; or the way in which Cervantes sets verses from popular ballads side-by-side with narrative vignettes drawn from pastoral novels and the chivalresque romances. The narrator of *Don Quixote* often speaks in the "plain" style we have come to associate with literary prose. The famous opening phrase of Part I, chapter I, is an example of literary language moving in the direction of ordinary speech: "En un lugar de la Mancha, de cuyo nombre no quiero acordarme . . . " ("In a town of La Mancha, whose name I do not care to recall . . . "). But in *Don Quixote* even so-called "plain" speech is resonant with literary associations. In the case of this opening phrase, the apparent "ordinariness" of Cervantes' prose masks a perfect octosyllable Spanish verse that echoes the cadences of the popular ballads of the time. And, indeed, we know that there was a theatrical farce based on the ballads (the *Entremés de los romances* [*Farce of the Ballads*]) that Cervantes may well have had in mind when setting out to write *Don Quixote*.[4] The farce centers on the mishaps of a character, Bartolo, who goes mad from reading the ballads, just as Alonso Quijano loses his wits from reading the books of chivalry. But, getting back to the language of Cervantes' text, this prose may just as well veer away from popular speech toward the "lofty" style that was associated with classical literature. This is especially the case with the most conventional poetic topics, such as Don Quixote's daydream-like description of the dawn in I, 2 ("scarcely had the rubicund Apollo brushed the strands of his lovely golden locks across the face of the broad and spacious earth, no sooner had the tiny, speckled fledgling birds begun to greet the breaking of roseate dawn with the gracious, mellifluous harmony of their sweet-toned tongues – what dawn which, slipping from her heavenly husband's soft couch, began to show herself through mortal gates and balconies, at the edge of La Mancha's horizon – when that notable knight, Don Quixote de la Mancha, rising from the inactivity of his feathered mattress, mounted himself on his famous steed, Rocinante, and began to ride across the fabled ancient fields of Montiel"), or his more rhetorical portrait of successful academics, "perched on a throne, their hunger transformed into satiety, their cold turned into comfort, their nakedness become splendid clothing, and the straw mats on which they once slept transmuted into sheets of fine Dutch linen and silk, all of which is the fair and proper size won by their virtue" (1, 37). The diction in passages like these is serious enough to sound convincing, yet incongruous enough to be funny. Don Quixote's nearly rhapsodic account of what he takes to be the beauties of Maritornes, a vulgar Asturian woman whom he encounters by mistake at the inn in Part 1, is drawn directly from Renaissance love poetry written in the style of Petrarch, subsequently filtered through the books of chivalry. The style is high but the matter is low, and the loftiness of the diction is undermined by the ridiculousness of the encounter:

> The hour arrived . . . when the Asturiana had agreed to make her visit, and so, barefoot, wearing only her chemise, her hair tied up in a cotton net, walking softly and carefully, she entered the chamber where the three men were lodged, seeking the muledriver. But she'd barely gotten through the doorway when Don Quixote became aware of her presence and, sitting up in bed, in spite of all his mustard plasters and the pain in his ribs, stretched out his arms to welcome the beauteous maiden. Walking furtively and half bent over, groping with her hands in front of her, the Asturiana bumped into his arms, and Don Quixote clasped her by the wrist and drew her toward him and, while she did not dare utter a word, made her sit on the bed. Then he felt her chemise and, though it was burlap, to him it seemed the finest and most delicate silk. She wore glass beads on her wrists, but they made him see visions of precious oriental pearls. Her hair, though it was more like a horse's mane, to him was strands of the most magnificent Arabian gold, so radiant that they darkened the sun itself. And though her breath surely smelled of garlic and stale salad, he thought her mouth gave off a delicate, gracious fragrance. In a word, he painted her in his mind exactly like all the other princesses who, as he had read in his books, would pay visits to badly wounded knights, princesses overcome by love, wearing all the prescribed adornments. And the poor gentleman was so far gone in his fantasy that neither the touch, the smell, nor anything else about the good damsel – which would have made anyone but a muledriver vomit – disillusioned him in the slightest. Indeed, it seemed to him that he was holding in his arms the very goddess of beauty. And so, clasping her tightly, he began to speak in soft, amorous tones:
>
> "Would that I were able, oh lovely and exalted lady, to repay the immense favor you have granted me, by the very sight of your great beauty, but Fortune, which never wearies of persecuting good men, has chosen to place me in this bed, in which I lie so weary and feeble that, no matter how my wishes might long to correspond with yours, it would be impossible. And what makes this impossibility still more impossible, I have pledged my faith to the incomparable Dulcinea del Toboso, the rare and singular lady who occupies my most hidden thoughts." (1, 16, pp. 89–90)

These examples give some sense of how sensitive Cervantes was to the enormous diversity of speech-types surrounding him, both in literature and on the street. But, whatever the level of the tone or the voice, and whatever the literary resonances, Cervantes was attuned to the ways in which all forms of speech were marked by their social, historical, and cultural worlds. And he was particularly alert to the fact that literature served both to transmit and to challenge those codes. As the first novel, *Don Quixote* undertakes a massive effort in the re-coding of inherited literary forms.

As for what Bakhtin meant by the specifically *social* dimension of those literary codes, the *Quixote* obliges us to construe "social" in the broadest possible sense, so as to include all the markings of gender, ethnicity, national language, religion, and regional politics, as well as education and class. In addition to the "discourses" of the epic and ballad, the pastoral and the chivalresque, the Petrarchan love lyric, the fable, and the proverb, Cervantes echoes the "feminized" language that was prominent in the sentimental novels, the street slang of rogues and criminals, the pretentious language of university graduates, and the hybridized forms of speech that circulated among Christians and Moors in places like Algiers. The time that Cervantes himself spent in Italy and as a captive in Algiers no doubt raised his sensitivity to the polyglot nature of the social landscape. (Unfortunately, many of the linguistic nuances of the *Quixote* are lost in any translation; historical distance tends to cancel others; but many can be recaptured through critical reconstructions and through training of the literary ear.) But perhaps most important is to understand that all these different speech types enter into the world of the *Quixote* as *utterances*, i.e., as speech-acts, and not simply as so many "objects" which Cervantes attempted to portray. To say this much implies that each type of speech is taken on by an individual character, who in speaking makes an intervention within the larger landscape of discourse. The world of the *Quixote* is formed as if from sheaves of language. There are, moreover, conditions of possibility (and impossibility) for the articulation of each of the many discourses that Cervantes inherited. What can be said by a rogue in a picaresque adventure cannot be said by a heroine in a sentimental novel, except in the mode of parody or farce, nor can a proverb be uttered by the hero of a chivalresque romance, who would no doubt exhibit other kinds of virtue. These seemingly obvious facts reach beyond questions of plausibility and verisimilitude to touch on the way in which every social context enables some types of speech and disables others. There are conditions of education, gender, class, etc., that are binding for each of these literary genres and these in turn form the horizon of possibilities for the interactions of Cervantes' characters with the world. The characters in *Don Quixote* are drawn as if from other fictional worlds, and Cervantes' novel in turn re-organizes these many different ways of wording the world – quite often in the mode of parody or farce.

As a result of Cervantes' re-fashioning of discourses, the horizon of the language-world becomes considerably more open than before. And yet this openness stands in stark contrast to the realization that the repertoire of discursive forms is always inherited from the past. Indeed, the *Quixote* begins with a frank acknowledgment of the weight of the literary past, which the writer bears as a burden. Cervantes imagines the problem of literary invention as a struggle between authority and innovation. On the one side is the accumulated weight of the past, which lends authority to the task of authorship but which can easily lead to stagnation; on the other side is the desire for invention, which seems impossible to achieve except as an exertion against the authority of the past. Not surprisingly, the narrator in Cervantes' prologue does not know exactly how to introduce his novel, but Cervantes allows this ambivalence to lend creative resources to the process of literary invention:

> I would have preferred to give this book to the world just as it is, plain and simple, not decorating it with a prologue or endless list of all the sonnets, epigrams, and elegies we put in the front of books. Because, let me tell you, though writing the book was hard work, nothing was harder than this preface you're reading right now. I kept picking up my pen and putting it down, over and over, not knowing what I was supposed to write, and once, when I was sitting like that, just hanging fire, motionless, with the paper in front of me, a pen stuck behind my ear, my elbow on the desk, my hand on my cheek, wondering what I ought to say...

Just then, an imaginary "friend" enters the scene and advises the stalled author not to worry about authority and originality: in the absence of distinguished colleagues to write prefatory sonnets, and lacking epigrams and elegies, the author can simply pen them himself and attribute them as he wishes. The text can be adorned with learned citations stolen from reference books. The concluding wisdom of the prologue is that "the better you copy, the better your book."

What the prologue to Part I concludes in irony is nonetheless full of truth. Throughout the writing of *Don Quixote*, Cervantes engages the genres that preceded him through different kinds of "imitation." I place this term in quotes because "imitation" is a notion with an exceptionally diverse and difficult critical history. Its philosophical pedigree extends back at least to Plato, where it has to do with the validity of likenesses. Plato's concern in *Republic*, x, was that any likeness was bound to stand at some remove from the truth, which lies in the realm the ideas. The more distant the likeness from the truth, the more inferior the imitation. Cervantes was well aware of the Platonic critique of mimesis, but over the course of the Renaissance "imitation" came also to mean the emulation of models; the notion thus supported the ethics of exemplary conduct. In its Christian mode, the imitation of examples meant the imitation of Christ. In *Don Quixote* imitation has both a literary weight and an ethical charge. (One of Don Quixote's predecessors, St. Teresa of Avila, was both a reader of novels of chivalry and a self-conscious imitator of Christ.) Imitation is at once a guiding thread in Don Quixote's mock-heroic project to emulate the virtuous heroes of the books of chivalry, but it was also the literary means by which Cervantes sought to re-cast the language and conventions associated with the pre-novelistic discourses available to him. These two modes converge insofar as Don Quixote's imitation of examples proceeds by the imitation of literary texts. Don Quixote's references to the chivalric models are nearly all references to specific books: *Amadís of Gaul, Palmerín of England, Tirant the White,* etc. It is their examples that lend a semblance of legitimacy to Don Quixote's madcap project. As for Cervantes, his goal was not so much to reproduce the style or form of the books of chivalry as to allow them to be spoken again, but undercut by irony, and in a mock-heroic way. The same holds true for the genres of the pastoral and the picaresque, and for all of the others already mentioned. They are all transformed in the *Quixote* by their displacement in time and space and by their situation relative to other discourses undergoing a similar process of rearticulation.

Cervantes' engagement with the panoply of discourses that preexisted *Don Quixote* (including the discourses of Renaissance literary theory) was facilitated by his keen sensibility for something beyond the tone and cadences of different styles. One important feature of *Don Quixote* is the realization that literary discourses are thoroughly historical. Their origins lie in time and in space, but they change their meaning, their temper, and their relative weight as historical formations around them change. While discourses are contextually placed, they can also be displaced. And so Cervantes "invents" the novel by moving the discourses of pastoral, chivalric, picaresque, etc., from their original locations in culture and into the domain of self-conscious parody and pastiche. In the context of their new, novelistic location, each discourse provides a critical perspective on the others, but none asserts itself as privileged. *Don Quixote* establishes the discourse of the novel as a linguistic plurality that cannot be reduced to any single form. The convergence of different literary and linguistic forms, and the fashioning of new from old, creates the effect of a dazzling, dizzying literary complexity that criticism *about* the novel has always had a difficult time tracking. Some examples may nonetheless help.

The protagonists of "El curioso impertinente" ("The Tale of Foolish Curiosity") in Part I speak and act like characters from a Spanish honor play. Their jealousies and suspicions, their fears and betrayals, would be at home in the world of Cervantes' contemporary Lope de Vega or, later in the seventeenth century, Calderón de la Barca. But in Cervantes they are set within a world where the discourse of honor is placed beside that of chivalric parody. The language of mock-heroic chivalry in turn is angled against the glancing desires of shepherds drawn from the world of the pastoral, not to mention the shadows cast by rogues like Ginés de Pasamonte, and the allure of "exotic" characters like Zoraida drawn from the genre of tales with a Moorish setting and characters (the so-called "Moorish novel," *novela morisca*). There are as well numerous non-narrative genres, such as epistolary writing and the literature of political advice, that are placed alongside these narrative forms, as are distinctively oratorical modes of speech, such as Don Quixote's discourse on the mythical Golden Age (I, 11) or his speech, following the model of rhetorical exposition *in utramque partem* (on both sides of the question) concerning the relative merits of Arms and Letters (I, 37–38). One consequence of this incorporation of multiple speech genres by means of imitation is the erasure of any sense of linguistic or literary normativity. There is no norm of speech in the *Quixote*, and certainly none that does not already come loaded with some literary or historical charge. As for what is supposed to be the "plain language" of the townspeople of La Mancha, attentive readers of Cervantes' text will come to see that there is nothing plain in this novel at all, at least if by that one means to indicate some form of speech that does not openly display its social, historical, and literary ties. On the contrary: Cervantes is at pains to show that every form of speech carries some context with it, and that every context likewise enables certain modes of speech. The somewhat pretentious "Cousin" whom we meet at Basilio's house (II, 22) before Don Quixote descends into the Cave of Montesinos (II, 23) speaks in the idiom of the Renaissance humanists. Cervantes deeply admired some things about Renaissance Humanism, but his admiration was no obstacle to ridicule, and the Cousin's discourse is not without its risible side. The Cousin claims to be writing a learned supplement to an already-too-long book published in 1499 by the Italian historian Polydore Virgil, *On the Invention of Things*, which he has filled with various sorts of arcane knowledge, trivia, and useless information (such as who the first person was to catch a cold, or who was the first to use mercury ointment to treat syphilis). The son of the Knight of the Green Greatcoat is an educated young man who has ambitions to become a poet. Grisóstomo, the shepherd who has left behind a poem of despair after apparently taking his own life, was in fact a shepherd because the poet-lovers of pastoral

novels like Montemayor's *Diana* were cast as shepherds. He and his beloved
Marcela self-consciously imitate them. Meanwhile, some of the more theoretically sophisticated characters in the novel worry over the enforcement
of norms for prose that conform sometimes to the protocols of history and
sometimes to fiction. But Cervantes blurs the lines between history and fiction and turns the question of historical accuracy into something of a joke by
insinuating that the "original" narrator of the story, an Arab by the name of
Cide Hamete Benengeli, shares with all other Arabs one trait: unreliability.
The discourse of "history" thus opens itself up to the editorial comments of
a second narrator, the book's so-called "segundo autor" ("second author").
Though a fiction, the translating and editing of the "original" text suggest
the ways in which all the many discourses in this novel are not simply juxtaposed, but layered. They constantly shadow one another, and this shadowing
creates a text that seems unfathomably deep in terms of what it will yield to
the probings of an attentive eye and ear. Because of the way in which *Don
Quixote* is formed, it establishes the novel as a genre that is textually subtle
and intertextually rich.

If the novel is built from the re-articulation of genres already in existence,
then what can be said about the unity of the novel's style and the coherence
of its narrative voice? Because Cervantes works by re-fashioning literary discourses and the conventions associated with them rather than by creating
a radically new style, there has sometimes been doubt about how the novel
could claim a properly "artistic" status for itself. If the novel does count as
art, then what kind of art is it? Is it a new form of "high culture," to be
regarded as an adaptation of the epic to modern existence, or is it a form of
popular literature, in the line of adventure stories and amorous romances?
In his influential *Theory of the Novel*, Georg Lukács took *Don Quixote* to
be an instance of the former, i.e., a transformation of the epic quest under
conditions that reflect a profound sense of homelessness. He writes, "the
first great novel of world literature stands at the beginning of the time when
the Christian God began to forsake the world; when man became lonely
and could find meaning and substance only in his own soul, whose home
was nowhere; when the world, released from its paradoxical anchorage in a
beyond that is truly present, was abandoned to its immanent meaningless-
ness... Cervantes, the faithful Christian and naïvely loyal patriot, creatively
exposed the deepest essence of this demonic problematic: the purest heroism is bound to become grotesque, the strongest faith is bound to become
madness, when the ways leading to the transcendental home have become
impassible."[5] The development of romance as a genre may be regarded as a
moment in the progressive degeneration of the epic, and its popularity may

be taken as a symptom of the degree to which the condition that Lukács described as "homelessness" was beginning to take root. But it is equally important to think about Cervantes' role in re-shaping the relations between epic and romance, as between "high" and "low" cultural domains. Cervantes was charting new terrain in the production of a genre that did not correspond to existing literary norms. Indeed, Bakhtin reminds us that there was a time when novelistic discourse was regarded as a kind of writing for which there was no "poetics" whatsoever.[6] Whereas epic and tragedy could aspire to the status of true art, both because of their cultural and historical pedigree and because of their relationship to the various precepts that theorists had drawn from them (much in the way that Aristotle's *Poetics* took *Oedipus Rex* as a model for tragedy) the same could not always be said for the novel. The novel was a new genre, and no principles of composition or rules of style were prescribed for it. As for whether literary precepts could be *drawn from* it, this is precisely where the *Quixote* had a profound impact on what our conception of "literature" could be. In contrast to what one finds in the neoclassical cultures of early modern Europe (for example, France), the heterogeneity of genres and discourses that go to make up the novel simply defy prescription. Bakhtin hazards some reasons for this. He suggests that the novel reflects de-centralizing tendencies during a period dominated by centripetal movements: "At the time when major divisions of the poetic genres were developing under the influence of the unifying, centralizing, centripetal forces of verbal-ideological life, the novel – and those artistic-prosaic genres that gravitate toward it – was being historically shaped by the current of de-centralizing, centrifugal forces."[7] But there is more to the picture than this, principally because the "centripetal" tendencies of Cervantes' novel assert themselves against the centralizing forces of a particular culture, time, and place. The scrutiny of the books in Alonso Quijano's library would not be the same were it not for the fact that Spaniards had the disciplinary model of the Inquisition and the Index of Prohibited Books in their cultural consciousness. Likewise, there would be no parody of the language of the galley slaves and no writing of the story of Zoraida and the Captive were it not for the fact that Cervantes had spent time in captivity, was living at the point of the expulsion of the *moriscos*, and was faced with the presence of an absolutist and imperialist monarchy that stood in tense conflict with its racialized others.

As for the question of the rules of art, it would likewise be wrong to think that just because the *Quixote* is so heterogeneous Cervantes had no engagement with questions of aesthetics or with the philosophical issues raised by them. He was fully aware of Aristotle's pronouncements about the unity of plot, he was conscious of Horace's demand that literature be at once pleasing and beneficial, and he was deeply concerned about Plato's exclusion of poets from the *Republic* because of the allegedly inferior status of art. Cervantes was likewise steeped in Renaissance debates about the alleged illegitimacy of the marvelous elements of romance, the demands of verisimilitude, and the differences between history and poetry, all of which had been part of intense literary polemics in Italy before they entered Spain. But, as with everything else that finds its way into the world of the *Quixote*, these "theoretical" issues are not merely ideas debated in the abstract, or rules impinging on the novel from some oblique, external angle. Rather, theoretical ideas become active forms of speech. Literary theory is one of the many speech-types that was "novelized" by Cervantes. Aesthetic ideas become utterances because they are spoken by characters who – like the Canon of Toledo and the Priest – orient themselves toward the world according to ways of thinking familiar from contemporary literary debates. Moreover, the introduction of "theory" draws these characters into a web of discourse from which they do not always know how to extricate themselves. Consider what the Priest has to say about his own rather surprising authorial involvement with the romances:

> I myself . . . was once tempted to write a chivalric book, keeping in mind all the points I've been making, and, if I must confess the truth, I actually wrote more than a hundred large sheets of paper. And to see if it was what I wanted it to be, I showed these pages to men who are passionate readers of tales of knighthood, some of them learned and wise, and others ignorant folk who only care about the pleasure of hearing nonsense, and they all thought my book easily passed muster – but, in any case, I didn't go on with it, quite as much because I didn't want to occupy myself with matters so alien to my proper profession as because I realized that there are many more fools than wise men. (I, 48)

Here, as elsewhere in the novel, beginning with the very opening scene, the practice of reading leads to imitation, and imitation reveals itself to be wildly contagious. Especially in Part I, a concerted effort is made to keep the process of imitation within "proper" bounds, just as the Priest here attempts to purify the romances by writing them according to sound precepts. But imitation is hardly containable by any of the theoretical means used to defend against it. When the Priest and the Barber set out to bring Don Quixote home in Part I, for instance, they end up entangled in a web of imitation that replicates some of the very kinds of "madness" they are attempting to correct. The Barber tries to dress up as a wandering maiden, with the Priest as her squire, hoping to convince Don Quixote to come to her aid. They eventually persuade one of the characters at Juan Palomeque's inn, Dorotea, to take the Barber's place and dress up as a distressed princess (Micomicona) from a fanciful place (Micomicón), in order to lure Don Quixote back home. Strategies of costuming, disguise, and "imitations" of this sort continue in Part II of the novel, especially as Sansón Carrasco takes on the role of the Knight of the Moon and engages Don Quixote in a battle of equals.

But perhaps the most compelling feature of imitation as a means of literary invention in *Don Quixote* is that it allowed Cervantes to breed a self-conscious kind of originality into the novel at a time when the old models seemed to have grown stale, that is, when forms like the pastoral and the picaresque no longer held a firm grip on the popular imagination. Because that grip had loosened, Cervantes was free to range over an exceptionally wide field of literary forms in fashioning the *Quixote*.

What stands potentially in the way of this view is the stubborn idea that the *Quixote* is first and foremost a parody of the romances of chivalry. The implication of this view is that the novel is a form of literary realism born from a critique of the fantasies of romance. The suggestion is that the realism of a work like the *Quixote* represents a maturation within the history of fiction, and that in order to yield a form of prose with the depth of characterization and complexity of plot we find in Cervantes' work it was necessary to find ways to move meaningfully beyond the episodic shape of romance to a form that gives a wide berth to subjective agency and self-consciousness. According to this view, Cervantes' engagement with all the other forms mentioned above – the sentimental novel, the picaresque, adages and proverbs, the *novela morisca*, etc. – was tangential to his critique of the romances. In spite of the tendentiousness of this claim, which disparages romance at the expense of the novel and which discounts the viability of romance as a popular genre well after the novel's rise, there is a certain plausibility to the idea. After all, Cervantes closes Part II with the explicit claim that his sole purpose in writing the *Quixote* was to bring the ill-founded edifice of the romances of chivalry tumbling to the ground ("all I ever wanted was to make men loathe the concocted, wild-eyed stories told as tales of chivalry, nor can there be the slightest doubt that this truthful history of my Don Quixote has already begun to pull those books to the ground, just as surely as it will bring down every last one of them," II, 74).

There is no disputing the fact that the *Quixote* is at some level a critique of the romances. The process by which Don Quixote comes to fashion himself as a knight errant amounts to a comic imitation of some of the more familiar rituals of the chivalric romances: dedicating himself to a beloved who is claimed to be without peer (Dulcinea), assigning a heroic-sounding name to his horse (Rocinante), keeping vigil over his armor (with the aid of the innkeeper), enlisting a squire (Sancho Panza). Some of the most memorable adventures in Part I – such as the battle with the giants/windmills and the encounter with the maidens/prostitutes at the inn – are clear parodies of the romances. This engagement reflects the fact that, for a time, the romances of chivalry had succeeded in establishing a clear set of possibilities for what fictional discourse in prose could or should be: a concatenation of episodes, with good doses of fantasy and little regard for verisimilitude, organized around the adventures of a protagonist whose virtuous efforts were dedicated to the preservation of heroic ideals. No doubt these novels helped shore up Spanish imperial ideology. The world of the chivalric romances was built around binary oppositions, and its episodic plots characteristically masked a single ethical contest: that of absolute good against evil. While the absurdity of such sharply drawn distinctions is everywhere apparent in Don Quixote's estimation of the depravity of all his imagined enemies, Don Quixote's imitation of the knights-errant nonetheless plays upon the lingering attraction to heroic ideals at a time when the social class to which they had been entrusted was no longer able to sustain them as genuine possibilities for action in the world.

And yet, by the time the *Quixote* was written, the "fantasy" element in romance was no longer so clearly the bearer of heroic ideals. In fact, it had become a reminder of everything that was unachievable about them. The rise of Machiavellianism in political theory and the displacement of knighthood from the sphere of military action to that of courtly conduct played a significant role in this process. The *Quixote* was written at a time when fiction was attempting to grapple with what seemed to be the disappearance of heroism and virtue from the world. Don Quixote pointedly invokes the contrast between the two spheres of knighthood just mentioned, lamenting the decline that has taken chivalry out of the world of action and into the world of the court. This is taken as a clear indication of a much larger malaise:

> Our depraved age does not deserve that blessing, as former ages did, when knights errant shouldered and took on themselves the defense of kings, the protection of damsels, the succoring of orphans and wards of court, the punishment of the proud, and the rewarding of the humble. With most of our knights, today, it's the damasks, brocades, and other rich fabrics they wear that rustle as they go, rather than any coats of armor; knights no longer sleep out in the fields, open to all the rigors of the heavens, lying there, armed and armored head to foot; no longer do they try to snatch forty winks, as it's called, without pulling their feet out of the stirrups, but only leaning on their lances, as the knights of old used to do. (II, 1).

The historical background for the interest in chivalric romance in Spain was of course the centuries-long effort on the part of the Christians to regain the Iberian peninsula from Muslim control and, later, to halt the advance of Turkish forces in the Mediterranean. Cervantes himself had gained first-hand experience in the effort against the Turks, and was part of the combined Spanish, Venetian, and Papal forces that gained victory just outside the Gulf of Corinth at the celebrated battle of Lepanto in 1571. It was in this battle that Cervantes lost the use of his left hand, earning him the epithet "El Manco de Lepanto." Cervantes' stated literary aim was to defeat the heroic romances, and yet he refers to the battle of Lepanto in the prologue to the *Exemplary Novels* (1613) with great pride – excessive pride, perhaps; his language borders on hyperbole, and one is hard pressed to know whether Cervantes did indeed regard the battle of Lepanto as the momentous occasion that historians have often claimed it was. The event seems mixed in Cervantes' memory with the same combination of admiration and irony that he associates with the romances of chivalry themselves. A further context for Cervantes' interest in chivalric literature was the tendency to view the Spanish conquest of America through the lens of narrative romances. The deeds of empire in America followed the patterns of the chivalric dreams of adventure in part because literature had supplied the Conquistadores with models of how they might imagine "new worlds," how they should fashion themselves, and how they might ask the claims of virtue to embrace a project that also served imperial ideals.[8]

On the literary front, one of Cervantes' most immediate points of engagement for the parodic treatment of the romance form was Ariosto's *Orlando furioso*, a poem published in 1532 which draws on the Charlemagne legends. In part through Ariosto, but also through the Spanish ballads, the *Quixote* is laden with Carolingian literary material. In Ariosto's poem it is Charlemagne's nephew Orlando who goes mad when he discovers that his beloved Angelica has been sleeping with the enemy, a Moorish foot-soldier named Medoro. Upon discovering Angelica's infidelity, Orlando flees to a forest where he is consumed by rage. Although there is no issue of infidelity to drive Don Quixote mad (Sancho Panza reminds Don Quixote of this fact), this particular episode from Ariosto anticipates Don Quixote's wild antics in the Sierra Morena (I, 25–26). Here, the process of "novelization" works by means of direct literary allusion, including mention of "Roland, or Orlando, or Rotolando" (I, 25). The fact that Don Quixote's model is explicit draws this allusiveness within the ambit of the parodic "imitation" of exemplary literary and cultural predecessors. (In contrast, one might cite the tacit presence of Sophocles' *Ajax* in the episode [I, 18] where Don Quixote takes a flock of sheep to be an advancing enemy army.)

But it is no accident that the figure to whom Cervantes entrusts the comic re-enactment of heroic ideals is drawn from the minor Spanish nobility, that he is a member of the landed class whose work no longer has a vital place in the national economy, and who consequently finds himself with time enough to assemble a library and to read books. Alonso Quijano is an idle gentleman, and his idleness reflects the condition of those readers to whom Cervantes addresses the *Quixote* (the "desocupado lector" of the prologue to Part I). It is as if Cervantes anticipates the middle-class transformation of idleness into the "leisure time" that enabled the reading of novels to put down broad cultural roots. In the *Quixote* the occupation of reading emerges where productive labor and adventure leave off. (In Cervantes' Spain, however, the activity of reading still involved many instances of reading aloud to small groups, such as happens at the inn in Part I.) And if one bears in mind that Don Quixote begins life as the fictional Alonso Quijano, who was a reader of everything from the philosophy of Aristotle to the Catalan romance *Tirant the White*, then it is also clear that the genre that this novel initiates is born from books. Alonso Quijano's imaginative space was crowded with ideas drawn from fictions. On the shelves in his study we find sequels to the *Amadís of Gaul* such as *The Exploits of Esplandián* (the legitimate son of Amadís), *Amadís of Greece*, the exotic *Florismarte of Hircania*, as well as Ariosto's *Orlando furioso*, which the Barber owns in the original Italian in spite of the fact that he does not know the language. The Barber pleads to save *Amadís of Gaul* from the flames of this literary inquisition because it is said to be not only the first book of chivalry printed in Spain but also "the best book of chivalry ever composed" (I, 6).

And yet a glance at Alonso Quijano's library confirms just how mistaken it would be to regard the *Quixote* as born solely from a critical engagement of the romances. The shelves of his library also hold copies of Jorge de Montemayor's pastoral novel *La Diana* as well as Cervantes' own *Galatea*. The library also contains several anthologies of lyric poetry as well as various examples of Renaissance epic verse; among them is a copy of the first colonial war epic written in America, Alonso de Ercilla's *La Araucana*. These epics, says the Priest, "are the best heroic verse ever written in the Spanish language . . . Keep them, as the richest jewels in all of Spanish poetry" (I, 7). Moreover, the process by which books engender books, either by emulation, by parody, or by critical response, is hardly restricted to what Don Quixote does in imitating the heroes of chivalric romance or what the Priest and the Barber do in criticizing them. In the relatively early chapters of Part I we meet a character named Ginés de Pasamonte. He has been sentenced to serve as a slave on the Spanish galleons. But this particular galley slave turns out to be authoring his own life, which he models upon picaresque narratives such as the *Lazarillo de Tormes*. Ginés claims that, when it is finished, his autobiography will vie with the *Lazarillo* for fame.

But since the story of his life cannot be complete until his life is finished, Ginés conceives of his story as open-ended. There is something subtle about Ginés's awareness of the co-equal status of text and life, but there is also something naive in what he imagines about the literary mapping of lived experience:

> "[My book] is so good," replied Ginés, "that it's going to be too bad for books like *Lazarillo de Tormes* and all those others they've scribbled, or they're still scribbling. All I'll say is that my book has the facts, and they're such fine and fantastic facts that lies just can't compete."
> "And what's the book titled?" asked Don Quixote.
> "*The Life of Ginés de Pasamonte*."
> "And is it finished?" asked Don Quixote.
> "How can it be finished," the galley slave answered, "if my life isn't? What I've written is from my birth up to the last time I escaped from the galleys."
> (I, 23)

There is another telling engagement of "naive" and "sophisticated" views about the mapping of literature and life in the *Quixote*, and it is Sancho's. Immediately following the encounter with the frightful sounds of the fulling-mills (I, 20), Sancho tells his master a story in order to keep him occupied and to quiet his nerves. Sancho obliges with a tale that raises questions about the relationship between narrative and the ordering of experience. The tale begins with a formulaic introduction that exaggerates the kind of beginnings characteristic of folk tales: "Once upon a time – may good things come to everyone, and bad things to anyone who looks for them . . . " This is followed by Sancho's own commentary on this beginning and a digression about the route of travel that he and his master might decide to take: "You should know, dear Sir, that the ancients didn't start their tales any way they wanted to . . . don't go looking for trouble anywhere, but let's find another road, because there's nothing forcing us to stay on this one" (I, 20). Don Quixote interrupts at once, insisting that Sancho proceed straight ahead with the matter of his story. Their brief exchange raises some of the same issues that will form the heart of the tale that follows. What degree of connectedness must narrative sustain in order to be valid? What degree of interruption can it tolerate?

The story goes on to dramatize these fundamental questions about narrative form. A shepherd, Lope Ruiz, is fleeing from a shepherdess, Torralba, who has pursued him as far as the banks of the Guadiana river. A fisherman's boat can ferry Lope Ruiz across the river, but the boat will carry only one goat and one person at a time. As Sancho imagines the tale, each crossing is distinct and must be related separately. Notwithstanding Sancho's tactical desire to delay, his underlying assumption is that the crossing of each and every goat must be recounted or the story will fail:

> "The shepherd got in the boat and took a goat with him; then he came back and took another one; and he kept coming back, and coming back, and taking another one each time."
>
> "But you'd better keep track of how many goats the shepherd carries across, your grace, because if we forget a single one that will be the end of the story, and it won't be possible to tell another word."
>
> "Anyway, let me go on. I ought to tell you that the place where they landed, on the other side, was all muddy and slippery, so it took the fishermen a long time to get there and then come back. Anyway, the shepherd came back for another goat, and then another, and then another."
>
> "Let's say he carried all of them," said Don Quixote. "You don't need to keep coming and going like that, because in a whole year you'll never get them all across."
>
> "How many has he carried over already?" said Sancho.
>
> "How the devil should I know?" replied Don Quixote.
>
> "Now that's just what I was telling you: you had to keep track. Because otherwise, by God, that's the end of the story, because I can't go on." (I, 20)

The elements of this episode derive from irrecoverable origins in the traditions of folklore, which likewise served Cervantes in the making of *Don Quixote*. According to one interpretation, Sancho sustains a naive commitment to narrative as a mapping of the world that finds its standard of truth in a complete correspondence to the facts. This is among the simplest and most perfect of narrative dreams. Following this view, counting and re-counting (which are both forms of telling made prominent in the story) occur in the shadow of a mimetic ideal that aims at a point-to-point transposition of the world into words. And yet as a more "sophisticated" reader, himself also a narrator, Don Quixote also knows that the expectation of absolute continuity is as impossible to achieve as that of an exact mimesis. In fact, narrative must tolerate a certain degree of *dis*-continuity in order to be effective.

A sophisticated approach to the mapping of life and literature is important to the *Quixote* because the process of making a novel involves not just the "imitation" of ordinary life, however critically one might understand that term, but also the ordering of prose. And *Don Quixote* is nothing if not a supremely complex text when it comes to narrative structure. Narrative does more than order experience according to a mathematical ideal; it also registers something about the ordinary quality of experience in the world, which is intermittently continuous *and* discontinuous. If the earthy realism of the book and its obvious critique of illusory ideals establish the paradigm for realism in the modern novel, its narrative inventiveness establishes a paradigm for novels of the self-conscious, experimental kind. Consider the development of Part I in this regard. The opening group of chapters, 1–8, can be imagined as a kind of short story, or what Cervantes might have called an "exemplary novel." Though it may have been inspired by the farce about the ballads mentioned above (the *Entremés de los romances*) the story of the gentleman who goes mad from reading books of chivalry is not too unlike the story from the *Exemplary Novels* about the man who thinks he is made of glass ("El licenciado Vidriera," ["The Glass Graduate"]). Moreover, the first eight chapters of *Don Quixote* are nearly self-contained. But between chapters 8 and 9 Cervantes draws on a stock device of literary suspension in order to depart on an entirely new narrative track. He pretends that the ending to the story we have been reading is lost and that the remainder of the original Arabic manuscript is only later found in the marketplace in Toledo. With this, Cervantes opens the sequence of narrative events to a series of interruptions that will not cease until we are very nearly at the conclusion of Part I. Following chapter 8, the narrative takes a highly experimental turn, such that the new, novelistic narrative of *Don Quixote* will be marked by the intrusion of the numerous other genres and characters mentioned above. Indeed, as we move through the sequence of interpolated stories that begins with the pastoral episode of Marcela and Grisóstomo (I, 12) and ends with the goatherd's tale about Leandra and Juan Vicente de la Rossa (I, 51), passing through the narratives of Cardenio, Dorotea, Fernando, and Luscinda, Zoraida and the Captain, and the reading of the "Curioso impertinente," it is only intermittently clear that Don Quixote's story constitutes the "main line" of the narrative plot. Unlike the romances of chivalry and picaresque narratives, which were mainly episodic, the *Quixote* is built around a plot that is woven of many, mutually interrupting strands. As the reader makes his or her way through the text, there is a temptation to become fully absorbed in each one of the interpolated stories, but there is likewise a requirement to see that each is but one part of a multi-layered whole. Indeed, the question is whether Cervantes offers us any position from which to survey this incredibly complex literary structure as a whole.

One answer to this question about the novel as a whole, not without its own complications, is that the perspective for viewing the multiple discourses of *Don Quixote*, Part I, is *Don Quixote*, Part II. At a distance of some ten years, Part II shows us Cervantes himself reflecting, not just on Part I, but on the public reception of it. Indeed, one of the most often noted features about Part II is that many of the characters in it have read Part I. Don Quixote and Sancho are received as familiar characters, but there is more to it than this. They are not only received but anticipated, which is to say that the world in Part II is sometimes "rigged" by the characters within it so as to produce the kind of effects that seemed spontaneously to happen in Part I. Sansón Carrasco stands a chance of defeating Don Quixote where the Priest and the Barber failed because he has read of Don Quixote and knows how to anticipate him. And Sansón Carrasco does indeed defeat Don Quixote. Not surprisingly, there is something less than innocent about the treatment Don Quixote receives at the hands of the Duke and the Duchess. Sancho is appointed governor of an "isle," but the isle is a sham and he is ill prepared to govern; the entire experience turns out to be a lesson in disappointment. Add to this the fact that while composing Part II Cervantes discovered the publication of an apocryphal sequel to the first part, written by someone who called himself Alonso Fernández de Avellaneda (the true identity has never been found), and it immediately becomes clear that Part II establishes possibilities for novel-writing that build reflectively, relentlessly, even incestuously upon the history of Part I. The novel begins not just from the incorporation of other preexisting discourses, but from a critical reception of itself.

Thus it is that the establishment of Cervantes' text as the beginning of the novel as a genre starts with *Don Quixote* itself. At the end of *Don Quixote*, Part I, Cervantes speculates about the possibility of a sequel to the book. He quotes a line from *Orlando furioso* that suggests, even invites, the possibility that someone else might continue the story ("Forsi altro canterà con miglior plectio" ["Maybe a different poet could sing it better"], I, 52). In the case of Avellaneda's *Quixote*, someone else did indeed try to "sing it better," and largely failed. Though Cervantes demonstrates some tolerance toward Avellaneda, the prologue to the "authentic" Part II nonetheless makes it clear that, in Cervantes' mind, Avellaneda grossly underestimated what it was to write a novel like *Don Quixote*. Cervantes likens Avellaneda's effort to the cheap and absurd humor to be derived from inflating a dog by putting a straw up its rear end, blowing it up, then letting it go and watching it fly around like a balloon. At the end of Part II Cervantes attempts to arrive at a more final ending in order to block any possible sequels. His hero dies and the narrator relinquishes his pen, but not without speculating on the ways in which the fantasies of chivalric action and the writing of fiction are mirrors of one another:

> Don Quixote was born only for me, as I for him; he knew how to act, and I only to write; only we two are a unity, in spite of that fake Tordesillian scribbler who dared – and may dare again – to record with his fat ostrich-feathered quill such badly drawn adventures for my brave knight, who is far too weighty for his shoulders to bear, and is a subject his frozen brains could never take on – so warn him, if you happen ever to meet, that he'd better let the weary, powdered

bones of Don Quixote rest in their tomb, and not even think of raising them up, against all Death's laws, and carrying them off to old Castile, yanking them out of that eternal resting place where, really and truly, they now lie stretched in moldering peace, incapable of making more journeys or sallying forth yet again, because in the cause of mocking knight errantry, as he has done, the two journeys he made are more than enough, and they gave immense pleasure and satisfaction to all who read them, whether here in Spain or abroad. (II, 74)

In so saying, Cervantes was partly right and partly wrong. *Don Quixote* has of course continued to give readers boundless pleasure. But his hero has by no means been allowed to rest in the grave. He has reappeared over the course of the novel's subsequent history, for better or worse, in incar-nations as different as Monsignor Quixote (Graham Greene) and Emma Bovary (Flaubert). He has been interpreted by those capable of great depth (Kierkagaard, Unamuno), and he has spawned interpretations that merely gesture at depth (*Man of La Mancha*). His influence on culture has been profound in philosophy and he has left a lasting impression in the visual arts (Goya, Daumier, Doré, Picasso). But the role of *Don Quixote* in the history of the novel extends beyond the quixotic hero's literary influence, to the very openness of form that Cervantes discovered in the course of writing this text. That openness became the source of a generic productivity that Cervantes himself could not foreclose, not even by having his hero renounce chivalry and die. And so Cervantes bequeaths to the history of literature a new form of discourse: that of the self-conscious, open text, whose lines can be traced to Pirandello, Proust's *Pastiches*, Nabokov's *Pale Fire*, and Cortázar's *Hopscotch*. As in the case of Borges' Pierre Menard, who sets out to re-write *Don Quixote* word for word, the example of Cervantes is one in which the originality of literary discourse derives from the very factors that would seem most to limit it: history, and especially that peculiar inheritance of the past that we call *literary* history.

NOTES

1 See Philippe Lacoue-Labarthe and Jean-Luc Nancy, *The Literary Absolute: The Theory of Literature in German Romanticism*, trans. Philip Barnard and Cheryl Lester (Albany, NY: State University of New York Press, 1988).

2 Bakhtin introduces the term in his essay "Discourse in the Novel," in *The Dialogic Imagination*, ed. Michael Holquist, trans. Caryl Emerson and Michael Holquist (Austin: University of Texas Press, 1981). It remains an important notion, though at least one recent critic has suggested that it ceased to be central for Bakhtin in the late stages of his career. See Matthew Roberts, "Poetics Hermeneutics Dialogics: Bakhtin and Paul de Man," in Gary Saul Morson and Caryl Emerson, eds., *Rethinking Bakhtin: Extensions and Challenges* (Evanston, IL: Northwestern University Press, 1989), pp.114–34.

3 Bakhtin, *Dialogic Imagination*, pp. 261, 262.
4 See Ramón Menéndez-Pidal, "The Genesis of 'Don Quijote,'" in M. J. Bernardete and Angel Flores, eds., *Cervantes Across the Centuries* (New York: Dryden Press, 1948).
5 Georg Lukács, *Theory of the Novel*, trans. Anna Bostock (Cambridge, MA: MIT Press, 1971), pp. 103–04.
6 "After a failure to find in novelistic discourse a purely poetic formulation . . . prose discourse is denied any artistic value at all" (Bakhtin, *Dialogic Imagination*, p. 260).
7 Ibid., pp. 272–73.
8 Diana de Armas Wilson writes about the question in her essay included in this volume, "Cervantes and the New World." See also Martin Green, *Dreams of Adventure, Deeds of Empire* (New York: Basic Books, 1979); and Irving Leonard, *Books of the Brave* (Cambridge, MA: Harvard University Press, 1949).

FURTHER READING

Alter, Robert. *Partial Magic: The Novel as a Self-Conscious Genre*. Berkeley: University of California Press, 1975.
Bakhtin, Mikhail. "Discourse in the Novel." In *The Dialogic Imagination*, ed. Michael Holquist, trans. Caryl Emerson and Michael Holquist. Austin: University of Texas Press, 1981.
Bernardete, M. J., and Angel Flores, eds. *Cervantes Across the Centuries*. New York: Dryden Press, 1948. Includes "An introduction to Cervantes," by J. Cassou; "The Genesis of 'Don Quijote,'" by R. Menéndez-Pidal; "The Composition of 'Don Quijote,'" by J. Casalduero; "The Style of 'Don Quixote,'" by H. Hatzfeld; "Social and Historical Background," by A. Morel-Fatio; "Of How Don Quixote Fell Sick," by M. de Unamuno; "Incarnation in 'Don Quijote,'" by A. Castro; "The 'Simpatía' of Don Quixote," by B. Croce; "The Career of the Hero," by W. Frank; "Critical Realism," by M. Casella; "'Don Quixote' and 'Moby Dick,'" by H. Levin; "The 'Persiles' Mystery," by M. Singleton; "Thematic Design," by P. I. Novitsky; "The Apocryphal 'Quixote,'" by S. Gilman; "Musical Settings to Cervantes," by C. Haywood; "Cervantes and English Literature," by E. B. Knowles; "French Translations of Cervantes," by E. J. Crooks; "Cervantes in Germany," by L. Bergel; "Cervantes in Russia," by L. B. Turkevich.
Fuentes, Carlos. *Cervantes o la crítica de la lectura*. Mexico City: Joaquín Mortiz, 1976.
Gilman, Stephen. *The Novel According to Cervantes*. Berkeley: University of California Press, 1989.
Hart, Thomas R. *Cervantes and Ariosto: Rewriting Fiction*. Princeton: Princeton University Press, 1989.
Johnson, Carroll. *Don Quixote and the Quest for Modern Fiction*. Prospect Heights, IL: Waveland Press, 2000.
Kundera, Milan. *The Art of the Novel*. Trans. Linda Asher. New York: Harper and Row, 1986.
Lukács, Georg. *Theory of the Novel*. Trans. Anna Bostock. Cambridge, MA: MIT Press, 1971.
Mancing, Howard. *The Chivalric World of Don Quijote: Style, Structure, and Narrative Technique*. Columbia, MO: University of Missouri Press, 1982.

McKeon, Michael. *Origins of the English Novel 1600–1740*. Baltimore: The Johns Hopkins University Press, 1987.

Menéndez-Pidal, Ramón. "The Genesis of Don Quijote." In Bernardete and Flores, eds., *Cervantes Across the Centuries*.

Rico, Francisco. *The Spanish Picaresque Novel and the Point of View*. Trans. Charles Davis with Harry Sieber. Cambridge: Cambridge University Press, 1984.

Reed, Walter L. *An Exemplary History of the Novel: The Quixotic Versus the Picaresque*. Chicago: University of Chicago Press, 1981.

Robert, Marthe. *Origins of the Novel*. Trans. Sacha Rabinovich. Bloomington, IN: Indiana University Press, 1980.

Watt, Ian. *The Rise of the Novel*. Berkeley: University of California Press, 1957.

Williamson, Edwin. *The Half-Way House of Fiction: "Don Quijote" and the Arthurian Romance*. Oxford: Clarendon Press, 1984.

5

ALEXANDER WELSH

The influence of Cervantes

The influence we are concerned with is that of *Don Quixote*. Without question Cervantes would be remembered for his other works, his romances, plays, and especially the exemplary tales. But the legend of the man himself – his life of hardship and imprisonment, the loss of the use of his hand at the battle of Lepanto – would not be memorable if it were not for the appearance of *El ingenioso hidalgo Don Quixote de la Mancha* in 1605 and its continuation, in defiance of a spurious sequel, in 1615. Part I was translated into other major European languages almost immediately, Part II thereafter. The completed work became not a staple of Western civilization but a renewable source of its literature.

The immense influence of the work is also remarkable for being twofold: even as Cervantes' method offered a flexible model for realism in the novel, his runaway hero, the self-created Don Quixote, became the model of rare heroism in the face of mundane reality. Both resources, the Cervantine method and the quixotic hero, have become closely associated with realism in the novel but need not be invoked in the same text. In truth, allegiances to the method and to the hero have generally been divided, as novelists and their critics have been engaged with the formal and philosophical problems of realism or with justice – not justice as a sustainable achievement, if there is such a thing, but as an ardent desire. Only very exceptional novels, original in their own right, draw upon both lessons from Cervantes.

The first such novel is *The History and Adventures of Joseph Andrews, and of his Friend, Mr. Abraham Adams: Written in Imitation of the Manner of Cervantes, Author of Don Quixote* (1742). I give the full title of Henry Fielding's experiment because it comprises both the method – reconceived as a parody of Samuel Richardson's novel about Joseph's sister, Pamela Andrews – and its reincarnation of Don Quixote himself as Parson Adams. The tribute in the subtitle is similarly divided between method, or manner, and the hero. The resulting novel is not, in either department, a mere copy of the Spanish original. Richardson's *Pamela* (1740), needless to say, was not chivalric romance in any case, but a more up-to-date fiction about domestic service, already ridiculed anonymously by Fielding in a pamphlet called *Shamela*. The fun-making celebration of the brother servant's male virtue is little more than a beginning for *Joseph Andrews*, which created in Parson Adams a plausible and not the least mad Don Quixote. As we shall see, the very name Abraham anticipates the plight of some of the more abstruse modernist descendants of Cervantes' hero.

The second exceptional – and utterly different – novel that embraces both Cervantine method and at least two quixotic heroes is Laurence Sterne's *The Life and Opinions of Tristram Shandy, Gentleman* (1759–67). Students of this novel have more often identified it with Lockean association of ideas than with *Don Quixote*, perhaps, yet the self-consciousness of its narrative modernized and intensified other aspects of Cervantes' method besides parody, and the experiment became even more influential, in its turn, than *Joseph Andrews*. The narrator-hero, Tristram Shandy, pays tribute in his own voice to "the peerless knight of *La Mancha*, whom, by the bye, with all his follies, I love more, and would actually have gone further to have paid a visit to, than the greatest hero of antiquity."

Whatever the reason Fielding and Sterne were so profoundly affected by Cervantes' achievement, eighteenth-century Britain proved especially fertile ground for the Spanish novel – though *Don Quixote* could be enjoyed, admired, and imitated on many different levels.[1] Just so, in the heyday of the reception of Spanish literature in Britain – and the picaresque was as popular as the quixotic innovation – Cervantes' example could be adopted for purely satiric purposes, as in Richard Graves's *The Spiritual Quixote* (1772), a satire on Methodism. The evidence on the face of it, however, is that the full significance of the parody of romance and the careers of Don Quixote and Sancho, their coming together and later even encountering readers of their adventures, were never wholly anticipated by the author himself. What may well have begun as a satire on bad literature became a powerful invitation to realism in fiction and a celebration of foolishness, even a necessary foolishness of human endeavor altogether. Spain's own literary culture, after the Golden Age and in the decline of Spanish imperial power, tended to neglect Cervantes until, at the end of the nineteenth century, the Generation of '98 revived interest. Miguel de Unamuno himself credited English and Russian writers with appreciating Cervantes more than the Spaniards had.[2]

At the core of Cervantine method is a repudiation of romance. His *Don Quixote* could be said to inaugurate the distinction between novel and romance that became commonplace in Britain by the end of the eighteenth century: romance was devoted to the faraway, the unusual, often the supernatural, and certainly the unbelievable; the novel, or new art of fiction, to the everyday, the expected, and the entirely plausible in human affairs. Opposing one narrative to another is a method by no means confined to literary uses: by similar procedures an historian or a scientist often persuades us of the superiority of this account of events over that. Even if one acknowledges the problematic relation of a narrative in words to events themselves, nothing is more effective in defending a narrative than demolishing – or at least ridiculing – a rival account. The method is crucial for literary realism, for which any evidentiary grounds of the asserted facts are a mere pretense. If a novelist skillfully exposes some other narrative as romance, the reader of the novel readily imagines the freshly narrated events as actually taking place. Hence Fielding in *Joseph Andrews*, true to the method of Cervantes, gains a purchase on his readers by amending *Pamela*; or Jane Austen in *Northanger Abbey* (completed 1803) persuades readers of the reality of its fictional world by having her heroine initially mistake that world for a Gothic romance by Ann Radcliffe. *Don Quixote* was seen to be not simply a satire on chivalric romance – the priest and the barber, after all, are quite selective in their burning of the hero's library after his first sally – but an alternative narrative of the kinds of things that really might happen if an elderly gentleman set himself up as a knight errant in the modern world.

Another procedure adopted by Cervantes and subsequently by eighteenth-century novelists is the authenticating of the manuscript, the document from which the author, editor, or printer supposedly reproduces the narrative in question. Such documentation, of course, is again not limited to literary uses, but it is especially tempting for the introduction of untruth or fiction. So popular was the device in the early generations of the European novel that it could be tedious – a dull pretense that the novel recorded real adventures of real-life persons. But Cervantes and his shrewdest followers *play* with such fictions of authenticity, teasing readers with layers of source materials until all narrative is called in doubt or readers' attentions are diverted elsewhere. In chapter 9 of the first part of *Don Quixote*, as the hero is about to deliver a tremendous blow to the Biscayan, the narrative seemingly runs out. We know the story is a fiction, but putting a sudden stop to it leaves us wondering what happened – that is, catches us attending the narrated events as if they were real. When we are thereupon assured that there exists a version by a different hand, that of Cid Hamete Benengeli, the suspense – our expectation that Don Quixote was about to strike the Biscayan – carries us willingly into the continuation. Though this fresh authentication of the action is as fake as can be, and entertains us in itself, Cervantes has quietly supplied new documentation of the knight's adventures. He treats of the reliability of this new author as one might of any historian. Cid Hamete's prejudices as an Arab would work against the Christian knight, therefore Don Quixote's glorious deeds are not likely to have been exaggerated. Most tellingly, just there in the manuscript is reported to be an illustration of Don Quixote striking the Biscayan. When the initial narrative stopped, time stopped; and we are presented with a graphic representation of that moment, as a sharp reminder of the temporal constraints governing the pictorial mode. Gratefully we can pick up the sequence of the action once more from Cid Hamete's verbal representation. The whole mischievous business earns respect because it instructs as well as entertains.

Fielding plays some similar games, especially in his *History of Tom Jones* (1749), but Sterne is the true manipulator of Cervantine self-consciousness. The hero of *Tristram Shandy* ostensibly writes his own life story; thus Sterne seizes upon one of the oldest ways of authenticating a narrative, by having it told by the main actor. Notoriously, Tristram has difficulty in advancing the narrative to the beginning of the action proper, his own birth – or is putting pen to paper the beginning of the action proper? Because this is a verbal representation of the life, the means of registering the temporal relations of events should be ample, but somehow sentences and tenses of verbs do not guarantee the chronology supplied by most novels. Then paradoxically, the impression of actual happenings intensifies. The more the reader too is distracted by the problems of Tristram the narrator, the more it seems the events to be narrated must be real. The usual result of quixotic adventures also carries over into *Tristram Shandy*, in the shower of blows endured by the well-meaning protagonists. The catastrophes of "geniture, nose, and name" befall Tristram because of Walter Shandy's obstetrical theories; the guillotine-like window sash falls when Susannah holds up the child to ****, because the sash weights have been removed for uncle Toby's cannon. The victim and narrator of these adventures begins to sound a little like an exasperated Sancho rather than the two quixotes who have brought them about.

The physical world and its human population retaliate so regularly and abruptly against Don Quixote's imagined exploits that the knight can sometimes only ascribe what happens to the work of inimical enchanters. But enchanters with their magic inhabit only a world of romance: readers of Cervantes' novel understand that the blows come from windmills or from people trying to go about their ordinary business. A century and a half later the enchanters have departed altogether and have been replaced by scientific theory – in Sterne reduced to minutiae of cause and effect precisely because of his fascination with Lockean epistemology and the way it argues from the smallest and most diffuse experience. Many of Tristram's difficulties of narration result from the sheer number of causes bearing upon any given outcome. Enchanters, endowed with malign intent, were not nearly so hard to understand as these small impersonal forces nudging events this way and that. "But need I tell you, Sir" – Tristram addresses his reader, sometimes Madame – "need I tell you, Sir, that the circumstances with which every thing in this world is begirt, give every thing in this world its size and shape; – and by tightening it, or relaxing it, this way or that, make the thing to be, what it is – great – little – good – bad – indifferent or not indifferent, just as the case happens." In the world of *Tristram Shandy* contingency has replaced enchantment as the explanation of last resort.

With his own astonishing originality, Sterne thus anticipates the immense weight to be placed on circumstances, both in fiction and in the human sciences, for two more centuries to come; but he also reads these lessons out of the beloved book by Cervantes. He reads instinctively there what Ortega y Gasset said of *Don Quixote* in 1914: that the book was to be celebrated for its demonstration of unpoetic reality, which cannot "enter into art in any way other than by making an active and combative element out of its own inertia and desolation. It cannot interest us by itself. Much less can its duplication [i.e., its representation] interest us." Don Quixote's very devotion to the ideal cedes this opportunity to the real. "Surrounding culture – as the puppet show of fancy was surrounded by the inn – lies the barbarous, brutal, mute, meaningless reality of things . . . Culture is memories and promises, an irreversible past, a dreamed future. But reality is a simple and frightening 'being there.' "[3] Sterne, Diderot, and other novelists assumed some such reading of Cervantes in their own practices. In Charles Dickens's first novel (of which more below), Mr. Pickwick exclaims, "We are all the victims of circumstances, and I the greatest!" And in Dickens's writings the modern victims of circumstances will suffer the contingencies of what Ortega calls culture as well as accident.

Part II of *Don Quixote* inaugurated still other devices of Cervantine realism. Avellenada's spurious continuation of the adventures of the true Quixote was in retrospect a godsend for the author and his readers. Now Cervantes was able to introduce in his own sequel characters who had read both the original and Avellenada's version; these supposed readers could then inform Don Quixote of putative further adventures that he could indignantly deny. Both sequels could not be true, and the one now in fresh readers' hands has the last word: again the credibility of one narrative is sustained by repudiating a false one. The presence in the foreground of veritable readers, themselves capable of nice critical discriminations, would seem to confirm the reality of Don Quixote and Sancho, of those earlier critics the priest and the barber, and of all the rest. Moreover, as Jorge Luis Borges has mischievously put it, "these inversions suggest that if the characters of a fictional work can be readers or spectators, we, its readers or spectators, can be fictitious."[4]

By the time of Fielding, Part II of *Don Quixote* had fallen into disfavor with many readers because, instead of the spontaneous sallies of Part I, the hero and Sancho now become almost exclusively the victims of practical jokes conducted by their admirers the Duke and the Duchess; and something similar results from the tactics of young Sansón Carrasco, who wants to help but is also a little irritated by the way quixotic undertakings succeed in spite of him. Practical joking became distasteful to some eighteenth-century sensibilities – and perhaps remains so except among children to this day. Fielding deliberately has a few jokes played on Parson Adams mostly, it seems, to expose the crudity of the jokers. But in the Renaissance such joking was not altogether frowned upon among gentlemen and it was a staple of Renaissance fiction, notably in Italian novellas. It should be remembered that narrated practical jokes provide the same sort of proof of reality as that expounded by Ortega: the come-down, it may be supposed, will at least provide a lesson to the victim. Particularly in the sequel to a popular fiction like *Don Quixote*, jokes might give a fresh thrust to the action. Direct responsibility for the action is assumed by a handful of characters, though the author is still at work behind the scenes.

Sterne's genius translated the practical jokes of Part II into a vision of human life as the endless sport of jokes of circumstance. The propriety and morality of conducting such jokes were not at issue, therefore, and better for the victims to be despairingly entertained than to despair outright perhaps. As belief in Providence waned in intellectual and literary circles, the notion that we are all victims of circumstance took on the dimensions of something like a cosmic joke. The irony of calling the universe "a vast practical joke," as Herman Melville does in *Moby-Dick*, becomes perversely satisfying. Some novels and poems by Thomas Hardy, or stories by Joseph Conrad, seem to derive comfort – victim compensation, as it were – from a perception that events unfold like bad jokes: if it is a joke, someone – some far-off Duke or Duchess – must be in control. In *A Passage to India* (1924), persuaded that "most of life is so dull that there is nothing to be said about it," E. M. Forster contrives a kind of joke at the Marabar Caves so slight that it may never have happened, yet so brutal that few realities of the English and Indian communities are left in doubt.

Unlike the Cervantine method, quixotic heroism is far from being a repudiation of romance. It is more like the cultivation of romance amid incongruous surroundings. Unless chivalry and adventure can be reduced to armchair sentiment, Sterne's initiatives in this area are disappointing, literally disarming. Neither of his quixotic heroes, Tristram's father Walter and his uncle Toby, will be found far from home; they have no present mission that would require them to sally forth. What they have in common with Don Quixote are fixed ideas: Walter Shandy's theories and Toby's model fortifications. Dedication to knight errantry has become what Sterne denominates a hobby-horse, with the strong implication that any gentleman afflicted with much leisure rides or is ridden by a hobby-horse and cannot do otherwise. The brothers are endearing in their kind but helpless way. Fielding's candidate for the modern quixote, on the other hand, does sally forth and is as valiant with his fist as Don Quixote with his sword. Parson Adams is another true knight errant: he may naively overestimate his own importance and credit with the world, but the essential thing is that he goes out of his way – it is his way – to help those in need. It is thus Fielding's novel that sturdily confirms the quixotic hero's desire for justice.

In the Romantic era it was common to identify Don Quixote, however loosely, with the quest for justice. In canto 13 of *Don Juan* (1823), for example, Byron imagined Quixote as, among other things,

> Redressing injury, revenging wrong,
>   To aid the damsel and destroy the caitiff;
> Opposing singly the united strong,
>   From foreign yoke to free the helpless native.

But in Cervantes' novel most of these things simply did not occur, unless the hero's good intentions are all that need to be taken into account. Quixote's two most obvious attempts to bring justice, his coming to the aid of Andrés the farm boy and his freeing of the galley slaves, are largely counterproductive. In fact Byron quite understands this, for he turns about and perversely attacks Cervantes for writing so about his knight errant. Well before Byron, however, the quixotic hero began to move more determinedly against injustice. Fielding at least made the injustices more palpable. When he first introduces the heroine of *Joseph Andrews,* she is on the ground defending herself against an unmistakable rapist: thus "the great abilities of Mr. Adams were not necessary to have formed a right judgment of this affair on the first sight"; and "he immediately levelled a blow at that part of the ravisher's head, where, according to the opinion of the ancients, the brains of some persons are deposited." In continuation of this same episode (and possibly expressive of his opinion of the treatment of Adams's prototype in Part II of *Don Quixote*) Fielding initiates a convention by which the quixotic hero who redresses wrongs becomes a victim of injustice in his turn, since the rapist manages to have Adams indicted for robbery. Institutions of the law, take note, may themselves enforce or create injustices. Byron and others may have exaggerated – not to say politicized – Don Quixote's exploits, but they were instinctively right to associate justice with the intentions of heroes and the longings of peoples. Neither governments nor laws can finally guarantee justice, for there can be rulers and laws that are unjust, and acts of good people may also be unjust. It is far easier for knights errant, and all of us, to recognize injustices than to know what is just.

The immediate heir of Parson Adams in this respect was Dr. Primrose in *The Vicar of Wakefield* (1766). Oliver Goldsmith's novel was admired and imitated by Goethe among others, and was immensely successful with Anglophone readers for more than a century after its first appearance. No doubt the sentimentality of this short work accounts both for its popularity and its later neglect, but its hero is no mean exponent of quixotic principles and an obvious precursor of Dickens's Pickwick. The law and the Vicar's debts result in his imprisonment, but the proximate cause is the power of the local squire, as crude in his way as the would-be rapist of Fanny in Fielding's novel. From within the prison, Primrose can address the reader as well as his fellow prisoners on the subject of justice. Whatever one thinks of the imprudence of Don Quixote's release of the galley slaves (which episode now looms much larger in the quixotic tradition than it did in the original), the hero interviewed one convict after another and determined that from each individual perspective justice had indeed been unevenly administered. Goldsmith's hero, blithely addressing an audience composed for the most part of hardened criminals, assumes that some among them are innocent or victims of oppression like himself. His reflections on the administration of criminal justice and opposition to the death penalty except for murder begin to spill over into a sentiment for distributive justice. "It is among the citizens of a refined community that penal laws, which are in the hands of the rich, are laid upon the poor." Dr. Primrose speaks, in the prison, of wretches "stuck up for long tortures, lest luxury should feel a momentary pang," and of heaven as a place where there is "no master to threaten or insult us." This is foolishness, of course. Goldsmith's hero is neither a philosopher nor a revolutionary, but one who lives through the imagination like a true descendant of Don Quixote. He thereby sets us thinking about the difference between ideals we share and the realities we nonetheless consent to.

Dickens seems never to have admitted to anyone that his first novel, *The Posthumous Papers of the Pickwick Club* (1836–37), was modeled upon *Don Quixote*, though after his death his friend and biographer John Forster could casually write that "Sam Weller and Mr. Pickwick are the Sancho and Quixote of Londoners" as if all understood this right along.[5] Dickens's book was written on commission in the first place, as letterpress to accompany illustrations by a well-known artist. But unquestionably *Pickwick* is an updated *Don Quixote* for the early nineteenth century. Mr. Pickwick and his friends sally out into the countryside from their accustomed urban existences, ostensibly for scientific inquiries duly to be recorded in the minutes of the club. The hero – initially ignorant of country matters – immediately becomes engaged in rescuing spinsters from the seductions and devious ways of an enchanter named Jingle. Indeed throughout, the asexual but chivalrous hero is embarrassed by his encounters with women. Such embarrassment was not a factor in the romances Don Quixote modeled himself on but was prominent in the far more genteel fictions – not to say repressions – of this almost Victorian era. Behold, just as Cervantes' novel took on new life and direction when the hero appointed Sancho his squire, so Dickens's enterprise took off when Mr. Pickwick hired the bootblack Sam Weller as his personal servant and, after the fifth installment, sales of the novel soared. Wise in the ways of the world where his high-minded master is naive, Sam measures out some of that wisdom in Wellerisms – the cockney equivalent of Sancho's proverbs. A Wellerism typically evokes the materiality or violence within cultural commonplaces, as in "It's over, and can't be helped and that's one consolation, as they always say in Turkey, ven they cuts the wrong man's head off"; or, "Business first, pleasure afterwards, as King Richard the Third said ven he stabbed the t'other king in the Tower, afore he smothered the babbies."

Because of its episodic design, which Cervantes originally adopted from romance, Dickens's novel is sometimes thought to lack a plot, but this is not the case. One adventure follows another until – after the Shandean mishap that prompts Pickwick to protest that we are all victims of circumstances – his housekeeper Mrs. Bardell, abetted by the lawyers Dodson and Fogg and regardless of the true case, sues the bachelor hero for breach of promise. The outcome of the trial is as predictable as Dickens's satire of the law and lawyers, but the hero's response to the verdict against him is not. Scorning the advice of his own lawyer, his friends, and Sam, Mr. Pickwick refuses to pay the damages and costs awarded the plaintiff and instead allows himself to be imprisoned for these charges. This is a determined sacrifice of his own person of the kind that is usually called civil disobedience, and it is a true quixotic protest against injustice – all the more impressive because Mr. Pickwick can readily afford to pay Mrs. Bardell and her lawyers' costs and call it quits. Then Sam Weller deliberately commits an offense so that he will be arrested and can join his master in the Fleet prison. "Pickwick and principle!" is not only Sam's appreciative slogan but at the same time his Sancho-like criticism of his master, whom he continues to urge to buy his release. But then the hero visits the poor side of the prison, whose prisoners are wholly dependent on charity for their food and drink. Instead of preaching like Dr. Primrose on the injustices he discovers there, Mr. Pickwick again chooses to protest with his own body. He confines himself to his prison bed and begins to die.

Don Quixote bravely challenged others with his sword over truths that sometimes only he had reason to believe in; Mr. Pickwick, in a later age and contending with forces of law as well as circumstances, without threatening others physically puts his own body on the line for justice and truths all too palpable to the reader. And Mr. Pickwick is a vigorous law-abiding citizen, notice, except where law and due process have created an injustice. Dickens duly extricates his quixotic hero from this position beyond the ethical, as Søren Kierkegaard would call it a few years later, and carefully sends him into retirement in order to bring his adventures to a close. This retirement is as sad and as forced as the perfunctory conversion and death of Don Quixote at the end of Part II in Cervantes' novel. For all that the so-called *Pickwick Papers* are thought to afford only light entertainment, Dickens never permitted any subsequent hero to go this far beyond what is lawfully and socially acceptable in the pursuit of justice.

The seriousness of this action is surely reflected in *The Idiot* (1868–69), Fyodor Dostoevsky's strange quixotic novel. We know from a letter from Dostoevsky to his brother, after he had begun the novel, that he had in mind as models for his hero not only Don Quixote and Mr. Pickwick but Jesus – all exemplars of wise foolishness.[6] Prince Myshkin is the one memorable quixotic hero who is mentally unstable since Don Quixote himself (whose powers of mistaking reality are mainly willed in any case, and who seems most mad when, in the Sierra Morena, he willfully decides to imitate the mad Amadís and Orlando). Dostoevsky dramatizes the idea of wisdom in folly, however, by confining the action of *The Idiot* to Myshkin's window of sanity between bouts of the illness in a Swiss asylum. Like Mr. Pickwick and more so he is endowed with enough wealth to make his quixotic undertakings plausible, and though younger than Pickwick his relation to women is similarly empathic and ideal rather than sexual. Two desirable Dulcineas, the fallen (in her own eyes) Nastasya Filippovna and the frustrated Aglaia, are attracted by his goodness. As heir to the fortune of Pavlishtchev, the Prince is also attractive to a fraudulent claimant to his wealth named Burdovsky. "We demand, we do not beg," chants Burdovsky, and even to this unfounded demand for justice Prince Myshkin readily yields. He patiently explains that there is no such person as the son of Pavlishtchev, his benefactor, but kindly observes that the scarcely articulate Burdovsky may actually believe that he is a son of Pavlishtchev. Chivalry has come to its quixotic extreme, which foolishness Dostoevsky associates with Jesus of the Gospels.

Mr. Pickwick and Prince Myshkin are the two foremost quixotic heroes of the nineteenth century who seek justice despite the law and beyond the ethical. Their disregard for their own material interest recalls what is also Christian in Don Quixote's knight errantry. But there are numerous other quixotic characters in Western literature who are notable more for their common humanity than any extraordinary selflessness. Some of these are true to the original because their minds have initially been turned by the reading of books, usually novels rather than medieval romance. One of the earliest such is Arabella, the heroine of Charlotte Lennox's *The Female Quixote* (1752), who continually misapprehends the real world until a familiar novel plot itself takes over and she marries. Jane Austen's *Emma* (1815) borrows some of its tone from Lennox, perhaps, though not the specific addiction to reading. Emma Woodhouse's quixotism consists of mistaken altruism, a belief that she is sallying about on behalf of others' romantic interests, when she is still unaware of her own. Marriage to a Mr. Knightley would seem to put an end to her errantry, for he represents the stable and responsible virtue of an English gentleman. Dorothea Brooke in George Eliot's *Middlemarch* (1871–72) has more often than Emma been thought of as quixotic, even though one chapter epigraph leads the reader to suppose that the author identified Mr. Casaubon, Dorothea's first husband, with Don Quixote. Yet Dorothea is the principal idealist in this novel; she does dream of helping others, so much so that she mistakes realities and misjudges Casaubon altogether. Because her marriage is not what she supposed, she is left for the remainder of the action to seek other objects for her charity. The most acclaimed female quixote, Gustave Flaubert's Emma Bovary, has derived her notions of romantic love from reading, and is disappointed with her husband accordingly. But Flaubert's novel has more to do with the impoverishment and constraints of bourgeois provincial life; the coolness with which the heroine is portrayed hardly differs from the coolness with which her opportunities are mocked. *Madame Bovary* (1857) is a relentless more than witty account of the modern heroine as victim of circumstances. Flaubert's devotion to Cervantes was complicated, and he seems himself to have identified with Don Quixote.

The truth is that the influence of Cervantes on the history of the European novel and its colonial offshoots is as broad as it is long. When Walter Scott anonymously began to write fiction with *Waverley* in 1814, he modestly dissociated this enterprise from his understanding of Cervantes' achievement. His own protagonist, he explained in an early chapter, would apprehend "occurrences indeed in their reality," yet with "romantic tone and colouring." Scott's very self-consciousness here should alert us to the fact that young Waverley and and his subsequent heroes are still cast in a quixotic mold, if that pattern is conceived broadly to include "more common aberration[s] from sound judgment" such as may be attributed to youth and inexperience as well as reading or dreaming. One of the incongruous and amusing things about the original Don Quixote, it seems, is that he was too old to be a hero and fashion himself as a knight errant. For youth to model itself on storied heroism is nothing untoward, and especially if we recall (or insist) that Don Quixote is cured and repentant of his imaginary role before he dies, a more ordinary quixotism, which can be grown out of, may be quite acceptable, even salutary. This broad definition of what may be quixotic is precisely what Hegel wrote about as the *difference* between chivalric romance and the modern novel:

> the knightly character of the heroes who play parts in our modern novels is altered. Confronted by the existing order and the ordinary prose of life they appear before us as individuals with personal aims of love, honour, ambition, and ideals of world reform, ideals in the path of which that order presents obstacles on every side . . . Conflicts of this kind, however, in our modern world are the apprentice years, the education of individuality in the actual world.

Hegel's words describe very well the experience of Scott's heroes, whose progeny were legion in the nineteenth century. But note the satisfaction, even complacency associated with this state of literary affairs. Hegel goes on to stress "the object and consummation of such apprenticeship," which is "that the individual . . . finds his own place, together with his wishes and opinions in social conditions as they are and the rational order which belongs to them."[7]

Until confined to his death-bed, Don Quixote might protest that *he* is not content with our modern world or social conditions but intends all along to revive the golden age of knight errantry. Indeed one feels that true quixotic followers like Parson Adams, Dr. Primrose, Mr. Pickwick, and Prince Myshkin must refuse to grow up or to accept the rational order assigned to them; too evidently they have to be put to death, forced to retire, or sent back to Switzerland by their worried authors. One key to the project described by Hegel (every novel something of a *Bildungsroman*) is the substitution of "personal aims of love, honour, ambition, and ideals of world reform" for disinterested chivalric motives and the quest for justice. A second key is the assumption that history is progressive: the social conditions to which the hero must adapt have themselves changed for the better, and to come to terms with these conditions need not therefore be regressive. The variously expressed belief in the nineteenth century that history either already had or would inevitably bring about a satisfactory, if not just, arrangement of things put quixotic heroism at odds with historical realism and tended to eclipse the former.

Though Scott did not single-handedly create the historical novel, he effectively assured the genre its considerable prestige. He could do so because his novels relegated violence to the past and aligned their young heroes with the present and peaceful constitution of society as it appeared to have been achieved in Britain. Toward the close of *Waverley*, its hero is persuaded "that the romance of his life was ended, and that its real history had now commenced." History here amounts to the hero and his bride living happily ever after on the proceeds of real property: whatever quixotism lingered in the "romantic tone and colouring" of Waverley's youthful associations has been outgrown. In France the Revolution and national wars created a less certain atmosphere, and as Erich Auerbach argued, a novelist like Stendhal had no such stable idea of history to work with.[8] Stendhal's Julien Sorel in *The Red and the Black* (1830) and Balzac's Lucien de Rubempré in *Lost Illusions* (1837–43) have often been recognized as quixotic types and no doubt deserve to be thought so more than any equivalent hero of a British novel. Both model themselves in passing upon that modern real-life hero, Napoleon. But if they are quixotic, obviously, it is only in that mode prescribed by Hegel for the youthfully and personally ambitious.

In the epitome of all historical novels, nevertheless, there would still be found room for Don Quixote's example, and for Cervantes' proven method as well. *War and Peace* (1865–69), perhaps because of Leo Tolstoy's rather more open-ended idea of history, harbors two heroes with quixotic plans to change the world. Early on, like his French brothers, Prince André Bolkonski even imagines himself as Napoleon. Though Bolkonski above all incarnates personal honor – it is as if he were twice fatally wounded, at Austerlitz and at Borodino – he also, until his disillusionment, plans to reform the Russian army by creating a new military code. Pierre Bezukhov is more nearly a true quixote in that he blunders, seems foolish to others, is free with the fortune left to him by his biological father, and and for a brief while plans to assassinate Napoleon. (It is hard to believe that Pierre was not also an inspiration of Prince Myshkin, since *War and Peace* had begun to be published just before Dostoevsky began to write *The Idiot*.) Tolstoy's two heroes are linked by friendship and by a single Dulcinea: Natasha Rostova, who, before her aborted elopement from the one and eventual marriage to the other, represents something like life itself to both men. As Tolstoy's epilogue makes clear, Pierre's discontent with the modern world, the restlessness of a man of ideas, continues even after his marriage. In this same historical novel, Tolstoy plays again and again the Cervantine game of mocking an existing narrative in order to validate his own. When it comes to public events – that is, the Napoleonic wars – and especially their ostensible causes, he never tires of telling the reader that they did not happen the way the historians want us to believe but the way they are described here. In this fashion *War and Peace* is like *Joseph Andrews* and *Tristram Shandy* in seizing hold of both branches of Cervantes' endowment of the novel, the hero and the method.

Tolstoy and to a lesser degree Scott are fond of attributing actions to the force of circumstances. But as the nineteenth-century faith in history, in all its variants, began to be challenged, another aspect of quixotism, its dogged individualism, could begin to reemerge. In an essay of 1874, Friedrich Nietzsche attacked the malady of history – which he associated with Hegel – for its "idolatry of the actual" and the contemptible expression "to adapt ourselves to circumstances."[9] Disenchantment with history thus begins with a kind of resistance, first to enchanters and then to circumstances, that has characterized true quixotism right along. But history, especially in its nationalist modes, creates an ethos as well as its account of reality, so that without it or a strong religious belief the individual may be at a loss. That is where the original Don Quixote's capacity for self-invention comes in. The creation of individual identities that, however minimal, are proof against ridicule is the principal contribution of quixotism to modernism.

Cervantes' hero willed himself to be Don Quixote. Only at first and superficially does it seem absurd for the aging *hidalgo* to declare himself a knight and embark on adventures. Once readers become accustomed to his inventiveness, the character becomes familiar and dependable, and a number of things become clear about a seemingly derivative life of imitation. For example, when confronted by his neighbor Pedro Alonso on his return from the first sally, Don Quixote insists on his new identity as both singular and multiple: "I know who I am and I know that I am capable of being not only those I have mentioned, but all the Twelve Peers of France, and the Nine Worthies as well." If Don Quixote believed he *was* a certain knight errant – his favorite Amadís, say – he really would be crazy; but instead he will emulate them all, and that means fictional as well as living heroes of other days. Elsewhere he freely admits that the poets exaggerated the virtues of heroes – and of Dulcineas – in any case. As a self-decreed hero with numerous possible roles in mind, he has prepared himself for numerous defeats, yet repeatedly shows that identity can be preserved and wrested from defeat. By two measures – the many adventures that Cervantes, with the help of the Duke and Duchess and others, has thought up for him and his resounding fame ever since – Don Quixote, despite all the human and material resources opposed to him, is Don Quixote. In the nineteenth century, in what is surely an early modernist narrative, *Bouvard and Pécuchet* (1881), Flaubert seizes on this precedent to display the number of professions theoretically free for the choosing in the modern world. The middle-aged Bouvard and Pécuchet take up one profession after another, always by careful study of the books and always encountering defeat before going on to the next, until eventually they return to their profession as copying clerks. Their story is both depressing and dignifying, their dignity somehow proved and tested by defeat.

Because James Joyce's *Ulysses* (1922) is cast as epic rather than romance, its debt to Cervantes' novel and its hero is seldom much thought about. In a typical modernist move, the work ingests a couple of classic stories, one ancient and one modern, and much other literature besides. The title *Ulysses* and Joyce's advance notice to his acquaintances express the debt to Homer's *Odyssey* that is never explicit in the text; allusions to Shakespeare's *Hamlet* are scarcely disguised and are prominent throughout. Both famous stories were about fathers and sons, among other things, and Joyce designed some analogous relation to hold between the unrelated characters Leopold Bloom and Stephen Dedalus. Don Quixote was not a father, nor was he apparently the son of anyone, for his family is never mentioned by Cervantes. He comes to life in middle age as a knight errant pursuing justice at large and not as having inherited anything. It would be easy to show that *Ulysses* owes more to Homer and Shakespeare, more to Dante and Aquinas, more to Flaubert and Sterne even, than to Cervantes; yet in the history of the novel it still owes its being to *Don Quixote*.

In a tale of metempsychosis at the end of the *Republic*, Plato floated the idea that the famed Odysseus might prefer to return to life as an ordinary man. As the tale goes, even though that was the only lot left to him, Odysseus would choose it anyway. In carrying out the metempsychosis, Joyce does not strictly employ a Cervantine procedure, since he does not imply that Homer's epic was false or misleading and his novel true: he wants his readers to watch him juggle with both narratives. Yet the contrast is there, since the reincarnation of Odysseus is Mr. Bloom, canvasser of advertisements who has difficulty getting himself to return home on June 16, 1902; and one of the effects is to insist on the superior representativeness of this day in Dublin. Even the bewildering styles of narration in the later episodes of *Ulysses* force readers to search for and hang on to the represented action as if only that were real. And surely Bloom is a quixotic hero whose identity is forged in defeat. Though he may be mocked for his theories, for his Jewishness, or his wife's infidelity, his fame is known to many who have never read the book. More knight errant than Homeric adventurer, in truth, he helps others as well as getting himself into jams. Instead of enjoying rare sexual conquests, he succors women of the like of Mrs. Breen, Mrs. Dignam, and Mrs. Purefoy. His interior monologues reveal still other practical – and not so practical – designs for the improvement of his world. Like other quixotes, he lives mainly in these dreams. Above all, he protests against injustices, with energy and directness that may be more effective than Don Quixote's sword.

Justice, one may feel, is always eluding even the best attempts to legis-late, to govern, or to behave well. Accordingly, heroes like Don Quixote, Mr. Pickwick, or Prince Myshkin not only have a role to play but may transgress the usual rules to play it. (When pressed, Don Quixote claims that knights errant have this exceptional warrant.) We owe to Kierkegaard, writing six years after *Pickwick*, a definition of heroism that may fairly be called quixotic. In *Fear and Trembling* (1843), to illustrate what he intends by a "knight of faith," Kierkegaard chooses the story of Abraham and Isaac from Genesis 22. He contrasts Abraham with other biblical and classical figures who sacrificed their children for ethical reasons: that is, Jephthah and Agamemnon were called upon to sacrifice their daughters, Brutus his sons, for some common good. Their tragedy was to meet with situations where family bonds came in conflict with tribal loyalties. According to Kierkegaard, no such conditions applied to Abraham, whom God commanded to sacrifice his only son Isaac – that is, to violate on God's command both his own love and human law. By obeying the command Abraham becomes not a tragic hero but something finer. "The tragic hero renounces himself in order to express the universal, the knight of faith renounces the universal in order to become the individual." Thus there is such a thing as "a teleological suspension of the ethical," both in certain situations an individual might face and in the response to these situations.[10] Kierkegaard's knight of faith is not just any knight of romance but Don Quixote. As Kierkegaard tells and retells the story, the situation Abraham faces is absurd or pointless, and Abraham meets it all the same with a power of will altogether uncommon. On the other hand, one may interject, his reward is great. According to Kierkegaard, although and because no conditions were set beforehand, Abraham becomes one with the absolute, with God. And he was leader of his people to begin with.

In truth the biblical figure of Abraham was admitted to the quixotic tradition by Fielding. Abraham is Parson Adams's name, and in reproving Joseph Andrews' impatience to marry and (as Adams sees it) his failure to submit to Providence, he invokes his namesake: "Had Abraham so loved his son Isaac as to refuse the sacrifice required, is there any of us who would not condemn him?" Before he can finish this impromptu sermon, moreover, someone rushes in to tell Abraham Adams that his youngest and favorite son has drowned. As in the story in Genesis, the son is not killed: Mr. Adams is apparently being tested, and he sticks to his principles, though not without a very human explosion of grief. Two differences stand out between this story of Abraham as Quixote that Fielding tells and Kierkegaard's version. Circumstances, such as might affect any of us, test Abraham Adams; and no teleology can be inferred from the incident. The quixotic tradition does afford a suspension of the ethical – the responses of Pickwick, Myshkin, and Bloom are illustrations of this. But there is no evident teleology, and these heroes begin and remain ordinary people, for all their extraordinary individuality.

Like Fielding but with a darker sense of humor, Franz Kafka could imagine a foolish Abraham whose quixotism was of a more ordinary cast. In a brilliant parody of Kierkegaard's meditations, Kafka could imagine an Abraham as an alert waiter who was unable to take time from his duties, an Abraham who was old and ugly or young and dirty, an Abraham who cannot believe that he is the one called and is afraid that "he would change on the way into Don Quixote":

> An Abraham who should come unsummoned! It is as if, at the end of the year, when the best student was solemnly about to receive a prize, the worst student rose in the expectant stillness and came forward from his dirty desk in the last row because he had made a mistake of hearing, and the whole class burst out laughing. And perhaps he had made no mistake at all, his name really was called, it having been the teacher's intent to make the rewarding of the best student at the same time a punishment for the worst one.[11]

The pain and foolishness of these metamorphosed Abrahams can readily be identified in the protagonists of Kafka's posthumously published *The Trial* (written 1914–17) and *The Castle* (1918–22). The command comes to K or to the imagined Abrahams as a meaningless test, like the requirement of an initiate to a club to commit some illegal act that, once he has signaled his willingness to perform it, is casually waived. Kafka's novels repeatedly expose the injustice of this double bind. His hero K trusts that his allegiance will be recognized, but he is left blindsided, as if there never were any club in the first place. Authority appears only as random signals, or as a projection of K's own fears.

What is finally unquixotic about Kierkegaard's Abraham is that he wins; his faith carries him beyond the ethical to a higher state. Typically, modernist heroes inherit more of the bewilderment of Don Quixote than his self-confidence and readiness for battle in any case. The heroes of Samuel Beckett are still more passive and bewildered than Kafka's, though the humor is lighter again. Part II of *Molloy* (1951), in fact, is still another quixotic reenactment of the story of Abraham, with Isaac very much present. Jacques Moran receives orders "to see about Molloy" and to take his son with him. "Where are we going, papa?" the son asks. "How often had I told him not to ask me questions" is the all too recognizable rejoinder. The purpose of the story and the nature of Youdi's hold on Moran are as mysterious and open to interpretation as Genesis 22. Though the messenger Gaber comes and goes like an angel, Youdi never appears in the foreground. With Kafka-like sentiments but Irish humor, Moran reports: "I had never seen any other messenger than Gaber nor any other agent than myself. But I supposed we were not the only ones and Gaber must have supposed the same. For the feeling that we were the only ones of our kind would, I believe, have been more than we could have borne... Thus I was able to say to Gaber, Let him give this job to someone else, I don't want it, and Gaber was able to reply, He wants it to be you." According to Georg Lukács, *Don Quixote* itself "stands at the beginning of the time when the Christian God began to forsake the world."[12] Of course, Lukács could only make such an observation as a twentieth-century intellectual looking back in time. Don Quixote did not have quite this problem and could repent on his death-bed if he did. But his modernist descendants seem to be stumbling beyond the ethical without even their authors knowing quite where that is.

Finally, one definition of beyond the ethical is the criminal. It would seem a perversion of quixotic striving, even of the kind that salvages an identity from defeat, to turn to crime for such a purpose. Yet an alternative quixotism in some modernist literature would seem to go so far to seize hold of an identity, or merely a sense of existence, by committing a gratuitous crime. And so is the death penalty for such a crime somehow an affirming of existence. "I had been right, I was still right, I was always right," Mersault in Albert Camus' *The Stranger* (1942) shouts at the prison chaplain. "I had done this and not done that. I had not done one thing when I was doing another. What then? It was as if I had waited all the time for that moment and that brief dawn at which I would be justified." This may seem a long way from knight errantry, but I suggest that Dostoevsky's Prince Myshkin was one of the first avatars of such a strange faith. Even if we did not know from the early plotting of *The Idiot* in the author's notebooks that the hero and the murderer Rogozhin were once the same person, in the action of the novel as published Myshkin still seeks out Rogozhin and spends the night with him in vigil over Nastasya Filippovna's body.

Don Quixote, whose adventures were not always without cost to others besides himself, never killed anyone I am thankful to say. His object in combat was usually to bring his adversaries no lower than their knees, from which posture they might rise to pay obeisance to the Lady Dulcinea. In this essay I have attempted nevertheless to name the most distinctive descendants of Don Quixote in the European novel and to take note of their considerable differences. Even so I have held to one side the far greater number of novels that may fairly be called quixotic because they tell of a hero's or heroine's disillusionment after initial misunderstandings about their world; and I have touched not at all on the influence of Cervantes in both Latin and Anglophone Americas. When it comes to the Cervantine method it is even harder to find limits, for it can reasonably be assumed that as long as novelists (and others) seek to impress one with the truthfulness of their narrative, they will make sport of other stories. The contribution of *Don Quixote* to realism in the novel is likely to last more than four centuries.

NOTES

1 See Ronald Paulson, *Don Quixote in England: The Aesthetics of Laughter* (Baltimore: The Johns Hopkins University Press, 1998).
2 Miguel de Unamuno, "On the Reading and Interpretation of *Don Quixote*," in *Our Lord Don Quixote: The Life of Don Quixote and Sancho with Related Essays*, trans. Anthony Kerrigan (Princeton: Princeton University Press, 1976), p. 461.
3 José Ortega y Gasset, *Meditations on Quixote*, trans. Evelyn Rugg and Diego Marin (New York: Norton, 1961), pp. 144–45.
4 Jorge Luis Borges, "Partial Magic in the *Quixote*," trans. James E. Irby, in *Labyrinths: Selected Stories and Other Writings* (New York: New Directions, 1964), p. 196.
5 John Forster, *The Life of Charles Dickens*, 2 vols. (London: Dent, 1948), vol. I, p. 11.
6 Letter of 1 [13] Jan. 1868, in *Letters of Fyodor Dostoevsky*, trans. Ethyl Colburn Mayne (New York: Horizon, 1961), pp. 142–43.
7 G. W. F. Hegel, *The Philosophy of Fine Art*, trans. F. P. B. Osmaston, 4 vols. (London: Bell, 1920), vol. II, pp. 375–76.
8 Erich Auerbach, *Mimesis: The Representation of Reality in Western Literature*, trans. Willard R. Trask (Princeton: Princeton University Press, 1953), p. 463.
9 Friedrich Nietzsche, "The Use and Abuse of History," in *Thoughts out of Season*, Part II, trans. Adrian Collins (Edinburgh: Foulis, 1909), pp. 71–72.
10 Søren Kierkegaard, *Fear and Trembling*, trans. Walter Lowrie (1954; rpt. Princeton: Princeton University Press, 1974), pp. 86, 67.
11 Franz Kafka, *Parables and Paradoxes in German and English* (New York: Schocken, 1958), pp. 42–45.
12 Georg Lukács, *The Theory of the Novel*, trans. Anna Bostock (Cambridge, MA: MIT Press, 1971), p. 103.

FURTHER READING

Alter, Robert. *Partial Magic: The Novel as a Self-Conscious Genre*. Berkeley: University of California Press, 1975.
Cascardi, Anthony J. *The Bounds of Reason: Cervantes, Dostoevsky, Flaubert*. New York: Columbia University Press, 1986.
Close, Anthony. *The Romantic Approach to Don Quixote*. Cambridge: Cambridge University Press, 1978.
Crooks, Esther Josephine. *The Influence of Cervantes in France in the Seventeenth Century*. Baltimore: The Johns Hopkins University Press, 1931.
Kundera, Milan. *The Art of the Novel*. Trans. Linda Asher. New York: Harper and Row, 1988.
Levin, Harry. "The Example of Cervantes." In *Contexts of Criticism*. Cambridge, MA: Harvard University Press, 1957.
Nabokov, Vladimir. *Lectures on Don Quixote*. New York: Harcourt Brace Jovanovich, 1983.
Paulson, Ronald. *Don Quixote in England: The Aesthetics of Laughter*. Baltimore: The Johns Hopkins University Press, 1998.

Robert, Marthe. *The Old and the New: From Don Quixote to Kafka*. Trans. Carol Cosman. Berkeley: University of California Press, 1977.

Serrano Plaja, Arturo. *"Magic" Realism in Cervantes' "Don Quixote" as Seen Through "Tom Sawyer" and "The Idiot"*. Trans. Robert S. Rudder. Berkeley: University of California Press, 1970.

Welsh, Alexander. *Reflections on the Hero as Quixote*. Princeton: Princeton University Press, 1981.

Ziolkowski, Eric. *The Sanctification of Don Quixote: From Hidalgo to Priest*. University Park: Pennsylvania State University Press, 1991.

6

MARY MALCOLM GAYLORD

Cervantes' other fiction

Don Quixote's siblings

In cultures of Fame, other writings of the author of a masterpiece are likely to suffer the same fate as siblings of a prodigy. Classed as unexceptional, for whatever reasons, they languish in the shadows while beams of admiring curiosity are trained on one who has been singled out for special attention. So it has been with the "other" works of Miguel de Cervantes, ever since the *History of the Ingenious Hidalgo* burst upon the literary scene in 1605, serving as catalyst for a series of developments in imaginative prose that would permanently alter the landscape of world literature. Given Cervantes' identification with the novel, modernity's genre of choice, it is perhaps not surprising that his dramatic and poetic works should be little known outside of specialist scholarly circles.[1] But general recognition of *Don Quixote*'s inventor as a founding master of the art of narrative makes quite conspicuous widespread neglect of his three other works of prose fiction: the pastoral romance *Galatea* (*Los seis libros de la Galatea*) (1585), the collection of twelve *Exemplary Novels* (*Novelas ejemplares*) (1613), and the posthumous *Trials of Persiles and Sigismunda: A Northern Story* (*Los trabajos de Persiles y Sigismunda: Historia septentrional*) (1617).[2] Taken together, these volumes more than double Cervantes' output in prose. Indeed, as scholars have observed, had only these three been left to posterity, the resulting corpus would accord Miguel de Cervantes Saavedra a place of no small importance in the early modern history of European letters.

Why, then, are these other works so understudied? Until recently not a few university course titles labeled them dismissively as "minor works." In the prologue to *Persiles*, Cervantes complains of "an error into which many of my uninformed admirers have fallen," namely the extent to which *Don Quixote* has overdetermined his image. "I, sir, am Cervantes," he protests to a young fan, "but not the delight of the muses or any of the other foolish things that you mentioned" (15). Are we to understand this distancing from the burlesque mode as an earnest renewal of his ironic rejection of "biological" paternity for *Don Quixote* in the novel's celebrated 1605 prologue? Do such disclaimers imply that the author considered his other works to be offspring in some way more legitimate, at least more publicly acceptable as such, than the more famous "stepchild"? Whatever its original intention, this death-bed valedictory, cited more often than any other passage of *Persiles*, has worked to perpetuate a schizoid vision of Cervantes, one which continues to influence which of his works we choose to read and how we read them. To be sure, reception history has engaged in its own brand of baby-switching, usually confirming *Don Quixote* as heir apparent and relegating his siblings to the condition of disinherited stepchildren. To address the question of the "other" works is both to acknowledge such assessments and to perpetuate them, if only functionally, by grouping some books apart from others. Yet in view of extreme readerly partiality toward *Don Quixote* in our day, it may also be argued that the less-known fictions need separate consideration to do them justice before they can enjoy their birthright to the full.

At the same time, since virtually every reader who approaches the "other" writings already claims some acquaintance with *Don Quixote*, any critical introduction to the less explored novelistic territory of Cervantes' other fiction must of necessity adopt a comparative frame. That frame suggests a number of questions. Why should we read these neglected works? Has the masterpiece not given us acquaintance with the author's most remarkable fictional offspring? Are we not courting disappointment by asking to be introduced to the rest of the family? Once the door to forgotten parts of the Cervantes Saavedra household has been opened, however, more probing questions must be asked. Are the "biological" children as different from the "stepchild" as we have been led to expect? Do the most famous son's privileges rest on superiority, or simply on differences which have been scripted over time into a hierarchical scale of literary value? Do differences among siblings suggest family planning, or unforeseen changes in parental circumstance and perspective? The partialities of generations of readers notwithstanding, it is important to remember that Cervantes repeatedly extends the benefits of proud paternal recognition to all of his literary progeny, owning his diverse offspring not only as very much his own, but as products of an ongoing creative endeavor. The present essay aims to make that pride understandable, whether or not we decide to share it.

Galatea's broken mirror

In 1585, Cervantes published his first book, and the first of his works that have come to be known as novels. Still a young man at thirty-seven, he had been back in Spain for only as many years as the more than five he had previously spent in an Algerian prison, following his capture after several years' participation in Christian campaigns against the Turks in the Eastern Mediterranean. For his formal debut in the world of letters, the novice writer chose the genre of pastoral romance, which had enjoyed an extraordinary vogue throughout Europe since the appearance of Sannazaro's *Arcadia* in 1504. *Galatea* follows the model of prose narrative irregularly interspersed with verse passages inaugurated by Jorge de Montemayor's *Diana* (c. 1558), which had already seen several Spanish imitations.[3] It is no accident that the small-town censors who survey the Ingenious Gentleman's library find numerous of these hybrid works about shepherds arranged alongside books of verse. Both are identified as *poesía*, a term which throughout the early modern period continued to carry the Aristotelian meaning of Literature in the honorific sense, to be distinguished from History rather than from prose. The small but significant private collection described in *Don Quixote* (I, 6) suggests that, like his protagonist, the author was no less avid a reader of pastorals than of the chivalric romances with which the Manchegan's library was more famously supplied.

"Custom dictates that *La Galatea* be swept aside as a weak effort, interesting only because it was Cervantes' first major work," observes the biographer William Byron, all too accurately.[4] Some critics have voiced dissatisfaction with the book's advertised generic affiliation, seeing it as too pastoral and insufficiently Cervantine. Others find the first book quite recognizably its author's work, but imperfectly pastoral. For anyone interested in the prehistory of *Don Quixote*'s parodic practice, however, writing off *Galatea* has its price. For here, while creating his first full-blown fictional world, Cervantes hit upon the formula which would become hallmark, heart and soul of his novelistic method. Architects of our day speak of "adaptive reuse" of structures inherited from earlier builders. Using another architectural trope more naturalized within our critical vocabulary, Peter Dunn speaks of the novelist's deconstruction and reconstruction of the building-blocks of literary genre.[5] Either figure will do to evoke much that is central to Cervantes' *modus operandi*. Engaging an established, well-worn literary genre, he explores what Rosalie Colie calls its "resources of kind", adopting formal and thematic conventions, yet never hesitating to interfere with prescribed workings or to expose contradictions betweem premises and aims. Above all, he works slyly to bend each traditional feature to some new purpose.[6]

Thus, in cultivating a mode whose central literary business in the Renaissance consists in talking and singing about Love, Cervantes presents most of his characters as polished poets whose plaints imitate preferred models of high culture: Virgil's *Eclogues*, the troubadours, Petrarch, sixteenth-century

Italian and Italianate poets, including the "Prince of Castilian Poets," the Toledan Garcilaso de la Vega. But that aristocratic standard is held up to the test of other codes. One of Galatea's suitors, Erastro, sports more rough-hewn expressions and a self-deprecating humor rarely seen in courtly pastorals; another, the old man Arsindo, extols the joys of marriage, fertility and long shared years in the homely tropes of a folk poetry out of tune with the songs about Love's torments that dominate the work. Cervantes' preface acknowledges the "doings of shepherds, primarily their love affairs" as the mode's proper subject; yet he imports into his own version of pastoral precisely those facets of sentimental life which the poet-critic Fernando de Herrera had made a point of excluding from the idyllic sphere of the eclogue.[7] Jealous rage, adultery, competition between rivals, bloodshed and death – all of these find their way into Cervantes' Arcadia. *Galatea*'s author also follows long-standing tradition when he peoples his book with creatures of different ontological status; but he accentuates diversity, letting the most unreal of beings, goddess-like and inaccessible Galatea (namesake of the mythic nymph beloved of Acis and the Cyclops Polyphemus) and the Muse Calíope of Book 6, come alive alongside both newly invented characters and historical poets, including Cervantes himself, in transparent shepherds' garb. To add to a confusion already fostered by these pseudo-shepherds' disguises, many figures come paired with a friend, rival, or even twin who may be seen slipping into the place of some look-alike. The contrary effects of heterogeneity and resemblance are compounded by the absence of a clear sense of priority among characters. The title figure and her mismatched admirers, the elegant Elicio and the rustic Erastro, dominate neither the action nor the discourse of a crowded field.

Cervantes delegates to his least polished character the task of summing up a picture of human identity at once specular and fragmented. In one of his first songs, Erastro compares the proliferation of lovers' cares to the way a broken mirror returns multiple, fractured self-images to anyone who looks at it: "One sees not so many countenances displayed / In a broken mirror, or framed by art; / If we look and see ourselves reflected, / We discern a multitude in each and every part. / How many cares on cares arise / All from one cruel care . . . " (8).[8] Placed in the work's opening scene (74), this arresting trope offers a key to poetic and psychic structures soon to unfold. What the character proposes as a metaphor for the suffering of individual consciousness articulates with unwitting precision the generative principal of the whole book's construction. *Galatea*'s singers and narrators not only produce multiple lyric images of themselves and their own cares; narrative arrangement lets them encounter their private thoughts and feelings many times over, refracted in the self-referential discourse of their fellows.

Some readers have implied that Cervantes' ingenuity in taking the pastoral genre apart was much greater than his skill at reassembling it. The unevenness of *Galatea's* represented world, which the text itself recognizes in the trope of the broken mirror, has also been blamed on the absence of a coherent plot. The title character, who could easily have supplied a strong story line – her initial search for independence from unwanted suitors, supplanted by the stronger desire to elude an arranged marriage – rarely appears in the fictional foreground. Her life stands instead as backdrop for the singing and telling of others. As these figures appear, alone or in pairs, each new song or story works its strand into a carefully woven pattern. The case of Galatea and her suitors is presented in Books I and VI; the story of the "Two Friends" is first told retrospectively by Timbrio in Book II, moved forward with a chance meeting in Book III, and finally concluded by Silerio in Book V. Books III and IV circle around the wedding for which most of the romance's characters have gathered. But having placed the solemn, socially significant speech act of matrimony at the vanishing point of his nested narratives, Cervantes treats the occasion in an unsettling fashion. Set conspicuously off-center in Book III, the wedding unites Daranio and Silveria, shadow figures who neither speak nor are fleshed out in narrative. Their marriage, like Galatea's sentimental trajectory, provides the occasion for other characters to speak: Mireno protests Silveria's rejection of him; four enamored shepherds perform an Eclogue; the old man Arsindo contributes a folksy epithalamion; Book IV's shepherds debate the nature of Love; Rosaura threatens suicide in order to win back a suitor. Here, where the romance seems mired in its own complexities, it becomes clear that Cervantes has subordinated both story and discourse to the signifying design of symbolic architecture. Relegated to the narrative background, marriage marks the half-way point in the shepherds' progress. From it, they move on toward Death, represented in the funeral rites of the poet Meliso in Book VI, where their own life journeys come to a temporary resting place.

At the level of story, interweaving of narrative strands depends on the random encounters typical of Greek romance, on overhearing of voices singing in the woods, and on so much peeping and eavesdropping that one critic calls this pastoral a world of "staring onlookers [*mirones*]".[9] Yet the narrator's formula – "Jane would have continued her song/story, had it not been for the appearance of Jill" – is repeated so insistently that it acquires the force of a symbolic narrative grammar, melding psychological and aesthetic concerns into linguistic form. One individual's longings are kept from fulfillment by the intrusion of another's wish or will, or by her words. *Galatea's* shepherds live in the linguistic limbo of the subjunctive mode, their desires and experience governed by the contrary-to-fact or unreal condition. The reader kept hanging on tales of erotic frustration is not surprised to discover many loose threads still untied at the book's open ending. In the refusal to tidy up his messy plot, we find yet another key to the particular brand of verisimilitude which *Galatea* introduces. Rather than recruiting a wise witch like Montemayor's Felicia to release his characters from their sentimental binds, Cervantes makes their narrative impasses his own.

Such meticulous attention to the potential of what might have been passed over as the most minute or the most obvious features of an inherited mode underscores the insistently metaliterary character of this work. As he dismantles and reassembles constituent parts, Cervantes turns a sharp eye to the convention's traditional links with poetry. Introduced in the prologue as "Eclogue", this version of pastoral launches its first scene with Elicio's unframed song, then passing to alternation between lyric, narrative, and naturalized dialogue. *Galatea* follows Montemayor's practice of sprinkling samples of contemporary poetic modes through the fictional fabric. But what elsewhere amounts to little more than respectful anthologizing becomes in Cervantes' hands a full-blown metapoetic reflection on the possibilities of forms and discourses. In Book III's eclogue-within-an-eclogue, strikingly presented as a staged entertainment rather than according to pastoral convention as "natural" singing, and in Book IV's debate, the assembled poets not only consider philosophies of Love; they also take up the *linguistic* and *poetic* dilemmas that beset lovers. Throughout the text, even the shepherds' most innocent diversions, all of them verbal (riddles, chains of communication, guessing games about sentimental secrets, poetic glosses), actively put language to the test of encompassing experience. In Calíope's song in Book VI, the text shows not just its shepherd characters, but none other than the Muse herself, wrestling with the reach of words. In this sense, *Galatea*'s shepherds, fashioning themselves in language and at the same time holding up for general scrutiny the very expressions in which they find themselves mirrored, presage the self-consciousness of later Cervantine characters and their signature linguistic perspectivism.

The post-Romantic presumption that literary conventions make for artificial expression has discouraged generations of readers from looking for traces of Cervantes' life and historical world in his first novel. Rejecting *Galatea* as Cervantine juvenalia, one critic complains that its characters add up not to a society, but to a debating society, concerned more with theories of love than with the experience of it.[10] Evidence that the work is fashioned out of Neoplatonic material gleaned from early reading of Leone Ebreo's *Dialogues on Love*, first translated into Spanish in 1568, well before Cervantes' acquaintance with Aristotelian literary theory, is used to support the view that *Galatea*'s world is an ideal, rather than a real one. Early readers might have found it "natural for a young poet to initiate himself by Pastorals, which, not professing to imitate real life, require no experience." Yet, as Frank Kermode cautions in citing the opinion of Dr. Johnson, the practice of this convention required considerable knowledge of literary models, which had from Virgil's day onward made urban public life very visible from within imagined bucolic space.[11] Although *Galatea*'s shepherds do not, like Virgil's, talk politics, and though most never stray far from the bosky banks of the River Tagus, Cervantes uses narrative and poetic means to bring cities, seas and nations beyond the borders of his fictional world into the heart of his pastoral. At the close of Book VI, the prospect of Galatea's reluctant marriage to an unnamed Portuguese shepherd threatens no less than the dissolution of the sentimental and discursive world over which she presides. The specter of physical conflict raised by Elicio's vow to leave off singing and take up arms in her defense and the bridegroom's nationality could not have been trivial details in 1585, when Spain was five years into the tenuous union of Castilian and Portuguese crowns that would last six decades. The most mobile of the book's fictional inhabitants are Timbrio and Silerio, who shuttle on sentimental journeys and missions of honor between Spain and various Mediterranean sites (Naples, Gaeta, Lipari, Stromboli, Pantelleria, Lampedusa, Zembra, Genoa, Carthage, La Goletta) which Cervantes came to know during his soldiering years in the 1570s. More tangible evidence of his Italian sojourn has been uncovered by the sleuthing of Geoffrey Stagg, who concludes that the writing of *Galatea* took place during two distinct periods of the author's life, one before and one following his travels outside of Spain. When he returned to Madrid and his birthplace Alcalá de Henares in 1580 after ten years abroad, Cervantes brought not only the stories of storms, battles with Corsair galleys and escape from Turkish captors recounted by Timbrio in Book v, but also a more direct and nuanced acquaintance with the literary scene of sixteenth-century Italy, previously known to him largely through Spanish translations. When Cervantes notes in his prologue that, although his book still leaves something even for him to desire, he does not want to keep it to himself any longer, he is probably referring to this lengthy period of gestation, much disrupted – *pace* Dr. Johnson – by some fifteen years of life experience.[12]

Galatea also offers detailed evidence of the author's acquaintance with Spanish poets, writers, fellow soldiers and political figures during these years. Various clues permit the identification of several pseudo-shepherds with historical persons. The Mediterranean traveler Lauso is taken by most to be the author himself; Damón to be Pedro Laínez, a poet friend from 1560s Madrid; Tirsi the accomplished poet Francisco de Figueroa; and Larsileo the Mateo Vázquez to whom Cervantes writes from Algiers a remarkable verse epistle which is alluded to and glossed in the novel. Also mentioned is Don Australiano, clearly Don John of Austria, commander of the Lepanto expedition and half-brother to King Philip II. When the Muse Calíope reviews the ranks of living Spanish poets, we are introduced to nearly a hundred more writers, including soldier-poets, not a few of whom had actually sailed and fought alongside Cervantes. Within this same House of Fame, we find future masters like Luis de Góngora, Lope de Vega and Francisco de Quevedo; the age's masters of epic verse (Alonso de Ercilla, Juan Rufo, Cristóbal de Virués, all celebrated in *Don Quixote*, I, 6); the Castilian translator of Camões' *Os Lusiadas*; and a solid contingent of more than a dozen "Antarctic poets" hailing from Peru and Guatemala. Contact with transatlantic poet contemporaries can only have deepened the interest that induced Cervantes to petition in 1590 for permission to cross the Atlantic. The very fascination with the pastoral mode of which *Galatea* is one among many sixteenth-century manifestations owed much, as Kermode reminds us (*English Pastoral Poetry*, pp. 40, 43–44), to European curiosity about Edenic spaces in the American territories.

Calíope's catalogue makes it plain that the figure of the soldier-poet who took up "now the sword, now the pen [ora la spada, ora la pluma]" was no hollow archetype, but rather the blueprint for many sixteenth-century youths who, like Miguel de Cervantes, aspired to fight and write their way to personal recognition.[13] Her song's explicit link of soldiering and versifying helps us make sense of the otherwise perplexing selection of a Muse who traditionally presides over heroic poetry to adorn a work about love among country-folk. In the prologue, speaking as apologist for his work, *Galatea*'s author describes the practice of poetry as a quasi-martial exercise of conquest through which writers strive to acquire verbal treasure and "sovereignty" over the art of eloquence. When Cervantes evokes the Castilian language itself as an "open field, easy, spacious," where daring spirits may run freely and make new discoveries with God's blessing (p. xi), readers may recognize in his conflation of knighting and writing the founding merger, Arms and Letters, of Don Quixote's project. The ideal of a spacious field for writing will occupy the writer for the rest of his career.

Galatea is not often celebrated as an important forerunner of its author's more universally appreciated creations. Yet early in *Don Quixote*, whose prologue notes the twenty years separating the author's two published books, Cervantes shines a spotlight briefly on *Galatea*. As the village priest of the book-burning episode renders his judgment of pastorals and tosses more than one into the backyard bonfire, this mock inquisitor finally turns to the work of a personal acquaintance. He treats the book and his "old friend" with kid gloves. Word play – litotes (it *does not lack* imagination ["invención"]), a pun (its author is "more versed in misfortunes than in verses [más versado en desdichas que en versos]"), and finally antithesis (the work "proposes something, but concludes nothing [propone algo, y no concluye nada]" [63]) – manages to save this first effort from the flames, but also relegates it to literary limbo. As the reader of *Don Quixote* soon learns, Cervantine self-reference is rarely transparent and never idle. *Galatea*'s author recalls his 1585 promise to finish her story in order to bring that unfinished literary business into an ongoing agenda. He lets a fictional library and its readers announce that pastoral will enjoy a prominent place among the many literary modes used to shape characters and experience in the novel. Knight and Squire are routed early on through explicitly Arcadian space (I, 10–15), where poetic shepherding first offers itself as an attractive alternative to knighting. A number of *Don Quixote*'s characters and events appear made over from their 1585 originals: Galatea as Marcela (I, 14); Timbrio and Silerio as the two friends of "The Tale of Foolish Curiosity" (I, 33–35); Daranio's shadowy wedding takes on shadier tones in Camacho's (II, 22). And in a new work that gives pride of place to prose narration, Cervantes reintroduces at every turn *Galatea*'s concern with the status of poetry, the reach of language, the truth of literary representation, the power of voices, the uses of epic. With *The Six Books of Galatea*, Cervantes has prepared the ground for generic hybrids, discursive experimentation, and self-conscious metafictions to come.

Tricks of example in the novellas

In the English-speaking world, after *Don Quixote*, the twelve short stories called *Exemplary Novels* are by far the best-known and most intensively studied of Cervantes' works.[14] Following the first part of *Don Quixote* by just eight years, their publication in 1613 could ride the coat-tails of a predecessor whose celebrity sufficed to guarantee public eagerness for whatever its author might put into print. The volume's prologue is penned by a writer conscious of his success, keenly aware of the "devoted reader [lector amantísimo]" he addresses, supremely confident of his ability to engage his audience. Rather than using the occasion to make good on pending promises – second parts for *Galatea* and *Don Quixote* – Cervantes uses the advantage of his fame to carry a career-long journey of generic exploration into another promising literary territory, the novella.

By this time he is no stranger to the genre, having interpolated novella-like stories into both of the earlier books. *Don Quixote*'s first part indicates that the writing of the *Exemplary Novels* occupied more than a few years. After "The Tale of Foolish Curiosity" has been read aloud to travelers gathered at an inn, another piece "by the same author" is produced, though not read on this occasion. This "Story of Rinconete and Cortadillo" figures in a historical manuscript compiled close to the time of *Don Quixote*'s first printing to provide after-dinner entertainment for the Archbishop of Seville.[15] It is not known whether others of the stories were written or begun well before 1613, but references to historical events from the 1590s on make it reasonable to assume that they represent many years of intermittent labor. During the last decade of Cervantes' life, which saw the publication of no fewer than five volumes of his work, they unquestionably shared the author's attention with other projects.

That the *Exemplary Novels* had taken the precise measure of contemporary tastes is evident. Within a decade, the collection had gone through a dozen editions in Spanish; nearly a dozen more would follow by the end of the century. Their popularity outside of Spain did not have to wait on translations into French, English, and German. Everywhere they found imitators, among novelists and dramatists.[16] The English translation of 1640 touts its versions of "Delight in Severall Shapes" as just what the reader would expect from the "elegant pen" of "one of the prime Wits of Spaine, for his rare Fancies, and wittie Inventions." If Cervantes bowed on occasion to the "comic monarchy" of Lope de Vega, he had firmly established himself, at home and abroad, as sovereign in the art of narrative.[17] The satirist Francisco de Quevedo acerbically advised one would-be look-alike to "leave the novellas to Cervantes."[18]

When the collection appeared, educated readers would have caught the title's clear allusion to two distinct kinds of narrative. The Spanish term "novela" rendered directly the Italian *novella* or short story, associated with Boccaccio and Bandello, while the qualifier "exemplary" pointed toward the medieval *exemplum*. One term evokes intrigues involving moral indiscretion; the other an openly moralistic kind of narrative. Separated, the modes suggest a generic division of labor between instruction and delight, Horace's famous goals for writers; together they make an oxymoron. Aware that he was effecting a purely symbolic reunion between a famous couple more separate in theory than in the practice of his day, Cervantes uses their fusion to put his personal copyright on a new form of storytelling. In the prologue he explains, with a flourish of paternal authority, that he has given his stories the name *novelas* because he is the first to write wholly original novellas in Spanish.[19] Disparaging unnamed stories previously "translated" from Italian, he declares that "these are my very own, neither imitated or stolen; my wit engendered them, my pen gave birth to them" (1, 52). When he goes on to insist that these tales offer "decent and agreeable exercise" ("ejercicios honestos y agradables") for the recreation of the spirit, the writer identified since 1605 with his best-selling burlesque romance may be seeking to cultivate a more dignified image. But the questionable morality of fiction in general and of novellas in particular is reflected in the titles of many seventeenth-century collections. In this new and still developing genre, which like the early modern *comedia* had not been canonized by ancient poetics, doubts about literary respectability compounded a potential for disapproval that moved writers like Cervantes to take refuge in claims of their stories' exemplary value.[20]

Cervantes' prologue does not spell out what sort of exemplarity he has in mind for his tales. But it stretches its commonplace promise that some sweetened profit lies waiting within the text (to be had, as it were, for the reading) into a more pointed challenge to the reader. "If you look carefully," he says, "there is not one from which may not be extracted some useful example," which, given time, he could spell out, not merely for each tale but for all of them. For the moment, he does no such thing. Instead he produces a new metaphor: his collection of stories is like a billiard table set up in the public square of society ("la plaza de nuestra república") (1, 52) where all comers are sure to find entertainment. The figure suggests that the stories will be contemporary in subject and thematically attentive to social and political concerns: "drawne to the life," as his English translator puts it. But the slippery Spanish name for the game on the table ("mesa de trucos") gestures beyond billiards toward other kinds of writerly tricks (the generic meaning of "trucos"), suggesting that the stories aspire to aesthetic as well as ethical exemplarity.

A first opportunity to gauge what intentions may be encrypted into Cervantes' novelistic practice comes sooner than we might expect, as the author uses the prologue to stage the fictional creation of one exemplary portrait: his own. The gesture of imagining that an anonymous friend has written an ekphrastic description of a non-existent likeness of Miguel de Cervantes Saavedra by the famous painter, Juan de Jáuregui (1583–1641), is pure whimsy of a sort familiar to readers of *Don Quixote*'s prologue. But this portrait's carefully drawn lines turn metafictional jest into autobiographical earnest. First reading out signs of mellowing in his features, Cervantes proceeds to pull out of physiognomy the decades of personal history crystallized there: more than five years' captivity and the proud service at the 1571 naval battle of Lepanto whose badge of honor is displayed in the veteran's maimed left hand. This self-staging, positioned in playful earnest between life and art, is the only moment of its kind in the *Exemplary Novels*. Unlike *Don Quixote*, whose author enters and exits at will, in many guises, the novellas proper have few trap-doors. In placing a fiction of his concretely historical self at the head of his book, however, Cervantes makes a gesture no less significant. Offered as example of his stories' enigmatic exemplarity, this portrait smilingly implies many things: that he could have chosen to tell his own story; that no history, once translated into fiction, should be taken for the real thing, no matter how often writers' tricks encourage us to do just that; that still and all, this author does write from lived experience. One early reader clearly caught the suggestion that the narratives walk a fine line between poetic imagination and historical reality. Translator James Mabbe responds in kind to Cervantes' playful invitation to enter the novellas' world of the possible by signing his own name in a witty reverse translation as "Don Diego Puede-Ser [Sir James May-Be]."

When Cervantes ends his prologue with the suggestion that his stories have "some hidden mystery that uplifts them" (1, 53), he sets the stage for spirited controversy over the meaning of individual stories, the coherence of the collection and its place in an unfolding novelistic vision. The prologue's offer of something for all customers makes textual variety a virtue in the cultural marketplace. Early readers, including Mabbe, who subtitled his English version "Delight in Severall Shapes," appear to have welcomed profusion of subjects and forms; the same diversity has proved more disconcerting to modern critics. Many have attributed to the collection, and its author, a personality split between the wishful optimism of uplifting love stories and a darker vision of grim social realities.

Students of the novellas have long engaged in ritual sorting of the tales into bins labeled idealistic, romantic, sentimental, Italianate (therefore imitated), ideologically conservative, generically romance narratives on the one hand; and realistic, picaresque, satiric, original, progressive and essentially novelistic works on the other. Into the "idealistic" bin are likely to go five tales of threatened love that ultimately triumphs over opposing forces (kidnapping, rape, rivalry, class pride, absence prolonged by war or weather): "The Generous Lover" ("El amante liberal"), "The English Spanish Lady" ("La española inglesa"), "The Force of Blood" ("La fuerza de la sangre"), "The Two Damsels" ("Las dos doncellas") and "Lady Cornelia" ("La señora Cornelia"). Into the "realist" grouping go another five stories of disorientation and failure whose edges have been sharpened by close observation of the world: "Rinconete and Cortadillo" ("Rinconete y Cortadillo"), "The Glass Graduate" ("El licenciado Vidriera"), "The Jealous Man from Extremadura" ("El celoso extremeño"), "The Deceitful Marriage" ("El casamiento engañoso"), and "The Colloquy of the Dogs" ("El coloquio de los perros"). Novellas that seem to move between the two realms ("The Little Gypsy Girl" ["La gitanilla"] and "The Illustrious Kitchenmaid" ["La ilustre fregona"]), sometimes called hybrid, have just as often been recruited to the "idealist" as to the "realist" camp: in the former case because their title characters, wrongly debased, are ultimately restored to rediscovered noble origins; in the latter because they and their aristocrat suitors spend most of their time in social underworlds.[21] While the perception that the "realist" novellas are more quintessentially Cervantine has awarded them the lion's share of modern readers' attention, too often foreclosing scrupulous analysis of the "idealist" stories, the grid-resistant diversity of the motley "hybrids" has pointed the way beyond preconceptions and pigeonholing toward more probing readings of all of the *Exemplary Novels*.

Scholars have also tried to graph the largely undocumented chronology of the novellas' composition against fictional typology, with mixed results. Those who consider novelistic realism typical of the mature Cervantes tend to set aside the idealistic novellas as throwbacks to an earlier period in the writer's career, even as hypocritical concealments. Others use evidence for pre-1605 composition of "Rinconete" and "The Jealous Man from Extremadura" as an indication that Cervantes worked through a mid-career dalliance with ironic realism, the better to embrace once again in his last years the high-minded mode of romance with which he had first entered the world of letters.[22] Virtually no account of the novellas' order of composition claims support from the sequence in which they appear in the 1613 edition.

That given order, perhaps not even the author's work, has resisted explanation.[23] When Renaissance theorists celebrated variety as central to Art's imitation of Nature, they referred to multiplicity within the unity of one epic poem or romance thought of as "a single fabric of variegated strands."[24] It may be that, in the novellas, Cervantes has set aside temporarily a problem he faces in all of his other fictions: that of weaving many fictional threads into whole cloth. Yet this author who explores so many other signifying possibilities of form, especially one who insists that the secret fruit of his book belongs to his whole book as well as to its parts, would almost certainly have taken some care with arrangement. Joaquín Casalduero found each idealistic narrative followed by a realistic one, but saw that pattern breaking down near the end of the collection, where two wishful stories grouped together precede a final two very dark tales. Albert A. Sicroff sees "The Glass Graduate," the fifth story, as a turning point, after which the novellas, marked by an obsession with honor, grow more pessimistic.[25] Strategic placements at beginning ("The Little Gypsy Girl") and end ("The Deceitful Marriage" and "Colloquy") seem certain, because of the way these stories recapitulate concerns of the whole group. By raising more questions than they answer, such discussions turn us back on the *Exemplary Novels* themselves.

Cervantes' titles appear to promise a focus on individual figures, yet only three identify their central characters by name. More surprising, in view of the collection's pretensions to exemplarity, just two invoke moral values explicitly (a jealous man, a deceitful marriage). The greatest number introduce their protagonists by type, in terms of gender, national or regional origin, social class, educational status, sentimental condition, sexual behavior (the Spanish "doncellas" makes "The Two Damsels"' protagonists explicitly virgins), even species. Characters frequently come paired (two boys, two damsels, two not-quite-spouses, two dogs), while others fuse contrasting traits (an *English* Spanish lady, an illustrious servant-girl, a generous lover, fraudulent marriage, talking dogs). Titles thus begin to sketch the outlines of a fictional universe whose inhabitants' identities become worthy of notice to the extent that they transgress boundaries or embody contradictions.

Cervantes has taken great care in assembling his kaleidoscopic world mirror. The novellas map an extensive territory, repeating place references rarely enough to suggest that varied topography was one of the collection's conscious aims. Geographical coverage, moreover, adds up to a whole greater than the sum of its parts. The novellas' fictional map overflows with significant sites: great urban centers (Madrid, Seville, Barcelona), commercial hubs (Seville, Burgos, Valencia, Murcia), former court cities (Toledo, Valladolid), seats of the Church (Toledo) and learning (Alcalá de Henares, Salamanca), pilgrimage geography (Guadalupe, Santiago), momentous places for Habsburg foreign policy (Cádiz, England, Cyprus, Italy, Flanders), breeding grounds of conquistadores (Cáceres and Trujillo in Extremadura), the capital of the Indies trade (Seville).[26] The collection's tour of social classes and occupations is no less grand.

The reins of geographical expansion are apparently pulled in in the last two stories. The connected tales of "The Deceitful Marriage" and the "Colloquy" hover around the Old Castilian city of Valladolid, twice home to Cervantes, where Ensign Campuzano hears or dreams a nocturnal conversation between two dogs. Despite the promise of travel latent in his soldier's rank, "The Deceitful Marriage" not only restricts the young man's movement, but shuts him up in interior space: first in the house where his erotic indiscretions play themselves out, later in the Resurrection Hospital where he sweats through bouts of syphilis. The "Colloquy"'s two interlocutors are said to belong to a known historical figure, Mahudes. Although the canines too are tied to the same night and place as the delirious Ensign, Berganza recounts his service to many masters, in a journey that spreads out across Andalusia (Seville, Cordova) and the northbound roads leading back to Valladolid. Spanning an extensive social territory in the process, the "Colloquy" has also by virtue of the species of its quadruped interlocutors reached beyond humanity. This extraordinary two-part finale, moreover, is routed through a large number of sites visited in earlier stories, calling attention to their cumulative itinerary.

Movement across various kinds of borders, and its destabilizing effects on the value of signs of identity, are not features of the whole contributed by stories of a particular "realist" stripe. They are, rather, insistent features of each of the stories, inextricably tied to the formal and generic diversity of the novellas' world. The collection advertises a broad range of generic affinities. Most conspicuous among these are links with the romance genre that will be called upon to structure the *Persiles*. "The Generous Lover" and "The English Spanish Lady" compress into the confines of the novella Byzantine romance's rambling sagas of lost-and-found lovers or relatives, whose testing in political conflict and stormy weather gives way to miraculous encounters and recognitions, ultimately sacralized by nuptial vows. Similar plot lines are projected onto less sweeping canvas in "The Force of Blood," "The Two Damsels," and "Lady Cornelia," stories which marshall the narrative trick of anagnorisis to return errant suitors to their conjugal responsibilities. With greater attention to underworlds traversed and transcended, romance structure also undergirds "The Little Gypsy Girl" and "The Illustrious Kitchenmaid" as they work to restore lost but resourceful noblewomen to their proper stations. Indeed, so pervasive is the romance paradigm that variations on its forms turn up everywhere in the *Exemplary Novels*.[27]

For some readers, notably El Saffar and Forcione, the structures of "inescapable romance" seem to seal the collection's commitment to stories where personal struggles culminate in self-knowledge, self-control, self-realization within a Christian humanistic universe.[28] But Cervantes harnesses the transgressive potential of romance structures to other less likely projects: for example, in Rinconete and Cortadillo's or the dogs' descents into underworlds of delinquency on open-ended journeys toward identity; in the inversions of "The Glass Graduate" and "The Jealous Man from Extremadura," whose trajectories fail to reach any resting place and instead spin off into some outer space; in the bankrupting of the marriage plot effected by "The Deceitful Marriage." These traces of romance forms and themes in stories often catalogued as realistic, ironic, or satiric, point up the hybrid technique that makes the novellas so resistant to one-dimensional classification. In "Rinconete" and the "Colloquy," resistance to standard features of picaresque fiction (linear episodic chronology, first-person narrative, exclusively negative perspective) has long been celebrated as the mark of creative freedom and originality.[29] In these novellas, Cervantes escapes picaresque determinism with help from dialogue, proverbs, folktales, theatrical techniques, and verse, using parodic appropriation and genre-switching tricks familiar from *Don Quixote*. As Forcione notes, the limit of this kind of transgression occurs in the "Colloquy of the Dogs," whose adaptive reuse of traditional genres achieves a density unknown outside *Don Quixote* (*Mystery*, pp. 194–204).

Many of these experiments bear traces of the intense theoretical discussions on epic and romance, history and poetry, verisimilitude and the marvelous, that marked Cervantes' writing lifetime. Although these issues will be explored more fully in *Persiles*, they have no small part in the composition of the *Exemplary Novels*. Resolution of "The English Spanish Lady"'s Byzantine design is scripted as a near-miracle in which a repatriated Isabela plays the part of the Virgin; the finale of "The Force of Blood" uses calculated effects of awed astonishment (*admiratio*), matched by clever manipulation of appearances, as characters bend "chance" (in fiction always a mask for authorial arrangement) to Providential purpose. Amid the novellas' insistent flirtation with the implausible, only the "Colloquy" makes room for the supernatural, in Ensign Campuzano's dream experience of hearing dogs talk, and in the dog Berganza's encounter with the witch Cañizares. Here a playful author puts credulity to the test by perversely framing his most naturalistic observations of life in and from Spanish society's underbelly as a combination of human delirium and canine sagacity.

The novellas explore no less vigorously the potential of dialogue and its implications for authorial control. Like *Don Quixote*, all the novellas but one are framed by a narrating voice that stands outside the represented fictional world. This is true even in stories, like "The Little Gypsy Girl," "Rinconete," and "The Glass Graduate," that rely heavily on direct speech. In the 1613 collection, only the "Colloquy" is given the appearance of a free-standing form: its two canine interlocutors begin to speak without introduction and talk the night away with no interruption from the author. Their independence, however, is a function of the story's status as a dream, told within a character's autobiographical narrative as part of another dialogue, all finally presented by the frame narrator. Cervantes' ubiquitous fictional conversations clearly reflect the thematic capaciousness of the Renaissance dialogue and its special hospitality toward metalinguistic and metaliterary subjects.[30] "The Little Gypsy Girl" takes up the nature and uses of poetry; "Rinconete" autobiographical narrative, lies, the jargon of thieves; "The Glass Graduate" the powers of the celebrated Spanish wit (*ingenio*) as well as the contingent authority of proverbs and satire.

The "Colloquy"'s arch-critic, Cipión, raises a host of issues including stylistic affectation, narrative digressions, slander, and proper use of the divine gift of speech. But this allegory, which, as Peter Dunn has noted, features canine actors in the familiar roles of Arms and Letters, has unexpected twists: literary criticism of the pastoral vogue and contemporary dramatic practice emerge not from study but from the active life recounted in Berganza's picaresque narrative; Cipión's critical distance on the world, conversely, makes him as much a literary descendant of the Stoics' favorite general Scipio, who wisely withdrew from conquests, as of Cicero. Metafictional moments like these do more than reflect spillage from contemporary theory. By giving characters a high degree of literary and linguistic self-consciousness, they also make Cervantes' texts multi-dimensional, self-consciously dialogic, and self-commenting. It is no surprise to discover that, by the time canine meditations reconnect with human conversation, the collection comes full circle, as the "Colloquy"'s fictional readers head back toward the public spaces of Spanish society where the whole wonder show began.

This gives us another opportunity to look over the prologue's billiard table. The figurative business of the table seems plain enough. The metaphor proposes a link between proffered wares and eager shoppers, wholesome entertainment and roving appetites, supply and demand. But if we see the writer, his merchandise and his activity set on one side of the figural fence, with the referential world of the plaza on the other side, we will miss the point of Cervantes' trope for publication. The writer's game – the "tricks" on the table, his novellas – is the same game he invites others to join as readers. His text takes in the scene in the plaza, including his own entertainment business venture, at the very moment when the real book (of which the prologue is a part) is on the verge of becoming part of that world. What we may separate in analysis – the novellas' fictional reference and their literary-theoretical concerns – comes in one package. Genres mixed, codes travestied, structures twisted almost beyond recognition – these are the formal corollaries of transgressive itineraries, identities in question, values in flux in the represented world.

What does all of this imply about the novellas' message? The author's no-nonsense offer of decent, safe, equal-opportunity recreation sits awkwardly with the slippery Spanish name ("mesa de trucos") for the whole set-up. What kind of tricks can this smooth-talker of a traveling salesman be hiding in plain sight? Many have argued that the novellas transmit ambiguous, ambivalent, even disturbing lessons. As a writer disenchanted with the literary models he inherits, Cervantes has often appeared to trade old messages for newer ones. A growing number of today's critics are digging deeper into the stories' rich referential dirt and finding that they yield more traces of the material contexts of early modern history than had previously been suspected.[31] To date, this work has brought to light a wealth of new sources of Cervantes' disillusionment (even anger) with military affairs, scorn for the nobility matched by scathing views of still-born capitalism, faith in marriage and love as sources of personal renewal eroded into bitterness, religious and cultural ecumenicism marred by inconsistency. It suggests further that the writer's distrust of inherited conventions (pastoral, picaresque, and others) is part and parcel of this pervasive malaise, that he saw exhausted forms and their contradictions as symptoms of his age's capacity for self-delusion and inability to make sense of itself. Where old models tumble, while even newer ones teeter in confusion, an art of exemplarity cannot help foundering. Whether this author was happy to let it fall, or whether what strained optimism his stories retain makes a bold proposal for mending a troubled world, will probably never be demonstrated beyond reasonable doubt.[32]

The spacious field of *Persiles*

Cervantes' last work of prose fiction appeared in print in the year following his death in Madrid, at the age of sixty-nine, in April of 1616. In other books published during his final years, the author had found many occasions to tout his "great *Persiles*" as the ambitious venture which friends assured him would culminate in his finest creation. That an eager public awaited this final instalment of his literary legacy is evident from its immediate public success, comparable to that of *Don Quixote*. Ten Spanish editions appeared in the seventeenth century, followed by translations into French, Italian, and English, and myriad partial imitations in prose and in drama. Reception history in post-Romantic centuries has shown a sharp decline in enthusiasm. Coming so close on the heels of two burlesque volumes, the 1614 *Journey to Parnassus* and the 1615 conclusion to Don Quixote's history, not to mention satiric novellas and thoroughly irreverent comic interludes, the unwieldy saga of the labors of wandering lovers appears to shift gears abruptly toward a more earnest kind of storytelling. Perception of *Persiles* as an anomaly has moved not a few modern readers either to imagine a death-bed conversion with the author imitating his most famous character's rejection of worldly fictions, or to speculate that its writing had commenced long before, which would explain why it seems more akin to *Galatea* than to later works.

Despite its scant appeal for modern tastes, *Persiles* has found many apologists in recent years. In two books devoted to the posthumous work, Alban Forcione accords it a place of honor as the most ambitious experiment in its author's aesthetic program. Forcione's studies reflect the prevailing interpretive tradition, which reads *Persiles* as an allegory of life as a journey upward from the depths of sin toward the salvation that ultimately rewards its toils.[33] The guiding trope of human existence as a spiritual pilgrimage which unfolds along the ascending trajectory of a Christianized Great Chain of Being is seen as bringing the mature Cervantes in line with the Counter-Reformation values some earlier writings appear to challenge. The resulting picture of a writer who became more experimental in his aesthetics while growing more conservative in ideology is a disconcerting one. It serves as a reminder here that all readers of *Persiles* face the challenge of reconciling formal and philosophical features.

There is no denying the grand conception of this Christian romance. In sheer scope, the "Northern Story" has no equal among Cervantes' writings, except perhaps in the once and future history Don Quixote vaingloriously imagines for himself. Its plot features the title's star-crossed pair – Prince Persiles, in love with his brother's promised bride Sigismunda – who flee Thule (Tile), the island realm of King Magsimino, and head for Rome, where they hope to secure a Christian blessing to their politically impossible union. Traveling as brother and sister, under the assumed names Periandro and Auristela, on occasion in transgendered disguise, they are subjected by Fortune to a seemingly endless string of separations, natural disasters, illnesses, and the like. From an *in medias res* beginning in barbarian captivity, their story takes them on several months of island-hopping in northern seas, then south to Lisbon, and across southern Europe to Rome. Despite the suggestion of its subtitle, only half of *Persiles* is set at the northern edge of civilization; the action of Books III and IV takes place in the "Midday [*le Midi*]" of Europe, moving from Atlantic outer limits steadily toward a Mediterranean center. But as the initial strangeness of distant islands, real and imagined, yields to a landscape of recognizable sites and cities, the backdrop of northern adventure continues to haunt the work's formal geography. Indeed, the *Persiles* may strike the reader as an "ocean of story" whose winds bring boatload after boatload of new characters into view, and with them the potential of their histories to engulf the protagonists or to blow them off their purposely charted course.[34]

For the early modern writer, the point of these waves of episodes was to intensify the effects of a principal action through repetition and variation. Whatever appearance of sameness several dozen stories of erotic passion tried by fire and water may have today, their selection and arrangement in a Renaissance romance would reflect compositional care and even sometimes an intricate design. The first book of *Persiles* tells a great deal about this romance's narrative logic. Its opening scene snatches Periandro (Persiles) from near death at the hands of the inhabitants of the Barbaric Isle, setting him back into the motion which captivity has interrupted. Troubles with these island wild men are not over. No sooner liberated, the hero volunteers to stand in for a young woman about to be handed over to the tribe's traffic in virgins, among whom he reencounters his beloved Auristela (Sigismunda). Both escape thanks to internecine strife among the brutes, who promptly self-destruct in bloody slaughter, and to the intervention of the half-breed

Antonio. The tale of this barbarian's Spanish father inaugurates a succession of three life stories which point toward the book's principal geographical and thematic destinations: the elder Antonio has fled an honor drama in Spain; the Italian Rutilio reveals the wages of his lust; the Portuguese Manuel de Sosa Coutiño, after plaintively singing the loss of his beloved to her religious vocation, dies a poet's death of love. With new encounters and more separations caused by shipwreck, the growing company of storytellers moves by various means toward the island of King Policarpo, whose enlightened republic of virtue nonetheless holds new dangers. The benefits of early rescue by Arnaldo prove to be as dubious as they are short-lived: the Danish Prince becomes the first of many characters to fall in love with Auristela; Policarpo soon follows, while one of his daughters, Sinforosa, conceives a passion for Periandro.

By the end of Book I, although large numbers of characters and places remain to be introduced, most of the defining features of the romance's narrative technique have been put forward: non-linear plotting, rapid-fire accumulation of melodramatic episodes, delayed indentification (via pseudonym, disguise, or unnamed voice), meteorological surprises, and dramatic foreshadowings of meticulously prepared "happenstance." Near-certainty is given to the principle of ironic reversal, as rescuers become pursuers, captors unwittingly liberate, allies become rivals, and vice versa. A second, closely related engine of Cervantes' plot is the power of attraction attributed to the protagonists in their progress through the geographical and psychic maze that is the world of their experience. This magnetic force draws others to them, making each of them and their story into objects of desire for many fellow characters. All of these serve the purposes of romance form, "which simultaneously quests for and postpones a poetic end, objective, or object" (Parker, *Inescapable Romance*, 4).

Once this narrative template is recognized, the densely packed structure of the remaining books becomes much less forbidding. Roughly half of Book II's chapters are devoted to the marital designs visited on Cervantes' dangerously appealing protagonists; the other half to Periandro's retrospective account of the pilgrims' journey from its beginnings. Their story catches up to the present just as the whole romance nears its midpoint. Here Policarpo's burning of his own palace combines with the annual arrival of a ship from the south to set Periandro and Auristela back on course toward their Mediterranean destination. Landing in Lisbon as Book III opens, the pilgrims undertake a tour of significant Peninsular sites, many familiar from the novellas (the Virgin's shrine at Guadalupe, Badajoz, Trujillo, Cáceres, Talavera, La Sagra of Toledo, Aranjuez, Quintanar de la Orden, Valencia, Barcelona), before crossing into France at Perpignan. As the journey moves ahead, two interests work insistently to organize a welter of detail. The love intrigues of the numerous personal histories told on the trek across Spain turn increasingly on social expectations and codes, rather than on purely erotic passions. Meanwhile, the text's interest in the dynamics of representation enlarges an earlier concern with narrative to encompass other arts like painting (in the canvas commissioned by Periandro to relay the pilgrims' story and in Auristela's portrait), theater (a director tried to cast Auristela as heroine of a comedy), and proverbs. As objects of representation Periandro and Auristela become increasingly complex and precarious objects of desire.

The pilgrims reach Rome in the first moments of Book IV, but with much social and spiritual distance left to cover, as material interests, the dangers of fame, rivalries, and new twists of passion threaten the protagonists' lives and liberty. Auristela is robbed of her beauty and brought to the brink of renouncing human love altogether to take the veil; Periandro faces the arrival of his brother, the only rival whose claims to Auristela's hand could conceivably survive the workings of poetic justice. Just when it appears that their two years' journey may come to naught, however, two final chapters restore Persiles and Sigismunda to their true identities, keep a failing King Magsimino alive long enough to bless the lovers' union and make them his successors, and marry off not a few pairs of their companions in pilgrimage.

As fictional case histories, the romance's myriad episodes explore many versions and perversions of love. Unsystematically but obsessively, they instance erotic love and lust, Christian charity, parental and filial devotion, idolatry, incest, homoerotic desire, gender roles, interracial marriage, public and private love duties, monastic vocation, friendship, jealousy, grief, homicidal rage. The author clearly means his text to join Renaissance dialogues on love, philosophical and theological. Many of the work's conceptual tropes (Love's fire as either destructive flame of the body or guiding light for the soul) and not a few lapidary phrases ("There is no woman who does not desire to make herself whole with her missing half, which is that of her husband [No hay mujer que no desee *enterarse* con la mitad que le falta, que es la del marido]" [399, my translation and emphasis]) gloss sixteenth-century Neo-Platonists like Bembo, Castiglione, Ebreo. Faulted more than once for surrendering to the "exemplary fallacy" (e.g., Entwhistle, "Ocean of Story," p. 163), *Persiles* has recently been celebrated for the richness and liberating perspectives of its numerous "allegories of love."[35]

If the concept of a Platonic ascesis that will eventually reunite separated halves of creation promises to govern this fictional trajectory, less ennobling impulses undeniably work to retard the pilgrims' progress. Countering more wistful readings of *Persiles*, Cesáreo Bandera Gómez finds, not only in diversionary episodes but in the main plot, the same structures of imitative or triangular desire that foster violence in *Don Quixote*. In Bandera's reading, Persiles' idolatrous love for Sigismunda holds him captive in the illusory realm of misplaced metaphysical desire for the length of their pilgrimage. Since the romance's characters are not released from desire's "romantic lie [mensonge romantique]" into "novelistic truth [vérité romanesque]" until their stories' eleventh hour, their story amounts to a fiction about the self-deluding fictions of desire.[36]

By making visible this connection between fictionalized mysteries of love and issues of literary representation, Bandera's study points to other links between thematics and poetics in *Persiles*. Cervantes appears to have found in the erotically driven sagas of Heliodorus and in Renaissance romances like Ariosto's *Orlando furioso* the scope and freedom that his most ambitious fictional venture demanded; but the model of epic seems to have been no less present to his thinking. When the Priest and Canon (I, 47) pick the books of chivalry to pieces, they find one jewel of a literary virtue among heaps of rubbish. We have seen it before. Romances offer a "wide and spacious field", like *Galatea*'s field of the Castilian language, where the writer can give free reign to his pen and his intellect, so as to explore a whole range of character types, actions, discourse, and disciplines. Although Cervantes never explicitly identified the "prose epic" of these fictional dicussions with his last book, many have assumed he meant it to embody that ideal. Toward the end of *Persiles*' first book, ceremonial games reminiscent of those in the *Aeneid*'s Book v sound Virgilian echoes which become clearly audible in the second book of the Spanish romance. Based like Books II and III of Virgil's epic in a foreign monarch's palace, Book II of our text recalls the Latin poem's lovesick ruler (Dido doubled into enamored royal father and daughter), Aeneas' retrospective narrative, and the Carthaginian queen's funeral pyre. Michael Armstrong-Roche sees Cervantes redirecting the Roman poet's celebration of military virtues and imperial dynasties to the ends of a no less heroic song of spiritual conquests and liberations, under the sign of Christian *caritas*.[37]

That Byzantine romance continued to be a source of imaginative energy throughout the writing of *Persiles* can be seen in the work's legendary prologue. As he had done when introducing the *Exemplary Novels*, the author makes himself the protagonist of a miniature of the very genre he is cultivating. Once again Cervantes honors a chosen model, but takes ironic and self-ironizing distance from it. In this caricature of a romance episode, a flurry of Byzantine motifs (chance encounter, mistaken identity, repudiation of masks and even naming) leave the famous writer and his young admirer on the road, still short of perfect recognition and closure, even as life ebbs and the traveler continues on his way to the next life ("la otra vida").

As much as a cornucopia of love stories, the *Persiles* reads like a two-year seminar on verbal representation. Cervantes' permanent predilection for self-constructing figures, as we have seen, includes characters who not only recount what has happened to them, or what they would like to happen, but also their views on how such stories, their own included, are or ought to be told. Without intruding into the ontological space of his characters, the author cultivates his resemblance to those among them who are critics and can be found questioning unreliable or prolix narrators, credibility of marvelous events, uncanny coincidences. As concern with literary modes of representation expands in Books III and IV to include other arts and new forms of discourse, it becomes clear that interest in representation does not rest on aesthetic concerns alone. What the text's metarepresentational moments make plain is that Cervantes shared his age's conception of literary and artistic activity "as intervening directly in human life – as imparting and empowering beliefs and as communicating truths (and of course also falsehoods) in a pleasing form," and the concomitant habit of judging works of art "instrumentally, in terms of their success (or failure) in serving these broad human purposes."[38] For Cervantes' characters, verbal expression is a mirror of identity, a strategic art, ultimately a survival skill. For his fictional storytellers, narrative makes existential connections on a communicative road that may lead either to freedom or to captivity, to fulfillment or to death, depending on efficacy and reception.

Yet Cervantes treats even such serious subjects as these with a measure of ambivalence: sooner or later, virtually every shred of advice or opinion put forward meets its opposite. Playing the omniscient, providential author, for example, the narrator ironizes that persona by never recognizing himself as character, yet permitting him an increasing number of editorializing intrusions. Self-critically, he aborts a harangue on jealousy in one place (II, 1), yet gives sermonizing impulses free rein elsewhere, in imitation of Renaissance epic *exordia*. Periandro is often urged to step up the pace of his story by avoiding digression, but just as often interrupted. Allegorical representation, whose interest for Cervantes is attested by the 1615 prologue to his collected dramatic works, is first treated as a ceremonial game (II, 10's regatta pits Love, Interest, and Diligence against the winner, Fortune), then naturalized into Periandro's vision (II, 15), where Chastity, Temperance (Continencia) and Modesty (Pudicia) appear, only to be dismissed quickly as a dream. The protagonist is at pains to warn his listeners (II, 9) that he should not be expected to tell the end of his story; yet the seer Soldino (III, 18) does just that, and more, as he not only augurs happy endings for the lovers, but "predicts" the outcomes of real imperial engagements (victory at Lepanto, 1571; defeat at Alcázarquivir, 1578) as well. Other forms receive the same kind of contrary, ironic attention. The canvas (*lienzo*) that presents the pilgrims' story in pictures, commissioned by Periandro to save narrative time, finds its exploitative counterpart in the money-making scheme of pseudo-captives (III, 10) and a dangerous spin-off in the painting of Auristela, which soon becomes the focus of a tug-of-war for possession of the icon and its subject. Portraiture is given a new twist of its own in the Roman gallery of "future portraits" (IV, 6), once again linking fancy to history. And the Extremaduran impresario's wish to recruit Auristela for one of his comedies comes full circle, as the rumor circulates that her portrait has inspired a new play (I, 8), at the very moment when Auristela comes face to face with the spiritual danger to her of her own dehumanized image.

In a great many of these vignettes, the author can be caught peering wryly out from behind one of his fictional masks. So it is with the proverb collector (IV, 1) whose project of sifting valuable verbal nuggets from the experiences of others, and selling them, mimics Cervantes' own. In the plum of this fictional collection, "Don't desire anything, and you'll be the richest man in the world," we find a homely version of the famous vision of perpetually restless human souls borrowed verbatim from St. Augustine's *Confessions* for Book III's exordium, and of neo-Stoic warnings on the self-destructiveness of greed. These ideas, treated with utmost seriousness elsewhere in *Persiles*, undergird the unwieldy bulk of the romance and support its philosophical ambitions. As opportunistic parasite of the book trade and a nascent writing profession, the maxim-monger stands too as the measure of Cervantes' care in his grandest project to continue to give the material world its due in imaginative accounts of human behavior. It is particularly striking, in a work whose principal metafictional interest has been assumed to attach primarily to experiments with the marvelous, to find matters of representation routinely piggy-backed onto social, economic, political, and religious issues. Traffic in portraits stands in for traffic in women; fantasy narrative canvases hint at other political misrepresentations; quasi-religious icons are found to undermine the integrity of individuals and families; and the publishing world creates the conditions for multiple manipulations.

Scholarship has only recently begun to take the measure of this scruple and to recognize, in a text heavily freighted with philosophical and religious symbolism, ubiquitous references and less transparent allusions to the author's historical world. *Persiles* offers in 1617 a far more telling mirror of European realities than do the previous century's preferred modes of fiction. Renaissance pastorals, heirs to the Latin poets' anti-commercial bucolic ideals, make no secret of their aversion to court politics and urban society, approaching that world rarely and always obliquely, by negation and from the margins. Chivalric romance, although it deals in such recognizable early modern phenomena as the martial and marital politics of dynasty-building and Christian messianism, even setting them in known territory, still fails to give its figures political or cultural specificity. The primary strategy of *Don Quixote* is to uproot chivalry's fictions from the *illo tempore* of myth and replant them squarely in a particular here and now. By contrast, Cervantes' last romance engages a striking number of pressing European concerns. Although it displaces some of them into exotic regions of apparent unreality, this text registers such phenomena as new mobility and mixing of populations, changing family culture (gender roles, bases of "honor"), competition between aristocratic and bourgeois values, the reach of the state and its laws into private life, questions about the temporal authority of the Church, practices of Christian monarchy, and much more. In giving fictional shape to these aspects of European culture and politics, Cervantes frequently shows his unorthodox and ecumenical leanings.

But the imaginative sweep of *Persiles* looks even farther afield. Just as many more of its themes were certain to set off American resonances for Cervantes' earliest readers: island-hopping, maritime commerce, shipwreck, captivity, slavery, Utopias, conversion, miscegenation, linguistic and cultural alienation, the impact of foreign excursions on domestic politics, barbarity and questions about the nature of humanity.[39] Michael Armstrong-Roche finds in the whole of the posthumous work, and not only its properly "Northern stories", a disturbing vision of "Europe as Barbaric New World" ("Cervantes' Epic Novel," pp. 22–67). Such a vision makes Cervantes heir to an intuition shared by Antonio de Guevara, Bartolomé de las Casas, and Michel Montaigne, that at its most alien, the example of America stood to reveal most about the strangeness and barbarity of European "civilization". Nowhere are the decentering effects of the fictional travelers' two years' experience of distances and differences more evident than in the long-awaited moment of arrival in Rome. A major symbolic act of the text's final book is to show the Holy City itself, and the pilgrims' relation to it, dramatically altered by discovery of humanity on the margins and barbarity in the heartlands of Christianity. As Cervantes ties up loose threads, he knows that it is his text, not his world, that is being made whole.

The novelist in the mirror of his offspring

This essay began by resurrecting the venerable rhetorical figure of artistic paternity, in order to press it into service as an emblem of aims and conclusions. Readers of the masterwork for whom other Cervantine texts are unfamiliar may expect on reading *Galatea*, the *Exemplary Novels*, and

Persiles something akin to the first meeting with family members of a friend. In such experiences, initial strangeness gives way to recognition of resemblances, similarities awaken a sharpened sense of difference, and comparative perspective lends new depth to someone we thought we knew. In the lifelines of other members of Cervantes' brood – that is, in the variety of their formal, thematic, contextual, and ideological features – we rediscover the inventor of imagined worlds of unprecedented complexity, the fashioner of narrative and rhetorical structures supple enough to encompass them, and the self-conscious explorer of the powers and limits of verbal representation. And in the mirror of these other fictions, we find new keys to aspects of Cervantes' novelistic practice – experimental approach to genre, attraction to parody, meticulous attention to speaking and narrating voices, enduring fascination with the idea of epic – that may have appeared up to this moment to belong only to his masterpiece.

What we may still miss is the side-splitting hilarity of *Don Quixote*. If we conclude as a result that the other fictions lack irony, we shall be mistaken. For what *Galatea*, the novellas, and *Persiles* teach, above all, is that this writer's irony comes in many shapes and guises. Cervantes' energetic engagement with such varied modes of representation shows not only openness to each of them, but ultimately a degree of detachment from them all. In this sense, the epistemological tremors that Foucault detects in *Don Quixote* also make themselves felt in the works we have been examining.[40] To the extent that the Knight's quest to restore lost connections between words and things allegorizes the writer's search for a literary language capable of taking the measure of a changing world, these other fictions deserve recognition as part of that project.

NOTES

1 The principal of these are one early historical tragedy, *The Siege of Numancia* (*El Cerco de Numancia*), an epic burlesque of poets and poetry; "Voyage to Parnassus" ("Viaje del Parnaso") (1614); and a collection of *Eight Comedies and Eight Interludes* (*Ocho comedias y ocho entremeses*) (1615).

2 In this essay I quote from editions and translations as follows, unless otherwise noted: *La Galatea*, ed. Francisco López Estrada and María Teresa López García Berdoy (Madrid: Cátedra, 1995); *Galatea: A Pastoral Romance*, trans. Gordon Willoughby and James Gyll (London: Bell and Daldy, 1867); *Novelas ejemplares*, 2 vols., ed. Harry Sieber (Madrid: Cátedra, 1986); *Exemplary Novels*, trans. James Mabbe, ed. S. W. Orson (London and Philadelphia: Gibbings and J. B. Lippincott, 1900); *Los trabajos de Persiles y Sigismunda*, ed. Juan Bautista Avalle-Arce (Madrid: Castalia, 1969); *The Trials of Persiles and Sigismunda: A Northern Story*, trans. Celia Richmond Weller and Clark A. Colahan (Berkeley: University of California Press, 1989).

3 For the history of the pastoral mode in Italy and Spain, see Amadeu Solé-Leris, *The Spanish Pastoral Novel* (Boston: Twayne, 1980).

4 William Byron, *Cervantes: A Biography* (Garden City: Doubleday, 1978), p. 274.

5 In "Cervantes De/Re-Constructs the Picaresque," Dunn offers a shrewd reading of the adaptive reuse of that mode in *Don Quixote: Cervantes* 2 (1982): 109–31.

6 Rosalie Colie, *The Resources of Kind* (Berkeley: University of California Press, 1973).

7 The famous dictum appears in the poet-critic's controversial *Annotations to the Works of Garcilaso de la Vega* (*Anotaciones a las obras de Garcilasso de la Vega*) (Seville, 1580; facsimile edn., Madrid: C.S.I.C., 1973), p. 507. Metaliterary aspects of *Galatea* receive more sustained attention in Mary Gaylord (Randel), "The Language of Limits and the Limits of Language: The Crisis of Poetry in *La Galatea*," *MLN* 97 (1982): 254–71; reprinted in Ruth El Saffar, ed., *Critical Essays* (Boston, MA: G. K. Hall, 1986), pp. 29–44.

8 The Spanish reads: "No se ven tantos rostros figurados / en roto espejo, o hecho por tal arte / que, si uno en él se mira, retratados / se ve una multitud en cada parte, / cuantos nacen cuidados y cuidados / de un cuidado crüel que no se parte / del alma mía … " (177).

9 Cesáreo Bandera Gómez, *Mímesis conflictiva: Ficción literaria y violencia en Cervantes y Calderón* (Madrid: Gredos, 1975), p. 124.

10 William C. Atkinson, "Cervantes, El Pinciano and the *Novelas ejemplares*," *Hispanic Review* 16 (1948); reprinted in El Saffar, *Critical Essays*, p. 126.

11 *English Pastoral Poetry from the Beginnings to Marvell: An Anthology*, ed. Frank Kermode (New York: Norton, 1972), p. 13.

12 Geoffrey L. Stagg, "The Composition and Revision of *La Galatea*," *Cervantes* 14.2 (1994): 9–25.

13 The expression was immortalized by Garcilaso de la Vega (1503–36) in the dedication of his third Eclogue. *Renaissance and Baroque Poetry of Spain with English Translations*, ed. Elias L. Rivers (Prospect Heights, IL: Waveland Press, 1988), 69.

14 Among important recent studies of the novellas in English are William A. Clamurro, *Beneath the Fiction: The Contrary Worlds of Cervantes's "Novelas ejemplares"* (New York: Peter Lang, 1997); Ruth El Saffar, *Novel to Romance: A Study of Cervantes's "Novelas ejemplares"* (Baltimore: Johns Hopkins University Press, 1974); Alban K. Forcione, *Cervantes and the Humanist Vision* (Princeton: Princeton University Press, 1982); the same author's *Cervantes and the Mystery of Lawlessness* (Princeton: Princeton University Press, 1984); Carroll B. Johnson, *Cervantes and the Material World* (Urbana and Chicago: University of Illinois Press, 2000).

15 The prebendary Francisco Porras de la Cámara copied "Rinconete," making no mention of its author, along with another future *Exemplary Novel*, "The Jealous Man from Extremadura" ("El celoso extremeño"). Juan Bautista Avalle-Arce provides details about the Porras manuscript and its variants in his *Enciclopedia cervantina* (Alcalá de Henares: Centro de Estudios Cervantinos, 1997), p. 383.

16 Data on publication, translations, and early imitations is supplied by Agustín G. de Amezúa y Mayo, *Cervantes, creador de la novela corta española*, (Madrid: Consejo Superior de Investigaciones Científicas, 1982), vol. I, pp. 561–601.

17 Cervantes refers to the "comic monarchy" of "the monster of Nature" who has usurped all power in matters theatrical in the prologue to his 1615 *Eight Comedies and Eight Interludes* (*Ocho comedias y ocho entremeses*), ed. Rodolfo Schevill and Adolfo Bonilla (Madrid: Bernardo Rodríguez, 1915), vol. I, pp. 7–8.

18 Quevedo's *Perinola* (*The Teeter-Top*), addressed to Juan Pérez de Montalbán, a dramatist imitator of Cervantes' rival Lope de Vega, may be found in *Obras completas: Prosa*, ed. Felicidad Buendía (Madrid: Aguilar, 1961), pp. 446–58.

19 The Spanish text ("Yo soy el primero que he *novelado* en lengua castellana" [I, 52]) requires this restricted sense of the verb "to novelize" (*novelar*). It is not historically accurate to turn this boast into Cervantes' claim to have invented the modern novel. For ease of reference, I follow critical custom in using the title *Exemplary Novels*, but I avoid anachronistic terms like "novel" or "novelist" in speaking of all of the "other fictions."

20 The justice of Cervantes' overstated claim has been challenged on many occasions. For the fictional and theoretical contexts surrounding the *Exemplary Novels*, see Marina S. Brownlee, *The Poetics of Literary Theory: Lope de Vega's "Novelas a Marcia Leonarda" and Their Cervantine Context* (Madrid: José Porrúa Turranzas, 1981), pp. 1–41 and *passim*.

21 Howard Mancing provides a useful compendium of proposals for classifying the twelve novellas in his "Prototypes of Genre in Cervantes' *Novelas ejemplares*," *Cervantes* 20.1 (2000): 127–50.

22 This chronological proposal receives its strongest statement in El Saffar's *Novel to Romance*. Américo Castro makes the case for a hypocritical Cervantes in "La ejemplaridad de las *Novelas ejemplares*," in *Hacia Cervantes* (Madrid: Taurus, 1957).

23 Few critics take on the ordering of the published tales, a notable exception being Joaquín Casalduero in *Sentido y forma de las "Novelas ejemplares"* (Madrid: Gredos, 1962). The twelve novellas in order of publication are no. 1, "The Little Gypsy Girl"; no. 2, "The Generous Lover"; no. 3, "Rinconete and Cortadillo"; no. 4, "The English Spanish Lady"; no. 5, "The Glass Graduate"; no. 6, "The Force of Blood"; no. 7, "The Jealous Man from Extremadura"; no. 8, "The Illustrious Kitchenmaid"; no. 9, "The Two Damsels"; no. 10, "Lady Cornelia"; no. 11, "The Deceitful Marriage"; and no. 12, "The Colloquy of the Dogs."

24 E. C. Riley sets Cervantes' practice of variety in the context of contemporary discussions in his classic *Cervantes's Theory of the Novel* (Oxford: Oxford University Press, 1962; rpt. Newark, DE: Juan de la Cuesta, 1992), pp. 118–31.

25 "The Demise of Exemplarity in Cervantes' *Novelas ejemplares*," in Joseph V. Ricapito, ed., *Hispanic Studies in Honor of Joseph H. Silverman* (Newark, DE: Juan de la Cuesta, 1988), pp. 345–60.

26 William Byron's biography offers useful accounts of Cervantes' biographical connections to these places.

27 Peter N. Dunn, "Shaping Experience: Narrative Strategies in Cervantes," *Modern Language Notes* 109 (1994): 187–203.

28 I borrow an enduring coinage from Patricia A. Parker's *Inescapable Romance: Studies in the Poetics of a Mode* (Princeton: Princeton University Press, 1979).

29 Américo Castro noted Cervantes' distance from hard-core picaresque fiction first in *El pensamiento de Cervantes*, 2nd edn. (Barcelona: Crítica, 1972), pp. 228–35, and later in "Perspectiva de la novela picaresca," in *Hacia Cervantes*, 3rd edn.

(Madrid: Taurus, 1967), pp. 118–42. Carlos Blanco Aguinaga's "Cervantes and the Picareque Mode: Notes on Two Kinds of Realism", in Lowry Nelson, ed., *Cervantes: A Collection of Critical Essays* (Englewood Cliffs, NJ: Prentice-Hall, 1969), pp. 137–51, has influenced readers of both modes, notably Walter L. Reed in *An Exemplary History of the Novel* (Chicago: University of Chicago Press, 1981).

30 The Latin *Colloquies* of Erasmus, by updating classical models for debate about religion, politics, social mores, education, and verbal behavior, launched an enduring vogue which in Spain spawned vernacular dialogues on many subjects. Forcione discusses the imprint of the *Colloquies* and other works of Erasmus on the *Exemplary Novels* in *Humanist Vision* and *Mystery*. The foundational study of Erasmus's influence on Spanish letters is Marcel Bataillon's *Erasme et l'Espagne* (Paris: Droz, 1937).

31 The work of Harry Sieber, William Clamurro, and Carroll Johnson is notable for its attention to Peninsular contexts. In "The Bonds of Patrimony: Cervantes and the New World," *PMLA* 109.5 (1994): 969–81, James D. Fernández uncovers *the* somber projection of New World expeditions onto commercial and domestic spaces in Seville in "The Jealous Man from Extremadura." A welcome recent study is Barbara Fuchs, "Empire Unmanned: Gender Trouble and Genoese Gold in Cervantes's the *Two Damsels*," *PMLA* 116.2 (2001): 285–99.

32 Sicroff proposes the former view. Anthony J. Cascardi mounts a philosophically grounded argument in favor of the latter in "Cervantes's Exemplary Subjects," in Michael Nerlich and Nicholas Spadaccini, eds., *Cervantes' "Exemplary Novels" and the Adventure of Writing* (Minneapolis: The Prisma Institute, 1989), pp. 49–71.

33 Alban K. Forcione's *Cervantes, Aristotle and the "Persiles"* (Princeton: Princeton University Press, 1970) situates that work with learned precision as a practical exploration of the theoretical concerns of neo-Aristotelianism. His *Cervantes' Christian Romance* (Princeton: Princeton University Press, 1972) interprets the work's message as an unambiguous expression of Christian idealism. In *Novel to Romance* and *Beyond Fiction: The Recovery of the Feminine in the Novels of Cervantes* (Berkeley: University of California Press, 1984), Ruth El Saffar reads *Persiles* as the endpoint of Cervantes' aesthetic and ideological trajectory. I explore these questions from a different perspective in "Ending and Meaning in Cervantes' *Persiles y Sigismunda*," *Romanic Review* 74 (1983): 152–69.

34 William J. Entwhistle, "Ocean of Story: el último sueño romántico de Cervantes," in *Cervantes* (Oxford: Oxford University Press, 1940), pp. 172–82; reprinted in Nelson, 162–68. For Greek origins of the trope, associations with Homer and epic, and ancient images of Europe's margins, see James S. Romm, *The Edges of the Earth in Ancient Thought* (Princeton: Princeton University Press, 1992).

35 Diana de Armas Wilson's *Allegories of Love: Cervantes's Labors of Persiles* (Princeton: Princeton University Press, 1991).

36 Bandera's study explores implications of René Girard's *Deceit, Desire and the Novel* (*Mensonge romantique et vérité romanesque*), trans. Yvonne Freccero (Baltimore: The Johns Hopkins University Press, 1965) for others of Cervantes' texts.

37 Michael Armstrong-Roche, "Cervantes's Epic Novel: A Study of 'Los trabajos de Persiles y Sigismunda' " (unpublished Ph.D. dissertation, Harvard University, 2000). My rethinking of *Persiles* for the present essay owes much more to Armstrong-Roche's visionary readings than can be accounted for in formal documentation.

38 Martha Woodmansee, *The Author, Art and the Market: Rereading the History of Aesthetics* (New York: Columbia University Press, 1994), p. 12.

39 For readings of Cervantes' American allusions, see "Cervantes on Cannibals," chapter 5 of Wilson's *Allegories of Love* (pp. 109–129); the same author's *Cervantes, The Novel, and the New World* (Oxford: Oxford University Press, 2000); and her contribution to the current volume. See also George Mariscal, "*Persiles* and the Remaking of Spanish Culture," *Cervantes* 10.1 (1990): 93–102.

40 Michel Foucault, *The Order of Things* (*Les Mots et les choses*) (New York: Vintage Books, 1973), pp. 46–50.

FURTHER READING

Atkinson, William C. "Cervantes, El Pinciano, and the *Novelas ejemplares*." *Hispanic Review* 16 (1948): 189–208. Reprinted in Ruth El Saffar, ed., *Critical Essays*. Boston, MA: G. K. Hall, 1986. Pp. 123–39.

Collins, Marsha S. "Transgression and Transfiguration in *La española inglesa*." *Cervantes* 17.2 (1997): 69.

Dunn, Peter N. "Cervantes and the Shape of Experience." *Cervantes* 5.2 (1983): 149–61.

El Saffar, Ruth *Cervantes: "El casamiento engañoso" and "El coloquio de los perros"*. London: Grant and Cutler, 1976.

Gaylord, Mary M. "*Don Quixote* and the National Citizenship of Masterpieces." In Marjorie Garber, Rebecca L. Walkowitz and Paul B. Franklin, eds., *Field Work: Sites in Literary and Cultural Studies*. London and New York: Routledge, 1996. Pp. 97–105.

Gaylord Randel, Mary. "Cervantes' Portraits and Literary Theory in the Text of Fiction." *Cervantes* 6 (1986): 57–80.

Gerli, E. Michael. *Refiguring Authority. Reading, Writing and Rewriting in Cervantes*. Lexington: University of Kentucky.

Hart, Thomas R. *Cervantes' Exemplary Fictions. A Study of the "Novelas ejemplares"*. Lexington: University Press of Kentucky, 1994.

Johnson, Carroll B. "Cervantes's *La Galatea*: the Portuguese Connection, 1." *Iberorromania* 23 (1986): 91–105.

Lowe, Jennifer. *Cervantes's Two "Novelas Ejemplares": "La gitanilla" and "La ilustre fregona"*. London: Grant and Cutler, 1971.

Márquez Villanueva, Francisco. "Erasmo y Cervantes una vez más." *Cervantes* 4.2 (1984): 123–37.

Murillo, Luis A. *The Golden Dial: Temporal Configurations in "Don Quijote"*. Oxford: Dolphin Book Co., 1975.

Renieblas, Isabel Lozano. *Cervantes y el mundo del "Persiles"*. Alcalá de Henares: Centro de Estudios Cervantinos, 1998.

Ricapito, Joseph V. *Cervantes's "Novelas Ejemplares": Between History and Creativity*. West Lafayette, Indiana: Purdue University Press, 1996.

Sears, Theresa Anne. *A Marriage of Convenience: Ideal and Ideology in the "Novelas ejemplares"*. New York: Peter Lang, 1993.

Weber, Alison. "Pentimento: The Parodic Text of *La gitanilla*." *Hispanic Review* 62.1 (1994): 59–75.

Williamson, Edwin. *The Half-Way House of Fiction: "Don Quixote" and Arthurian Romance*. Oxford: Oxford University Press, 1984.

7

MELVEENA MCKENDRICK

Writings for the stage

Known above all for his great masterpiece of prose fiction, Cervantes himself aspired perhaps more than anything to success as a playwright and a poet. In late sixteenth- and seventeenth-century Spain, drama and poetry were the two connected areas of artistic endeavor which dominated literary output and in which literary reputations were made. The sixteenth century had seen the rise of prose fiction but, although fiction yielded the century's best-sellers in the domain of the secular, the status of imaginative writing in prose was still uncertain in that it lacked the authority of the classics. One of Cervantes' chief concerns in his prose works was to adapt classical pre-scriptions for poetry – creative as opposed to factual writing – to the new genre, but the ultimate accolade he sought, the respect and admiration of the literary establishment, was still fully accessible only through the traditional channels. Cervantes' trouble was that in his intellectual conviction early on that poetry and drama must continue to observe the classical precepts, he was slow to understand that the new commercial theatre being pioneered by Spain's first great dramatist Félix Lope de Vega Carpio, which abandoned the constraints of neoclassical theory, could contrive to combine popular-ity with art. In chapter 48 of the *Quixote* the priest and the canon pour scorn on the contemporary theatre and the way it has sacrificed art to profit, and on the evidence of his *Viaje del Parnaso* (*Voyage to Parnassus*, 1614) Cervantes never lost his misgivings about Lope de Vega's popularizing, anti-classical influence on poetic activity in Spain. By the time he realized that Lope's national drama was indeed a new art form rapidly achieving status and respectability, and acknowledged that art must change with the times, it was too late.[1] He reworked some of his old plays and possibly wrote a few new ones, making concessions to the spirit of the new drama, but no actor-manager would perform them. Playhouse politics almost certainly played a part here. Lope, whose theatrical authority was paramount, did not forgive Cervantes' criticism of the *comedia nueva* from so public a platform as the *Quixote*, and if the offensive nature of some of his attacks on Cervantes is anything to go by he was perfectly capable of ensuring that within his own sphere of influence Cervantes did not flourish. At the same time Cervantes was in all likelihood perceived by then as an old-fashioned playwright. In the collection of eight plays and eight comic interludes he published in 1615 there are no political or chronicle plays,[2] no plays about monarchs and their favorites, no plays about class conflict, no rural plays, no plays about marital honor, all now popular with the theatre's public. Most of them are instead plays of the sort favored above all in the 1580s and 90s, with their roots in a world of adventure and romance largely unconstrained by time and place, albeit with a pronounced element of Islamic exoticism. They are efforts to experiment with and render performable the configurations of an existing dramatic habit rather than a wholehearted engagement with the conditions and demands of a new theatrical world.

This can be attributed to a lack of vision on Cervantes' part but it would be unjust to blame him for it, because to be a poet-playwright was not his true métier, for all that he wanted to be one, and by the time he tried to reconstruct himself as a dramatist his real literary energies were firmly channeled in the direction of prose fiction. The fact that success in the theatre eluded him, however, does not mean that we can afford to ignore his theatrical writing, not least because twentieth-century experimental theatre has encouraged a degree of latitude in the constitution of a play that now makes Cervantes' so-called deficiencies seem less real. The *entremeses* (comic interludes), written to accompany full-length plays, stand comparison with the best in any language. And both the full-length plays and the interludes not only illustrate his experiments with the theatrical representation of modalities, preoccupations, and ways of seeing present elsewhere in his work, but throw light on the indebtedness of his major prose works to the genre of drama itself. Indeed his interest in the theatre goes a long way to explaining some of the outstanding characteristics of his fiction, for as the commercial outlet for his dramatic aspirations was cut off, his theatrical imagination and instincts found ample expression instead in his prose, above all in the *Quixote* itself. Narrative there is delegated to a multiple layering of narrating characters, including an elusive 'I' who makes a provocative appearance in the opening sentence of the novel by laying down the terms of its involvement: "In a place in La Mancha, whose name I do not care to remember" ("En un lugar de la Mancha, de cuyo nombre no quiero acordarme"). Dialogue becomes increasingly dominant and, freed of the constraints of verse and dramatic action imposed upon the playwright, grows into brilliance on the expansive page. Role play and the staging of illusions and masquerades are central to the novel's literary identity and epistemological purpose, inhabiting the text with spectators as well as with actors – in the episode of the courts of death (Part II, chapter 11) real professional actors who have neglected to take their costumes off. An intensely pictorial imagination gives to principal characters and narrative episodes the definition and iconic plasticity of performance, as the myriad non-literary representations of them over the centuries serve to illustrate. At times an alienating use of dramatic irony positions the reader critically apart from the characters, at others a willful withholding of dramatic irony temporally makes the characters' perception of events the reader's own. Repeated climaxes and catastrophes multiply use of a dramatic *modus operandi* in order to guarantee interest and maintain pace throughout a protracted literary plot. In short, it would be difficult to conceive of a more extensively theatrical novel. When Avellaneda, in the prologue to his spurious sequel to Cervantes' Part I, declared the entire story of Don Quixote to be "almost a play" he was saying more than he knew. The theatre-in-fiction of the novel is without a doubt triumphantly more original and more successful than the dramatic pieces, yet a productive synergy between the two genres, with fiction and drama contributing to each other's inspiration and composition, is detectable. Lope's *comedia nueva* is in Cervantes refracted through the prism of a supremely self-conscious literary intellect, intent on achieving its own novel effects, that reached its full potential and highest elaboration in and through the process of writing the *Quixote*. The satirical interludes, for their part, while of their very nature lacking the complexity and subtlety of the *Quixote*, are self-evidently the product not only of the same acute ear for dialogue and the meaning-laden nuances of human discourse, but of the same comic vision – Rabelaisian in scope and ebullience though not in tone, intensely human yet restrained, robust and often sharp but never vicious.[3] Not for Cervantes the grotesque dehumanizing humor of the contemporary satirist Francisco de Quevedo y Villegas and the picaresque, even in the arena of parody and farce.

By Cervantes' own testimony, the circumstances of his dramatic career were particularly galling. He claimed in the prologue to his *Ocho comedias y ocho entremeses* (*Eight Plays and Eight Interludes*) of 1615 that in the mid-to-late 1580s twenty to thirty plays of his were staged in Madrid and received "without cucumbers or other missiles . . . without whistles, shouts or uproar." Subsequently, he says ruefully, since he had other things to occupy him, he abandoned his pen and the theatre, and "then there appeared that monster of nature, the great Lope de Vega, and he made off with the theatrical crown." He goes on, "Some years ago I returned to my former pastime and, thinking that the days when my praise ran high were still with us, I went back and wrote a few more plays, but I found no birds in the nests of yesteryear; by which I mean that I found no theatre-company manager to ask me for them, for all that they knew I had them, and so I tucked them away in a chest and consecrated and condemned them to eternal silence." The vagueness of his chronology makes it impossible to identify precisely the period in which he tried to re-launch his dramatic career, but the evidence points towards the first decade or so of the next century – possibly in response to the reopening of the playhouses in 1601 after their closure with the death of Philip II, quite plausibly after he had finished Part I of the *Quixote* (1605) when the Madrid playhouses started picking up again after the return of the court from its five-year sojourn in Valladolid. The implication that he waited to be asked for the plays may be the truth or it may be a face-saving way of avoiding an admission that the plays were offered and turned down – it is difficult to believe that, hard up as he was, he did not try actively to interest managers in the plays he spent valuable time revising or writing. Either way, his words offer a revealing glimpse into the professional scruples and distaste for commercialism of a man who frequently complained about the effect upon the quality of contemporary plays of the merchandising atmosphere in which they were written. Cervantes goes on to say that some years after he gave up the theatre for the second time, a bookseller remarked to him that he would buy his plays had a distinguished writer not told him that much could be expected of his prose but nothing of his verse.[4] Stung by this revelation, he took another look at the plays and some interludes stored away with them, judged them certainly good enough to see the light of day, and decided to let the bookseller publish them for a reasonable sum.[5] And but for that fit of pique they would almost certainly not have survived. The space Cervantes devotes to this story, despite its characteristically wry tone, is the indication of what it meant to him. He would only have undertaken to compete with Lope on his own ground if he were confident of success, and his inability even to get the plays performed when he quite clearly entertained hopes of their commercial success must have cut very deep indeed.[6]

Cervantes' unwillingness or inability to pour his later plays fully into the Lope mold is a measure of the difference between them. His concessions to the recipe of the *comedia nueva* were by and large the formal ones necessary to give the plays the familiar configurations and some of the pace and sophistication audiences had come to expect. Jean Canavaggio has identified the typical *comedia nueva* characteristics which infiltrated Cervantes' play texts: complicated love affairs, coupled characters (lady and gallant, maid and comic side-kick), an increasing tendency to locate situations in time and space, the use of different verse forms for different situations, moods and characters, dialogue flexibly attuned to circumstances and intentions rather than rigidly dictated by role, and the use of spectacular effects (denounced by Lope himself in his manifesto, *Arte nuevo de hacer comedias en este tiempo* [*New Art of Writing Plays in Our Time*], as a public-driven fashion resorted to by lesser playwrights).⁷ What makes the two thereafter so distinct – putting aside the undisputed facts that Cervantes, unlike Lope, was neither a great poet nor a great dramatic craftsman – is their different ways of looking at and understanding the world. This difference has in the past been represented as the stark divide between a Lopean view of a given, static world peopled by men and women determined by biological and social role (in dramatic terms, stereotypes) and a Cervantine view of an ambiguous world in process where individuals negotiate their own destinies (and hence may apparently be called characters). This polarized representation is the creation of two long traditions of Lope and Cervantes criticism. Neither of these sweeping assessments, however, is borne out by the evidence of the texts themselves. There is much more recognition of predetermined boundaries in Cervantes' writing than many Cervantine critics would care to concede – he was far from being a twentieth-century existentialist – and work done on Lope in recent years shows that there is much more ambiguity, flux, and complexity of characterization in Lope's plays than has hitherto been recognized. The crucial difference between Cervantes and Lope de Vega is that Lope understood that it was precisely in the gulf between self-determination on the one hand and social and religious prescription on the other, between self and role, that the potential for dramatic conflict lay. His plays are more successful largely because they recognize that self-fashioning and self-realization are only painfully and partially won, if at all, because they concede that role and duty are immanent aspects of human experience, simultaneously provoking and containing conflict and rebellion. It is an understanding of the world, rooted in realism, which paradoxically chimes closely now with our own although the terms and terminology are different, and which reached its highest dramatic expression in Spain with Pedro Calderón de la Barca. Cervantes' own experience would certainly have taught him that to choose one's life and to define oneself are difficult goals to achieve – *Don Quixote* is, amongst many things, the narrative of just such a journey of self-discovery, and some of the bleaker *Novelas ejemplares* (*Exemplary Novels*) carry the point as well. But his philosophical and literary allegiance was to optimism and the ideal. He was intellectually and temperamentally a product of the Renaissance, qualifying the Aristotelian view that man's first duty was to society with the Erasmian belief that through virtue and education man could learn to exercise his free will in such a way as to determine his own path through the world with the help of Providence. Accordingly the characters in his fiction and his full-length plays do by and large achieve enlightenment and, after negotiating impediments and adventures, "come home" emotionally, psychologically, and spiritually in a way that is very different from the restless compromises and reluctant submissions so typical of endings in the mainstream seventeenth-century theatre. Even in Cervantes' perspectivist, often inconsistent, world there is always the sense of a definable self to be discovered, cultivated, and adhered to in the face of the world's pressures which is quite different from the *comedia*'s typical presentation of the self as something unstable and negotiable that becomes what it is necessary for it to become in order to extract maximum advantage from a problematical situation.

Only two plays from Cervantes' early theatrical phase in the 1580s have survived, and it is one of these, *El cerco de Numancia* (*The Siege of Numantia*), that is normally judged to constitute his most impressive dramatic achievement. It is proudly neoclassical in inspiration and in form, a tragic epic commemorating the heroism in 133 BC of the citizens of Numantia who committed mass suicide rather than surrender to Scipio. It has four acts, a large cast list, and is metrically more uniform than the *comedia nueva*. It was admired by such as Goethe, Schopenhauer, and Shelley for its grandiose theme and sublime vision of communal self-sacrifice and was performed in 1809 to raise the spirits of the besieged inhabitants of Zaragoza during the Peninsular War. It is a play which sets out to squeeze every last drop of horror and pathos out of the predicament of a stubbornly proud but starving people, and in its attempt to capture a sense of both momentous tragedy and personal pathos it wanders at times into excess. A Greek chorus of allegorical figures – Spain, the river Duero, Hunger, Disease, Fame – make long rhetorical interventions simultaneously bewailing the inevitable fate of the Numantians and prophesying a glorious future for a united Spain; priests identify dreadful omens; a sacrificial goat is spirited away by a devil; and a wizard's attempt to reveal the future by resuscitating a dead youth ends with both of them being swallowed up by the grave. The purpose is to induce awe and terror and no doubt the heady cocktail of spectacular effects, doom-laden rhetoric, and patriotic triumphalism held its contemporary audience spellbound. But the impression is of an imagination unwilling to exercise the restraint necessary to suppress the potential for parody. A similar lack of sureness of touch is evident in the handling of the Numantians' suffering. The intimate interchanges between them often have a very powerful charge and the articulations of their desire to die free rather than live enslaved are irresistibly affecting. But after the truly harrowing scene with a mother and her two starving children at the end of Act III, a quick succession of histrionic deaths at the beginning of Act IV threatens to descend into farce, not least because two of them were declared earlier on in the play to have already taken place.[8]

The play, however, is more impressive than all this would suggest, for although it has always been taken as a exercise in patriotic fervor and an inspiring tribute to human endurance it has nuances which suggest a much more complex vision of the world. Heroism in *Don Quixote* is a problematic thing and so it is here. There is something repellent about the energy with which the Numantian men put their wives and children and then one another to the sword when starvation is about to claim them anyway, instead of dying in battle after their loved ones have succumbed to hunger.[9] And Marandro, Lira's lover, rejects her plea to be allowed to sink into death alongside him in favor of an act of futile heroism on her behalf which predictably leads to his violent end. Instead of dying in his arms she now has to bury him and, with her family already gone, face death alone. What value courage when there is nothing to be lost? How pointless has valor to be before it ceases to be valor and who is served by it, the rescuer or the victim? Marandro's is a heroism which, like Don Quixote's own, we admire but find difficult to condone. The Numantians' debates about how best to confront their perilous situation are themselves a recognition of the problematical claims of pride, courage, duty, and family ties, and the fraught psychology of shifting attitudes and emotions is very well caught. As for their sublime refusal to surrender, even here Cervantes trails a niggling doubt. At the start of the play, after sixteen years of armed resistance, Numantia offers a truce to the newly arrived Scipio in the knowledge that he is fair and just, a man who believes in the efficacy of prudence rather than force in the exercise of governance.[10] Angered, however, by the toll the Iberian wars have taken on Roman lives, Scipio refuses to make peace and resolves to subdue Numantia, little knowing what the consequences will be. The horrifying discovery of the Numantians' chosen end astounds him. Eager as he is for victory, he is appalled to think that they have so misjudged his capacity for restraint as to prefer starvation and suicide to surrender. Should they perhaps have trusted him in surrender as they were prepared to trust him in a truce? Was it not worth the risk? The questions are not answered, but they combine silently to weigh the reality of human suffering and loss against an ideal of glorious self-sacrifice which has achieved nothing but its own immortality. What we have here is an unexpected glimpse of the perspectivism and provisionalism of the *Quixote*. The contrasting points of view are external as well as internal to the play-text. Within the text Scipio and the Numantians, as well as the men and the women, see the situation in different ways, and we ourselves take the force of that polyvalency in our sense now that the fate of Numantia was honorable and necessary, now that it was honorable but futile and wrong-headed. Our ambivalence is the ambivalence provoked by the play of pragmatism and principle that inheres in human life, and the features that produce it add a dimension to the play that rescues it from pious jingoism.

Rather than a play, *Numantia* is a succession of scenes. Its parts are infinitely better than the whole, and that pattern repeats itself throughout Cervantes' drama. His talent was for narrative and the extended exploration of theme and character, not for the taut, cumulative action and dense poetic short-hand of the *comedia nueva*. And the natural formal basis of his writing – the imaginative building block of his inspiration – was the singular unit, so that his most successful works are his dramatic interludes, his short stories and a very long novel which is itself an organic succession of scenes and episodes strung into an extraordinary odyssey. The other of Cervantes' two extant early plays, *Los tratos de Argel* (*The Traffic of Algiers*), which is also in four acts, similarly lacks the suspenseful, concentrated action of a play, and its principal interest now is autobiographical. It is the vehicle for a cathartic evocation of his own life as a slave in Algiers, after the galley in which he was returning home to Spain in 1575, following six years as an infantryman in Italy, was captured by Barbary pirates. With him he carried testimonials in support of a petition to the king for a captaincy, which would have given him the status of a gentleman. Not only did the corsairs put paid to Cervantes' hopes of preferment, thereby changing the course of his entire life, but the very letters his hopes were pinned on convinced his captors that he was a prize worth holding on to until they could secure a substantial ransom in exchange. It took five arduous years for his family to raise the money and secure his freedom, so it is scarcely surprising that the experience provided the inspiration for one of his first attempts at writing for the stage.[11] He even inscribes a shade of himself within the text in the guise of a captive soldier called Saavedra, although his own experiences clearly inform those of other characters in the play as well – the Trinitarian friar Juan Gil who arrives to ransom the protagonist Aurelio at the end is the very same Juan Gil who ransomed Cervantes himself. He creates for himself, in fact, a series of different voices through which he recreates a range of moods and emotions – anger and indignation, resentment and frustration, despair and longing, optimism and resolve, patriotic and religious fervor, even temptation – provoked by those years of hardship, humiliation, and confinement. As in *El cerco de Numancia*, where the voices interact in dialogue the scenes can be very effective – psychologically convincing and spiked with irony – but too often long, declamatory pronouncements weigh the play's progress down.[12] Things he lived through, saw, or heard about are described with almost documentary precision – a slave's preparations to escape, for example, reflecting Cervantes' own four escape attempts, and the burning alive of a Valencia priest to which Cervantes must surely have been witness, so painfully vivid is the detail with which the episode is related.[13] The love interest, on the other hand, which Cervantes had already realized was indispensable to a contemporary play and which he uses to thread the succession of disparate episodes together, is swamped by the inclusive cavalcade of characters that further contributes to the overloaded busyness of the play – Christians, Moors, masters, renegades, slaves, lovers, parents, children, a lion, a devil, and two allegorical figures, Necessity and Opportunity, who try to undermine the protagonist's virtuous resolve and clearly represent the exteriorization of an inner conflict. Cervantes' predilection for the proliferation of episode, character, and detail – which would always handicap his dramatic writing, although his later plays are certainly more disciplined in this regard – only came into its own in his prose fiction.

Cervantes may well have been of *converso* (Spanish Jewish) descent as some have argued, but of his passionate allegiance to faith and country *The Traffic of Algiers* leaves us in no doubt. The same patriotism and religious fervor reappear later on in *Los baños de Argel* (*The Bagnios of Algiers*), one of the eight plays he published in 1615, which revisits his period of captivity but now with the somewhat surer dramatic touch that resulted from exposure to the *comedia nueva*. The slavery theme possessed an intense fascination for Spanish audiences at a time when the sea crossing between the Peninsula and the Spanish lands in Italy carried with it considerable risk of capture, and Cervantes would have considered it a promising subject on which to use his newly honed skills. He liked in any case to weave episodes, people, and experiences from his own life into his writings, and the trauma of his loss of liberty in Algiers was something he was repeatedly drawn back to, most famously in the captive's tale in Part 1 of *Don Quixote* (chapters 39–41). The plot of *Los baños de Argel* in part coincides with this tale and, although there is no character called Saavedra in this play, Cervantes, rather like Hitchcock in his films, passes through in the guise of an unnamed multiple escapee. This is a more vigorous and altogether more successful play, freed by the passage of time from the raw intensity of feeling and more subject to the fashioning of the artist. The static rhetoric is gone, the action (as in all eight later plays) is divided into three acts, the dialogue is brisk, some of the scenes are expertly crafted, and the plot, although essentially still episodic, has pace and excitement with events enacted rather than narrated. Other elements taken from the *comedia nueva* recipe are included – a *gracioso* or funny man, comic business, songs, *doubles entendres*, metatheatrical self-referentiality, a complicated love intrigue, borrowed identities.[14] Thematically, like *The Ways of Algiers*, *The Bagnios of Algiers* is predicated upon the traditional Christian virtues of loyalty, steadfastness, chasteness, fortitude, and piety, and both plays set out to dramatize the clash of religious cultures which not only shaped events in the Mediterranean as a whole in the sixteenth century but posed a severe problem within Spain itself. This came to a head in 1609 when Philip III issued a decree of expulsion against the abstemious, hard-working but largely unassimilated *moriscos* of Spain, in a move both to pander to Christian prejudice by obliterating the last trace of the Moorish occupation of the Peninsula and to quell widespread fears that they posed a threat to the country's security. Cervantes' representation of the Moor is noticeably ambivalent. The lusty mistress and importunate master in *The Traffic of Algiers* are guilty of sexual harassment, and it is clear from his other writings that, although Cervantes was aware of what the expulsion meant in terms of human suffering, the popular conception of the *morisco* as treacherous, avaricious, and unchaste was by and large his own. But these characters are by no means monsters and both are allowed the pain of passion as opposed to unadulterated lust. This willingness to concede the humanity of the Other is scarcely detectable, however, in *The Bagnios of Algiers*. Cervantes' representation of the Muslim, in other words, seems paradoxically to have hardened with the passage of time, succumbing perhaps to the stereotype – now distanced from close reminders of a shared humanity – and perhaps also to the build-up of animosity toward the *moriscos* that led to their expulsion. While there is praise for a king of Morocco and a Turkish janissary who never appear, the events of the play present Muslims as treacherous and cruel in the extreme. They are explicitly represented as an inferior and barbarous race and there is an on-going insinuation of sinister homosexual practices which culminates in the beating to death of a small Christian boy who refuses to abandon his faith. This is a deliberate process of demonization, and the fact that much of the play's comic business revolves round the humiliation and tricking of a Jew adds to what would now be perceived as a heavily racist atmosphere. Clearly these prejudices were the pervasive prejudices of Cervantes' time and cannot meaningfully be judged by the sensibilities of today, particularly in view of his own suffering in Algiers. However, the intensification of religious and racial animosity in the later play does make one wonder whether Cervantes was not, in part at least, deliberately pandering to the prejudices of his audience in an attempt to make the play more marketable.

The Moorish women in *The Bagnios of Algiers* – Halima the unchaste Moorish mistress who falls for her captive, and Zahara the secret Christian who combines piety with a provocative worldliness that equips her admirably for her double life – are, it has to be said, treated much more sympathetically than the men, no doubt because romantic rather than historical values and perceptions dictate their roles. *El gallardo español* (*The Gallant Spaniard*), another play about Christians and Moors set this time in Oran – where Cervantes had gone in 1581 to pick up dispatches during temporary employment as a king's messenger – moves further away from the contingent world and into the novelesque. Arlaxa is another variation on the sexually assertive Mooress. Capricious and willful, she is so caught by what she has heard of a certain don Fernando de Saavedra (note that name again) that she strikes a perverse bargain with her suitor Alimuzel to marry him if he brings Fernando to her as a trophy. Alimuzel, by contrast with his co-religionaries in the other two plays, is himself honorable and courageous, the Moorish equivalent of Fernando's Christian knight. Away from painful memories of the bagnios of Algiers, Cervantes, it seems, felt able to incorporate a very different contemporary literary representation of Spain's traditional enemy – that of the Sentimental Moor, an exotic heroic figure simultaneously emasculated and ennobled by defeat. The two linked forces at work in the play are Venus and Mars, the empowering and distorting effects of love and passion entwined with the heroisms and betrayals of war. For his heroine Margarita, who leaves home and homeland in disguise to find and ransom her former suitor (Fernando), Cervantes has recourse to one of the *comedia nueva*'s most popular female figures, the woman who cross-dresses as a man. In fact disguise and role play, so central a feature of the seventeenth-century Spanish theatre and its engagement with reality, are keynotes of the play, for Fernando himself has assumed another identity on being captured by a party of Moorish scouts, in order to infiltrate Arlaxa's household and get the better of Alimuzel. He claims to be the friend and companion in arms of the famous don Fernando, and the opportunities for irony and obfuscation which ensue are amply exploited. Later on both Fernando and Margarita assume third identities when they appear as Moors, a cumulative process of dissimulation which begins to destabilize Fernando's sense of self and make him wonder whether he will be able to recuperate his true identity. Cervantes clearly enjoys the joke of a surrogate Saavedra inside the "real" world of the play who assumes a fictional identity within which he then has to adopt a disguise. It is a fusion of real and imaginary dimensions worthy of the *Quixote*. The game intensifies later on when Fernando, Margarita, and her guardian all deny their real identities when confronted by her bemused brother and succeed for a while in threatening his grip on reality. Interestingly enough, Cervantes does not use the cross-dressing motif in the usual way to engineer sexually ambiguous love scenes. It suggests that this might be an early play from his later period, an impression supported by a certain rhetorical surplus in the dialogue and some awkwardness and lack of rigor in the crafting of the plot.

Arlaxa and Margarita are strong women's parts in a theatre full of them – in this respect, too, Cervantes had absorbed Lope's example. In *La gran sultana* (*The Grand Sultana*), the last of Cervantes' surviving plays with an Islamic setting, and again with a historical basis, a woman actually takes center stage, this time a Christian gentlewoman, doña Catalina de Oviedo, who after being taken captive as a child enters the harem of the Great Turk of Constantinople and ends up marrying him. At the heart of the play there is a serious and well-drawn ethical dilemma – whether Catalina is justified in marrying an infidel in exchange for being allowed to keep her faith and her Spanish identity – and the subtext throughout is provided by the bedrock of Christian values, patience, resignation, and endurance, that sustain her and her fellow captives. But otherwise the piece is a glorious festive romp, with its Turkish exoticism, splendid costumes, singing and dancing, and above all its comedy. Much of this is provided by the wit and nonsense generated by a very ingenious funny man, another captive, in his efforts to stay alive. When Madrigal vows at the end to become a dramatist so that he can go home to Madrid and turn Catalina's story into a play in which he will play the same character he is playing now, the boundaries between the worlds of fiction and fact, text and author, for a fleeting moment melt away as they do in the *Quixote*. Cervantes has found another way of initialling his text – the creative jester within the play is after all the creating jester outside it. Humor is also provided by the extravagant plot, which has a very pronounced risqué character. The Islamic setting allows Cervantes the opportunity once more to introduce Jewish characters who become the butt of jokes (since the expulsion of 1492 there were no longer any Jews in Spain itself). Setting it within a Turkish harem gives him further license to exploit a vein of sexuality and its consequences more explicit than would normally have been met with in romantic comedy at the time. Not only is there the frisson provided by the prospect of a reluctant pious virgin being bedded by the Great Turk, but unbeknownst to the eunuchs the harem harbors captive lovers – Zelinda, a young man cross-dressed as a harem girl and his pregnant girlfriend Zaida. When the Great Turk is persuaded by his Cadi that it is his duty to "sow in more than one field," the harem girl he chooses from the line-up is of course the terrified young man. He is rescued only by Catalina's belated admission that her period is three months late. The homosexuality motif reappears here too, when Madrigal taunts the Cadi with chasing a beautiful youth. The play's audience, had it ever had one, would have loved all this titillation, and it is entirely possible that it was not performed partly because it overstepped the bounds of decency or at least decorum. Theatre companies needed two-yearly licenses to perform, and the theatre's opponents were always on the look-out for dramatic material which supported their contention that the playhouses represented a danger to public morals and should be shut down.

The undoubted merits and actability of Cervantes' later plays as a whole do suggest that it was largely his reputation as a playwright, or rather lack of it, which let him down rather than the plays themselves, and it is quite likely, as we saw, that Lope de Vega had some part in what amounted to the blackballing of Cervantes' dramatic works. Nonetheless it remains the case that what Cervantes wrote were essentially dramatized narratives rather than dramatic actions, reminiscent in a way of television serials and dramatizations with their linear, episodic development and relaxed crafting. He was a (hi)story-teller, combining tales of life and the imagination to explore the complexities of human experience and the power of narrative. In *El gallardo español* both Arlaxa and Margarita desire a man they have never met but have been told about. They fall in love, as Margarita herself points out, not with their eyes (as Platonic theory would dictate) but with their ears. In other words they have been seduced by narrative and description – an idea central to Cervantes' fiction. These dramatized narratives have their own inner unifying elements in the form of recurring motifs, themes, and preoccupations. The four captivity plays are built round cultural difference, religious faith, and national identity, with the business of war and military life always hovering on the margins. They contain traces of other seventeenth-century topics – the theatre of the world, the apparent fluidity of self, the binaries of appearance and reality. At their core, however, is one of the *leitmotifs* of Cervantes' entire work – the idea of liberty, both physical and spiritual, the freedom of the will and of the spirit to surmount restriction and confinement. Given that he had lost five years to slavery its importance to him is predictable, as is the psychological rootedness of three out of his eight published plays in that period in his life. But confinement takes many forms and in his other plays exploration of it diversifies. At the same time some of the minor motifs mentioned above come to the fore.

None of Cervantes' plays better illustrates the primacy for him of content over form than *La casa de los celos y selvas de Ardenia* (*The House of Jealousy and Woods of Ardenia*). It is a patchwork of the chivalric, pastoral, and allegory, with Venus, Cupid, the shade of Merlin, an angel, a devil, a warrior maid, several savages, a serpent, and a lapdog for good measure. It gives every sign of belonging to his early theatrical period, and any efforts he made to refashion it for performance later on must have been half-hearted at best.[15] The world of the play is an enchanted world where little is as it seems and where good and evil fight for control of human minds and hearts. Flights of inflated rhetoric mingle with dialogue that is sharp and true, and supernatural nonsense with moments of finely modulated realism: the portrayal of the knight Reinaldos, haunted by his poverty and his insecurities, irremediably mean-spirited and constantly squabbling with his cousin and rival Roldán, is very good indeed. Sometimes the mixture of the two dimensions borders on the surreal in a manner suggestive of the *Quixote*, such as in the parodic scene where the evil Angelica's aged duenna first complains about the effect the interminable traveling is having on her complexion, and then attributes the pain in her womb to the cold draught produced by her short stirrups. Reminiscent of that novel too, and indeed of the *Novelas ejemplares* and *Los trabajos de Persiles y Sigismunda* (*The Trials of Persiles and Sigismunda*) is the pivotal role of physical beauty, not only with its power to turn men's minds for good and ill, but also for its capacity to belie its Platonic identity as the mirror of an inner goodness. Angelica's beauty is treacherous and causes discord and strife. And it is a beauty that induces confinement of mind and spirit. The prison is the prison of love, a favorite metaphor of medieval and Renaissance literature, and the play's allegorical figures represent its tortures – fear, impertinent curiosity, suspicion, jealousy, desperation – for knights and (in parodied form) shepherds alike, and the ill fame to which it can drive noble men by distracting them from duty and reason. Once the error of their ways has been pointed out to them in a series of supernatural apparitions, they exert their will and see sense, but it is only a temporary recovery and the play ends in as much discord as it began. The triumph of reason and virtue through the exercise of free will is one of the constants of Cervantes' work, not least in his pastoral romance *La Galatea* (*Galatea*, 1585), and for all the play's supernatural interventions the serious point is lurking here that human beings create their own fates. Nonetheless there is a very strong case for seeing the entire play as driven by the spirit of carnival. This is festive drama with a burlesque undertone that gets markedly stronger as the play progresses. In the enchanted wood of Ardenia nothing is as it seems, characters and stage effects appear and reappear, and the worlds of classical myth, late Medieval romance and Renaissance pastoral merge into a timeless world of the imagination controlled by a magus who delights in his own ingenuity and in poking fun at them all.

Cervantes' other dramatic excursion into the chivalric world, *El laberinto de amor* (*The Labyrinth of Love*), is a good deal less idiosyncratic and sprawling, but it is even more complicated, as its title promises. While its plot pays lip-service to the chivalric motif of the unjustly traduced lady whose honor has to be defended by a champion in single combat, the play in its unraveling owes much more to the extremely complex romantic comedies so beloved of seventeenth-century audiences. Transformation and disguise are its currency, and just as the *Quixote* is an experiment in seeing how far the boundaries between literature and reality can be destabilized without loss of control, so here Cervantes pushes to its limits the multiplication of identities and ironies in the creation of a comic plot in which nothing is as it seems. The heroine Porcia adopts no fewer than three male and three female identities in the course of the play – creating the sort of bewildering complexity that only really works on stage, where the true identity of the characters is accessible to the eye. Cervantes' grip on his cat's cradle never falters and the play, with well-differentiated characters and some excellent dialogue and scenes, is very successfully crafted apart from its rather limp dénouement and too generous an admixture of knock-about comic business – some of the humorous inserts are almost skits in their own right (one of them must be one of the earliest literary examples of a female brawl). Typically of Cervantes, the layered fictions within the plot are self-subverting. Disguise is revealed as theatrical convention by means of constant indications of its fragility – not only the repeated observations that speech register and accent do not fit appearance and assumed identity, but the difficulties experienced by characters in trying to be consistent to their surrogate selves. Its importance, however, is substantial as well as formal. The characters move within a labyrinth of love created by their own desires in conflict with the desires of others. Sexual attraction, jealousy, self-esteem, and competitiveness lock them into a maze where ingenuity, courage, pretense, and deceit are all necessary if they are to find their way to some sort of personal fulfillment. Confinement in the play, however, is not just the 'libertad rendida' (surrendered liberty) of love, a part delicious, part painful hijacking of mind and senses.[16] It is physical restraint as well. Julia and Porcia flee their home in order to escape the excessive confinement to which they were subjected by an overbearing father/uncle and find the men they love. Rosamira is locked up by her father when she is accused of being unchaste – a charge desperately trumped up by herself and the man she loves in order to delay a marriage arranged without her consent. The disguises resorted to in all these relationships are attempts to seize control of situations where individual freedoms are denied. Since these ends cannot be achieved within existing constraints, disguise allows the temporary transformations necessary to alter the ordered course of events. Disguise after all is the freedom to be someone else, a liberation from the given – a prescribed self, an ordained life, an allotted social or biological identity. Little wonder that it was so popular with audiences in a hierarchical system predicated upon social role. Little wonder too that it plays so prominent a part in the writings of a man who knew the value of freedom and the power of the human will.

If *The Labyrinth of Love* is romantic intrigue in a setting that owes much to Ariosto, Cervantes' *La entretenida* (*The Comedy of Entertainment*) is ostensibly a cape and sword play, a love intrigue in the much more familiar seventeenth-century setting of upper-class Madrid. The genre produced some of Golden Age Spain's most scintillating comedies. Cervantes' version, however, is a spoof from beginning to end, a mischievous denial or reversal of the very assumptions and procedures that give the genre its identity. There is always some comic business in a cape and sword play, with the servants' antics normally parodying those of their masters and mistresses, but here the characters from downstairs outweigh and outplay those from upstairs. There are far more of them than is usual, they take as prominent a part in the action as their superiors, they are extremely well differentiated, and the humor and nonsense they generate, firmly rooted as it is in the socio-economic realities of everyday life, is brilliantly done. A large part of the third act is even taken up by a comic interlude, performed by the servants, which degenerates into a brawl in which fact and fiction become indistinguishable. This parodic note, however, permeates the entire work and nothing turns out as we expect. There is more than a suggestion of Don Quixote in the rhetorical and emotional excesses of all four gentlemen lovers, and their behavior is mocked by other characters. Antonio's desperate search for the woman he believes is being kept from him by her father collapses into bathos when her father approaches him with a view to arranging a marriage, but their cosy masculine bargain is subsequently itself punctuated by the discovery that she has already committed herself to somebody else. Marcela seems all set to marry her real cousin from Peru instead of the impostor who has taken up residence in her house but stays in bed all day, only to learn that the Pope after all will not grant the awaited dispensation for them to marry. It does not seem to bother her very much, fortunately. Even the play's incest motif is still-born. Marcela, not realizing that there is another Marcela who looks very much like her, fears her brother Antonio is in love with her. We the audience know from the start that this is not the case, and the whole Marcela misunderstanding is cleared up very prosaically in the middle of Act II. In the process another complication, that of Ambrosio's love for a Marcela he assumes to be Antonio's sister but is in fact Antonio's beloved, rearranges itself so that Ambrosio now has reason to be jealous of Antonio whereas before he had none at all. Such discoveries are normally reserved for the end of a play, and their position here is a deliberate sacrifice of structural tension to comedic subversion. Similarly, the audience is deprived of its expectation of a happy ending. Of the seven characters who wish to marry, only one – unexpectedly Ambrosio – discovers that his feelings are reciprocated, and since he absents himself from the stage long before the end of the play and since the "other" Marcela is as omnipresent and invisible as Dulcinea, any hope of a knot being actually tied is frustrated. The dénouement is a self-declared cluster of frayed ends – the audience is in on the joke until the last. There are traces of serious matters of humanity in the work, notably the resentments and hardships of servants and the ubiquitous motif of confinement – the "other" Marcela's father tellingly refers to his daughter as "an ermine fettered with religious chains"[17] before he learns the lesson that captivity merely nourishes the desire for freedom. Nonetheless, in its essence, the play is exactly what its title proclaims it to be.

146

For the Renaissance the lowly were the appropriate target of humor in literature. In the seventeenth century, comedy's ruthless eye roved further up the social scale, as we have seen in some of Cervantes' own works, and little there escaped his gaze unscathed. But he was also enduringly fascinated by what are now called the lower and under classes – not just servants and peasants, but those who lived on the social margins and used their wits to survive – women of easy or no virtue, chancers, rogues, bully-boys, even criminals. In his fiction and in his drama he captures mind-sets, customs, speech patterns, insults, and jokes, and effortlessly turns them into comedy. He brought this interest in picaresque low-life to his single religious play, *El rufián dichoso* (*The Fortunate Ruffian*), one of a group of "saint plays" written for the secular stage that typically dramatize the conversion of some historical figure from sinner to saint – the ultimate transformation of all. The genre produced some extraordinary works but Cervantes' is not one of them, largely because he makes no attempt to provide the conversion with any psychological plausibility. Cristóbal de Lugo is a delinquent youth given to gambling, trickery, and carving up other thugs, albeit partly redeemed by his piety, a charitable instinct, loyalty toward his own kind, and a somewhat contemptuous gallantry toward the women that chase after him. At the end of Act I he arbitrarily decides to become a religious rather than a highwayman. The only precipitating circumstance is that he has won (by cheating), rather than lost, a game of cards, and plausibility has to make do with the scraps of virtue he has previously shown. The point of Act I for Cervantes lies elsewhere – in creating a vivid picture of the Sevillian underworld reminiscent of his exemplary tale "Rinconete y Cortadillo" ("Rinconete and Cortadillo"). It works particularly effectively here because the vehicle is dialogue, and here, as in the short story, Cervantes is especially good at conveying the sordid glamor of the criminal underworld. The rest of the play takes place in Mexico – a geographical displacement that provides striking proof of its author's own conversion to some of the ways of the *comedia nueva*. So conscious is he of this radical volte-face that he arms himself against criticism by inserting at the beginning of Act II a dialogue between Drama and Curiosity which not only brings us up to date with Lugo's life but which makes the point that art must change with the times. Curiosity declares herself only partly convinced – an indication of continuing misgivings on Cervantes' part. Acts II and III, as Drama explains, deal with the newly named Friar Cristóbal de la Cruz's holy life and saintly death respectively. They are threaded with banter and grumbles from his irrepressible side-kick, who would much prefer to be a petty criminal again rather than a poor Dominican friar, and by miracles and demonic visions the historical truth of which is affirmed in the accompanying stage directions. The play's narrative is taken from a contemporary account of the Dominican order in Mexico and in view of the Canon's denunciations in the *Quixote* about the absurdities of much contemporary religious drama Cervantes clearly wanted to stress the veracity of his own account. Since Cervantes, following his narrative instincts as usual, has chosen to display the life rather than to concentrate on the psychological conversion at its heart, there is space in the action for a more protracted verbal articulation of the centrality of faith and hope in the Christian scheme of redemption than is usual in such plays. The moving eloquence and passionate intensity of these passages make the attribution of the play to the years around the end of the first decade of the seventeenth century very convincing, for at that time religious life in the Cervantes household intensified, with his wife and two sisters, and eventually Cervantes himself, all becoming lay members of the Franciscan Order. What seems to have captured Cervantes' interest above all was the outer incongruity and inner coherence of a vicious life transformed by a Tridentine act of will into an iconic statement, and conventional dramatic considerations give way before this driving purpose – Cruz's death is as hasty as his conversion – as they so often do in his theatre.[18] For Cervantes the play was not really the thing.

In the eighth play published in 1615, *Pedro de Urdemalas* (*Peter Mischief-Maker*), Cervantes' comic realism takes complete control. Using as his linchpin a glamorous master fixer and trickster from Spanish folklore, he constructs a richly varied rural community whose inhabitants take center stage rather than playing supporting parts. It is his most original play and significantly it is the most completely conceived and achieved. While his other plays represent to varying degrees a distracted compromise between personal inclination and precept or formula, here one feels that Cervantes was working fully in his element. This is a literary shaping of a real world with which Cervantes was well acquainted, a world peopled by minor officials, sacristans, scribes and servants, laborers, shepherds, gypsies, and strolling players, all recognizable from the *Quixote*, from the interludes and from many of the *Novelas ejemplares*. The sub-plot of the lowly girl of noble birth appears again in two of his best-known tales, "La gitanilla" ("The Little Gypsy Girl") and "La ilustre fregona" ("The Illustrious Kitchenmaid"), while Pedro's tricks would be entirely at home in the farces. Although typically linear in form, the work is artfully put together and tonally consistent in its satirical portrayal of the foibles and absurdities of human nature. Here the lure of idealism and romance is invoked only to be willfully refused. This little gypsy girl-turned-princess is self-opinionated, arrogant, and ungrateful to the last, and her aunt the queen, who assumes that the discovery of the girl's real identity will douse the king's desire for her, is slyly shown as the play closes to be foolishly mistaken. While the play's comic business succeeds extremely well, the *tour de force* is the ingenious, seductive Pedro himself. An ubiquitous, protean figure who has lived many lives and occupied many selves, he continually changes clothes and identities in his negotiation of the opportunities and dangers that present themselves, paradoxically without ever being false to his own nature. He is the ultimate self-fashioner, admitting no indelible definitions, responsive to chance and change, free and in control of himself and his life because he is a realist who knows both the power and the limits of illusion, a lucid Don Quixote. And at the last he recognizes and grasps the perfect way of living a life of continuous transformation without ever losing sight of himself – he becomes an actor. Or rather he becomes a professional actor, because an actor is what he is all along, an actor conscious of the parts he plays and proud of the reputation he has won by playing them well. The play is Cervantes' most finely modulated and most successful venture into metafiction outside the *Quixote*.[19]

Cervantes' surviving full-length plays paint a composite picture of a highly self-conscious, experimental, and iconoclastic writer captivated above all by the interplay of the transcendental and the ordinary in life, by the serious mediated through the comic. His vision is an amused ironic one tinged with satire and occasionally with jaundice, but it is rarely overtly judgmental and never cruel. The pleasure he took in the risibility of life found its purest distillation, however, in his farcical interludes, eight of which he selected for publication along with his eight plays, though we know he wrote more.[20] Albeit minor pieces, in their snapshot length and nature they are the perfect instrument for producing an intense and vivid simulacrum of the routine absurdities of the human condition.

Since their pared-down form inevitably produces caricature, the satire of the interludes is more trenchant than the satirical element in the plays and, protected as they are by their farcical identity, their substance is sometimes stronger. Acutely observed, with dialogue full of puns, irony and bawdy innuendo, they give flesh and vigor to the stock themes and characters of the genre at the time: country bumpkins, cuckolded husbands, strident wives, mischief-making servants and neighbours, lusty sextons, student tricksters, swaggering soldiers, even pimps and prostitutes. Many of the characters have comically symbolic names or no names at all, since they represent types, roles, or qualities. There is nothing half-hearted or hidden about these pieces. Emotions and language are as aggressively energetic as the action itself, and for the audience, who are always allowed a strong sense of what is to come, anticipation is a major part of the pleasure. Endings are either deferred or merely provisional, because nothing has actually been achieved or changed, and are accompanied as was usual at the time by singing and dancing – which serves to neutralize acerbic or potentially offensive elements that have gone before. The interludes have been variously read as anti-establishment and pro-establishment, anti- and proto-feminist. Cervantes certainly uses them to grind some of the axes he grinds elsewhere – there are swipes at mixed-age marriages, at sexual jealousy, at the ineptitude of minor officialdom, at a corrupt judiciary, at a society obsessed with lineage and the constitution of its blood. Some of this is undoubtedly subversive. If they simultaneously appear conservative it is because their principal target is human nature itself, the sheer stupidity, shallowness, and gullibility of human beings, which necessarily prescribes a return at the end to the *status quo*. Their continuing focus is perception and deception, the capacity to deceive, to be deceived and to deceive oneself – all eight pieces are variations on those seventeenth-century binaries, illusion and reality. And if Cervantes sometimes seems to condone deceit, it is only to show that it is human foolishness that gives deceit permission to operate. It is, of course, in the nature of the satirical interlude that graver implications or repercussions be held sufficiently at bay to allow laughter to take its course, and it is in the crucial balance between the two that the extraordinary deftness of Cervantes' interludes lie. His satirical eye is unerring, and the pitch, pace and tone of the dialogue are precisely right, but it is the way they sit so perfectly poised between representation and caricature, between disclosure and fun, that makes them magisterial examples of their kind. Cameo portraits of the underbelly of seventeenth-century Spain – particularly of the hugely expanded capital which had become a magnet to riffraff, adventurers, and the poor from all over the country – they combine the rich specificity of a social documentary with the enduring comedy of human nature.

Of the eight interludes, only two are written in verse, which became a common vehicle for comic sketches from the end of the sixteenth century on. A more significant formal distinction relates to their structure. Four of them have little by way of action, relying on the dynamics of the dialogue for their comic effect, while the other four use plots of varying degrees of complexity as well in order to generate humor. The two verse pieces, *El rufián viudo llamado Trampagos* (*Trampagos the Widower Pimp*) and *La elección de los alcaldes de Daganzo* (*Electing the Magistrates in Daganzo*) belong to the first group. *The Widower Pimp* is not only a sparkling satire of the seamy world of sexual commerce but a mischievous parody of the values and rhetoric of sixteenth-century Neoplatonic love poetry. The golden-haired prostitute that Trampagos so eloquently mourns between bouts of fencing practice turns out to be a diseased fifty-two-year-old with dyed hair, false teeth, and rotten breath, and when three other prostitutes brawl over which of them should inherit his protection he promptly selects his new source of income and pawns his widower's weeds. A well-known folkloric *pícaro* who has just escaped from slavery in Africa (the shadow of Cervantes again) then turns up to lead the assembled pimps and their whores in singing and dancing. In *La elección de los alcaldes de Daganzo* (*Electing the Magistrates in Daganzo*) a band of gypsies draws proceedings to a close in a similar way. This sketch depicts the village worthies of Daganzo discussing the nominations for the office of magistrate for the coming year and then interviewing the candidates. As in *The Widower Pimp*, the repartee between the characters constitutes the comic business. The ineptitude and corruption of local government was a favorite complaint of Cervantes and a good deal of fun is poked here at both the selection committee and the nominees, most of them cut from the same cloth – at their ignorance, their unsuitability, their prejudice against literacy and learning. The suggestion that they actually interview the candidates rather than merely going on anecdotal evidence is regarded as revolutionary; Cervantes seems to have had a bee in his bonnet about professionalization, for in *Pedro de Urdemalas* he makes a plea for the proper selection and training of actors. The committee has just decided to postpone the election until the next day when the gypsies arrive. The ensuing noise provokes the arrival of an indignant sexton who is then tossed in a blanket for his pains – the sort of mayhem with which contemporary interludes often ended but which Cervantes himself resorted to only in one other of his eight farces.

The other two dialogue-centered sketches are *La guarda cuidadosa* (*The Watchful Guard*) and *El juez de los divorcios* (*The Divorce-Court Judge*). The first presents two rival suitors trading insults. Both are literary stereotypes – the swaggering soldier inherited from Latin comedy via the *commedia dell'arte*, and the lusty sexton – but both soldiers and sextons of course were extremely common figures in city life at the time. Against the bustle of everyday life in Madrid – the soldier sends packing a young beggar, a pedlar and a shoemaker who all call at Cristina the kitchen-maid's house – the ragged, self-deluding military man and the ill-favored sexton spring vividly to life as they quarrel over Cristina's hand. Sextons, like friars, had the reputation of being priapic, and soldiers for their part, since they were infrequently paid and foot-loose, and traded on their real or fictional military exploits, were regarded as louche and unreliable. Both are risible figures. Having been a soldier himself Cervantes was often swift to defend the soldier's life, but here the soldier in particular is heavily caricatured. When Cristina's master insists that she must choose for herself – self-determination in the selection of a life partner is a recurring theme in Cervantes' work – she makes the materialistic but sensible choice, opting for security with the sexton rather than for the dubious glamor of the threadbare braggart with his forged testimonials. The matter is resolved, the cast exits singing and dancing, but with the two men still at loggerheads. *The Divorce-Court Judge* achieves the same sort of compromised resolution. The three couples who appear before the judge to sue for divorce are all eager to be rid of each other and each has her or his own perspective on events. Mariana is sick of seeing to the needs of her decrepit old husband while he maintains she is a scold and a nag. Guiomar denounces her soldier spouse as a layabout gambler with aspirations to being a poet – the worst-paid occupation in the world, she claims. He first goes along with this version of their marriage in order to convince the judge he is indeed an unsuitable husband, only to be driven by her denunciations into retaliation, proclaiming her an arrogant, ill-natured spendthrift. Aldonza claims that her barber husband married her under false pretenses by claiming to be a fully qualified doctor, that he is jealous and that she dislikes him, while her husband suggestively counters that he dislikes her just as much for reasons he cannot possibly mention. There is only one single plaintiff, a porter foolish enough to have married a prostitute and set her up as a market trader, who now spends his life on the receiving end of her aggression and his neighbors' gossip. The laughter, in other words, is provoked by the traditional motif of the animosity between inadequate husband and harridan wife. Truth is shown to be a complex and elusive thing, changing its shape according to the point of view, although all the litigants are revealed as less than attractive human beings. The judge finds no faults serious enough to justify divorce – if incompatibility, disapproval, and distaste were sufficient grounds, he observes, the courts would be overwhelmed. A sour view of the married state, or perhaps just a warning about unwise pairings, but that we are not supposed to take the applications for divorce seriously is clear from Mariana's suggestion that marriage become a three-year renewable contract. To the accompaniment of a kiss-and-make-up song the judge goes off to a party being held by an estranged couple he has recently reunited, after asking for depositions in writing. So resolution is once more deferred, and with the attorney's cynical expression of support for divorce cases on the grounds that while most of them come to nothing they still put bread in the mouths of lawyers, the impression of human foolishness and venality is amply confirmed.

Those interludes which use comic plots as well as comic dialogue to achieve their effects are inevitably the most memorable because they work with story and images as well as with words. The cleverness of verbal interchange is harder to recall than a vivid arrangement of events. It also tends to suffer more from the passage of time, for words, jokes, and anecdotes carry a weight of reference and association which soon become culturally invisible, and this in turn makes them more difficult to perform. For these reasons amongst others the remaining four interludes are Cervantes' best known. The simplest is *La cueva de Salamanca* (*The Cave of Salamanca*), a somewhat oblique title in that it reflects a passing reference in the play to a cave in medieval legend where the magic arts could be learnt. Cervantes works here with the familiar types of the cuckolded jealous husband, the sexually active sexton, the bored wife, the complicit maidservant and the roguish student with an eye for the main chance. The piece opens with a scene of farewell between Pancracio and his wife, where Leonarda's exaggerated dismay immediately alerts the audience to her eagerness for his departure. As soon as Pancracio has left it becomes clear that during his absence Leonarda and her maid Cristina are expecting a visit from their admirers, the sexton and the barber, and that a large hamper of delicacies has been sent round by the two men in preparation for dinner. A student enters seeking shelter for the night, the sexton and the barber arrive and, after a great deal of lewd chit-chat and some humor at the expense of the pedantic sexton, they go off to prepare supper. The scene switches to Pancracio, whose coach has broken down and who is on his way back home. Consternation ensues when he is heard thundering at the door, the two men hide in the attic, while the student retreats to the hayloft. A few moments later he shouts to be let out, but defuses Pancracio's indignation at finding a young man in his house by offering to conjure up for him two devils carrying a hamper full of delicacies who will take the form of the sexton and the barber. The outcome will by now be obvious. Leonarda expects the worst, but she has underestimated her husband's gullibility. The interlude ends with them all going off to tuck into the food, so eager is Pancracio to discover whether devils actually eat or not. The effectiveness of the piece lies in its very simplicity and in the play of predictability and surprise – the audience are privy from the start to the build-up of tension with Pancracio's departure and return, but excluded initially from the secret of how that tension will be resolved. When they find out, they can laugh unrestrainedly at the credulity of the self-important Pancracio and enjoy being in on the deception. It has, furthermore, the whirlwind verve and the perfect pace of the very best farces.

So too does *El viejo celoso* (*The Jealous Old Man*), an interlude with a similar plot which is more sophisticated in conception, and at once more polished and more daring in execution. It is a high-profile piece in that it is a farcical version of Cervantes' exemplary tale "El celoso extremeño" ("The Jealous Man from Extremadura"), a strikingly memorable story about the pathologically jealous husband of a child bride whose attempt to protect her virtue by locking her up in a fortress-house from which everything male is excluded merely precipitates disaster. The predicament of the traditionally ridiculous figure of the cuckold is there seen in a somber, even tragic light, and the narrative, which is laden with expectant sensuality and rich in symbolism and psychological exploration, engages directly with the Cervantine theme of the relationship between freedom and virtue. The farce on the other hand does what its genre requires of it. The husband Cañizares is not only jealously over-protective but old, incontinent, and impotent, while the wife Lorenza, who was lured into the match by the thought of riches and an early widowhood, is now entirely complicit in her neighbor's plan to have her "serviced" by a handsome young stranger. And that is exactly what happens. The young man slips into the house behind a large tapestry unrolled for Cañizares's inspection – his outrage at the sight of the male figures on it rendered doubly absurd by his obliviousness to the presence of the real man behind it. The ending is extraordinarily provocative. Lorenza and the young man disappear into a room off-stage from which she gives a suggestive running commentary on what is happening inside, while Cañizares believes it is all a pretense to punish him for his jealousy. When he insists on bursting in nevertheless to pacify her, he has water thrown in his eyes, the young man makes his exit and Lorenza denounces her husband for believing her "lies." She has won both the practical and moral advantage with a trick that is a perfect example of that technique so beloved of Renaissance comedy – deceiving with the truth. And since Cañizares is forced to apologize for his allegedly ill-founded suspicions of the neighbor's influence, the scene is now set for similar visits in the future. The censor who granted the collection of plays and interludes its publication license on the grounds that it contained nothing against public morals must have paid scant attention to this little sketch, for its instantly readable message is that the old man has got his comeuppance and that his wife's sexual unruliness is acceptable. This is carnival, values are upturned, and the wife comes out on top. While there is no permanent resolution of a deeply unsatisfactory situation, however, the dénouement carries a forceful ethical charge. Not only is the folly of May–December marriages an obvious given of the piece – Lorenza is fifteen, Cañizares in his seventies – but there is a sinister undercurrent in Lorenza's very real desperation over her constricted life and in her mention of suicide. Cervantes knew the despair of confinement because he had lived it. He knew what extremes it could drive people to, and he knew that it was not the soil in which moral responsibility flourished. The brazen amorality of *El viejo celoso* is paradoxically a reaffirmation of belief in the absolute morality of freedom.

It is also a way of making mock of one of the social neuroses of the day – the obsession with honor. *El retablo de las maravillas* (*The Miracle Show*) pokes hilarious fun at a related, more oppressive, and more maleficent neurosis, the obsession with racial purity – like that with honor, rooted in insecurity and bound up with notions of image and immaculacy.[21] Given that anti-Semitism was enshrined in many statutes governing admission to military orders, cathedral hierarchies, university colleges, government bureaucracy, even to residence in certain areas of the country, to be able to claim pure Christian blood was essential not only to peace of mind but to social and economic well-being. To send it up as openly as Cervantes does, therefore, was sufficiently daring to justify the suspicions of some critics that his interludes were considered too risky to perform. *The Miracle Show* is an inspired variation on the theme of the emperor's new clothes. Three confidence tricksters arrive in a provincial town, pretending to be puppeteers, and offer to put on a miraculous puppet-show visible only to those born inside wedlock and with no Jewish blood in their veins. It is agreed that a performance will take place in the alderman's house to celebrate his daughter's wedding in advance of a public performance the following day. Of course there is no show at all. The tricksters demand payment in advance and, when the show begins, proceed to tell the assembled townsfolk what they should be seeing and hearing. What follows is a scene of collusive self-delusion. The audience consists of the socially aspiring members of the town who cannot afford to let others think that they are not legitimate Old Christians. Even the rational Governor, who admits to himself that he sees nothing and is totally confident of both his legitimacy and the constitution of his blood, feels compelled to play along. So eager are the more gullible to prove that they can see what they ought to be seeing that they respond verbally and physically to the supposed plot – pleading with Samson not to bring the roof down on their heads, running away from an invisible bull, lions, and bears, shouting because they can feel mice running over them and water flowing down their back, and generally running amok. The tricksters temporarily lose control at the end when the quartermaster arrives. Unaware of the circumstances, he insists he sees nothing, is promptly denounced by the spectators as being *de ex illis* (one of "them"), the biblical euphemism often used of those of Jewish descent, and sets about them with his sword for their effrontery.[22] But the con men calmly take down the blanket they use as a stage curtain in preparation for the next day's show, confident in the knowledge that theirs is the perfect sting because nobody can afford to admit the truth. The miasmic and illusory nature of racial prejudice is wonderfully caught, but so is its power over people's minds. The coruscating exposé contains a heart of darkness.

If *The Jealous Old Man* and *The Wonder Show* have the polished completeness of a cut diamond, the last of the interludes, *El vizcaíno fingido* (*The Sham Biscayan*), has an ambitious brilliance all its own. It weaves together a number of literary and contemporary themes, figures and issues: the idea of the biter bit, the confidence trickster who replaces a gold chain with a worthless imitation, as in Cervantes' exemplary tale "El casamiento engañoso" ("The Deceitful Marriage"), the figure of the Biscayan as a gullible fool, the layabout young noble, prostitutes and prostitution – these last motifs inspired by a law passed in 1611 to control female prostitution and combat effeminacy amongst men by restricting the use of coaches to upper-class women and forbidding the use of veils in the street. The little plot is cleverly complicated, with a sting inside another sting. Outwardly the rascally young noble Solórzano, with the help of a gold chain and a base-metal imitation, conspires with two prostitutes to fleece a Biscayan impersonated by his friend Quiñones, when in fact it is Solórzano and Quiñones who are conspiring to trick one of the prostitutes, Cristina. They confuse the women with a kind of situational sleight of hand complicated enough to bemuse the audience as well, and it is never clear when the chains are swapped or indeed whether they are swapped at all – since Solórzano has previously shown the silversmith the genuine chain he need only now give Cristina the duplicate. Truth and illusion are indistinguishable. The interlude is a window on the venal and morally bankrupt world of the capital. The prostitutes are deceived by their own greed, the police constable is bribable, the silversmith is cheating on his wife, and the young men whose motive is supposed to be merely amusement end up in profit at the prostitutes' expense. Even more revealing is the view it gives us of a society in flux, upside down even. Prostitutes with the airs and graces of ladies – reflected in the way they address each other as *doña* – ply their trade in coaches, bedecked with fine clothes and jewels. The two young aristocrats behave like *pícaros* in a way inappropriate to their station and responsibilities, as is suggested by the use of their surnames to refer to them in the text as if they were commoners. Young noblemen generally abandon their horses and the arts of war for the pleasures of carousing round the city day and night, ten or twelve to a coach. All this speaks of a breakdown of traditional values and structures – hence of course the legislation. Since the tricksters are not vicious and since Cristina, notorious for her own tricks, is fair game, what seems to be turning into a swingeing portrait of a corrupt and decadent society detumesces into an amiable recognition of the true state of affairs, and then into singing and a slap-up dinner for everybody. But the interlude has amply exploited its license as farce to tell some truths, to con the audience by making them laugh at others into seeing themselves with new eyes.

Cervantes' dramatic works, both interludes and plays, bear ample witness to his awareness that while all story, including the dramatic kind, is illusion and deception, the boundaries between fact and fiction are permeable. It was his abiding concern, consequently, that literary illusion and deception should be underwritten by the identification of a recognizable truth, that the realities of human nature and experience should shape and inform the constructions of the imagination. Equally significant, however, for the identity of his drama, as well as his prose, was his counter-intuition that within the workings of the imagination less visible, profounder human realities are already embedded, and it is in his ironic openness to the play of these two perceptions that the distinctive character of his writings for the stage lies.

NOTES

1 At the beginning of Act II of *The Fortunate Ruffian* and in the prologue to the *Eight Plays and Eight Interludes*.

2 E. T. Aylward points out that Cervantes carefully avoided political topics in his writings. See *Cervantes: Pioneer and Plagiarist* (London: Tamesis, 1982), p. 80.

3 The work of the French writer François Rabelais (?1494–1553), author of *Gargantua and Pantagruel* (1534), is renowned for its exuberance and bawdy humour.

4 The likeliest candidate is Lope de Vega, who had in 1605 denounced Cervantes in a letter to a friend as the worst poet of the age.

5 In his *Adjunta al Parnaso (Postscript to Parnassus)* of 1614 Cervantes stated that he had six plays and six interludes available for publication. Either he misremembered or he wrote or revised two further plays in the following year in time for publication of the *Eight Plays and Eight interludes* of 1615. Given that he was in ill health, must have been completing Part II of the *Quixote*, and had possibly already started the *Persiles*, it seems likely that the two plays at least already existed in earlier versions.

6 That he intended them for performance is clear from the detailed stage directions.

7 Jean Canavaggio, *Cervantès dramaturge: un théâtre à naître* (Paris: Presses Universitaires de France, 1977).

8 Lira's brother, who dies on stage, and the mother whose death he reports, were declared dead by Lira in Act III, *Obras completas*, ed. A.Valbuena Prat (Madrid: Aguilar, 1975), vol. I, p. 192. All references to the texts of plays and interludes are to this edition.

9 Interestingly enough, this is what happens in Rojas Zorrilla's later play *La Numancia destruida*, an extremely rare text which seems to have made some borrowings from Cervantes' play. See Manuel García Martín, *Cervantes y la comedia española en el siglo XVII* (Salamanca: Ediciones Universidad de Salamanca, 1980), pp. 190–91.

10 In Act I, 171b and Act III, 187a. The second occasion is riddled with dramatic irony as Scipio prides himself on the use of prudent non-violence toward Numantia, little knowing what is going on within the city.

11 It has often been assumed that Cervantes wrote the play in 1580, but since he did not sail for Spain until October 24 of that year and then spent a month in Valencia settling his affairs after an absence of ten years, it is unlikely if not impossible that the play was written that soon.

12 There is a noteworthy example of the irony toward the beginning of Act II (140b) where Cervantes has a dig at the concern for their honor which prevents Spaniards under attack at sea from grabbing an oar and rowing themselves out of danger.

13 Act I, 136–38.

14 The core of the love intrigue – the crossed passions of Moorish master and mistress for the Christian lovers who are their slaves – is faithfully lifted from *The Traffic of Algiers*, albeit rewritten.

15 There is some textual evidence that the play, now in the customary three acts, was previously divided differently, but Cervantes could have done little to make his material more thoroughly dramatic without virtually rewriting the whole work. The heavy reliance on stage machinery and other effects indicated in the stage directions suggests that the play in its present form belongs to the 1600s.

16 Anastasio's phrase in Act I, 496a.

17 Act III, 600b. The ermine – the stoat in its white winter coat – was a symbol of purity. It is, of course, only white in the season of darkness and cold.

18 The Council of Trent (Tridentum) during the period 1545–63 deliberated the doctrinal differences between Catholicism and the new Reformation groupings in an attempt to prevent religious schism. The initiative failed but out of it grew the Catholic or Counter-Reformation, which aimed at countering the rise of Protestantism by reaffirming and reinforcing Catholic orthodoxy and by encouraging religious zeal.

19 Metafiction is self-referential fiction which displays an awareness of its own identity as fiction; metatheatre like *Pedro de Urdemalas* typically exploits and explores the relationship between stage and world.

20 It is not obvious that Cervantes' interludes were written for the plays with which they were published. The reference in the 1615 edition to eight plays and "their" interludes might well have been a rationalization of the publisher's, Juan de Villarroel.

21 See McKendrick, "Honour-vengeance in the Spanish *comedia*; A Case of Mimetic Transference?" *Modern Language Review* 79 (1984): 313–36. A reference in the text to a shortage of actor-managers in Madrid almost certainly dates this interlude to 1610.

22 The phrase occurs in Peter's denial of Christ in the Gospels.

FURTHER READING

Aylward, E. T. *Cervantes: Pioneer and Plagiarist*. London: Tamesis, 1982.

Canavaggio, Jean. *Cervantès dramaturge: un théâtre à naître*. Paris: Presses Universitaires de France, 1977.

Canavaggio, Jean, ed. *Los baños de Argel*. Madrid: Taurus, 1984.

Close, A. J. "Characterization and Dialogue in Cervantes's 'Comedias en Prosa.'" *Modern Language Review* 76 (1981): 338–56.

Cruz, Anne J. "Deceit, Desire and the Limits of Subversion in Cervantes's Interludes." *Cervantes* 14 (1994): 119–36.

Friedman, Edward H. "Double Vision: Self and Society in *El laberinto de amor* and *La entretenida*." In Michael D. McGaha, ed., *Cervantes and the Renaissance*. Easton, PA: Juan de la Cuesta, 1980.

The Unifying Concept: Approaches to the Structure of Cervantes' "Comedias". York, SC: Spanish Literature Publications Company, 1981.

García Martín, Manuel. *Cervantes y la comedia española en el siglo XVII*. Salamanca: Ediciones Universidad de Salamanca, 1980.

Hermenegildo, Alfredo, ed. *La destrucción de Numancia*. Madrid: Editorial Castalia, 1994.

Lewis Smith, Paul. "*La gran sultana doña Catalina de Oviedo*: A Cervantine Practical Joke." *Modern Language Studies* 17 (1981): 68–82.

"Cervantes' Numancia as tragedy and as tragicomedy." *Bulletin of Hispanic Studies* 76 (1987): 15–26.

López-Vázquez, Alfredo Rodríguez, ed. *El rufián dichoso. El rufián viudo*. Kassel: Reichenberger, 1994.

Mariscal, George. "*La gran sultana* and the Issue of Cervantes's Modernity." *Revista de Estudios Hispánicos* 28.2 (1994): 185–211.

Martín, Adrienne L. "Images of Deviance in Cervantes's Algiers." *Cervantes* 15 (1995): 5–15.

Reed, Cory A. *The Novelist as Playwright: Cervantes and the "entremés nuevo"*. New York: Peter Lang, 1993.

Smith, Dawn, trans. and ed. *Miguel de Cervantes: Eight Interludes*. London: Everyman, 1996.

Syverson-Stork, Jill. *Theatrical Aspects of the Novel: A Study of Don Quixote*. Valencia: Albatros Ediciones, 1986.

Zimic, Stanislav. *El teatro de Cervantes*. Madrid: Castalia, 1992.

8

ADRIENNE L. MARTÍN

Humor and violence in Cervantes

In two of his recent books on the canon, *The Western Canon* and *How to Read and Why*, Harold Bloom echoes numerous literary historians when he asserts that Cervantes and his contemporary, Shakespeare, occupy the highest eminence as "wisdom writers" and that the Spaniard's *Don Quixote* is the first and best of all novels.[1] At the same time, Bloom notes that "No two readers ever seem to read the same *Don Quixote*, and the most distinguished critics have failed to agree on most of the book's fundamental aspects" (*The Western Canon*, 120). His words allude to the long-standing debate surrounding both authorial intent and readers' reception: is *Don Quixote* a fundamentally serious, philosophical work, or is it primarily a comedy? While Bloom is historically correct in arguing for Cervantes' novelistic genius, he is, as he himself admits, one of the Romantics who "see Quixote as hero, not fool; decline to read the book primarily as satire; and find in the work a metaphysical or visionary attitude regarding the Don's quest that makes the Cervantine influence upon *Moby-Dick* seem wholly natural" (*The Western Canon*, 121). Because of this debate's continuing relevance both in Cervantine studies and the general history of the novel, any volume exploring the critical tradition surrounding Cervantes' novelistic genius must address the topic that has critically subsumed many other themes and is of vital structural and thematic importance to *Don Quixote*: humor. At the same, it is essential to explicate humor's paradoxical relationship to violence in the novel.

Humor is so fundamental to Cervantes' conception of prose fiction that he opens his novel with a brief yet unmistakably explicit comic *ars poetica*. In the prologue the friend offers him the following advice regarding the effect his book should produce in the reader: "And see, too, if your pages can make sad men laugh as they read, and make smiling men even happier; try to keep simple men untroubled, and wise men impressed by your imagination, and sober men not contemptuous, nor careful men reluctant, to praise it."[2] Thus for Cervantes the risible should not be inconsistent with intelligent, witty inventiveness and when done well, it is worthy of the highest praise." The novelist repeats this thought at the beginning of Part II when he extols self-reflexively his own understanding and wit by having Don Quixote acknowledge that, "To talk wittily, and write pleasantly, are the talents of a great genius only" (II, 3).³ And finally, in his perhaps most autobiographical work, the *Viaje del Parnaso* (*Voyage to Parnassus*), Cervantes validates his comic achievements in *Don Quixote* as follows: "With *Don Quixote* I have provided amusement for the melancholic and unhappy breast on any occasion, at all times."⁴ This textual history makes it abundantly clear that humor and the risible, guided by appropriateness and discretion, are the rubrics under which Cervantes composed his novel.

The presence of humor and the therapeutic function of comedy to which Cervantes alludes in the above quote from *Voyage to Parnassus*, which Stephen Gilman has called "comic prophylaxis," have been an endless source of critical insight and blindness, and controversies continue to resurface in specialized discussions.⁵ If it is true that, for example, an arc can be traced regarding realism from Cervantes' novel to Joyce's *Ulysses*, it is even more feasible that humor allows readers to trace a conceptual link between those two masterpieces and the intertextual dependencies they continue to create. Of course it is mainly other novelists, such as Carlos Fuentes and Milan Kundera, who have intuited the all-encompassing role of humor in *Don Quixote*. Kundera, whose *The Art of the Novel* is quite dependent on Cervantes and his work for its elaborations, states in his introduction to the Oxford World's Classics edition of *Don Quixote* that

> We have entered the sphere of that other kind of comedy, subtler and infinitely precious, that we call humour. We laugh not because someone is ridiculed, mocked, or even humiliated, but because suddenly the world shows itself in its ambiguity, things lose their apparent meaning, people are revealed to be different from what they themselves thought they were. Octavio Paz said, correctly, that humour is a "great invention" of the modern era, one linked to the birth of the novel and particularly to Cervantes.⁶

Yet despite those familiar and emblematic assessments, at the dawn of the twenty-first century we are still trying to explicate the nature and the potency of Cervantes' four-hundred-year-old legacies, among which humor is as sacred as violence. Because of this productive indeterminacy, I think it important to begin this discussion of Cervantine humor by examining our immediate critical past. During the second half of the twentieth century, in their attempts to determine the novel's meaning, literary scholars increasingly resorted to considerations of *Don Quixote*'s original reception as a work of humor, whether that mode of expression be construed as parody, irony, wit, burlesque, satire, or even slapstick.[7] In large measure their studies contest nineteenth-century Romantic criticism (that has often continued into the twenty-first century, as we have seen with Bloom), which tended to disregard the comic aspects of Cervantes' prose in favor of a more philosophical-symbolic interpretation. They also respond to inherited neoclassical canons of literary good taste, which devalued comic literature as both shallow and frivolous. This recent line of criticism acknowledges that, to a lesser or greater degree, *Don Quixote* was composed to be, and was originally read as, a "funny book" (to use Russell's term). Such an assumption, however, has never diminished the novel as a serious, reflective work of literature, one profoundly and intimately engaged with its time and with literary history. *Don Quixote* is neither shallow nor frivolous and, as Kundera, Paz, and other writers have intimated, it is the first Western novel to elevate the comic tradition to the level of humor. Unlike much medieval comedy, humor has not only a serious intent, but also a strong critical and ideological bent and determined social function. The novel is undoubtedly a funny book written to entertain, but its humor has a profound and liberating significance as a vehicle for communicating issues of great social and literary transcendence. *Don Quixote* has proved that humor and profundity are in no way mutually exclusive.

The critical tradition has thus established that Cervantine humor is complex and multifaceted; it encompasses and integrates a multitude of diverse, yet complementary and overlapping comic currents or types. More than any other literary work of its time, therefore, *Don Quixote* provides a compendium of Renaissance comedy. One major comic current that defines the essence of the risible in Cervantes is the humanistic, classical vein of humor conveyed by irony, satire, burlesque and "fool literature." Another obvious current is parody; the novel is a parody and pastiche of the artificial chivalric world of the insidiously popular romances whose authority and influence *Don Quixote* attempts to destroy, if we are to believe the book's prologue. A third vein is the broadly comic strain of laughter and slapstick that evolved from the popular tradition. A further comic current underlying *Don Quixote* is linguistic in nature and consists of humorous speech acts, be they verbal jokes, wordplay, or Sancho's prolixity and prevarications. Yet another type of comedy is composed of subtle allusions and personal invective. All of these currents are perfectly interwoven to produce a novel that has been acknowledged to be a comic masterpiece. In the pages that follow I address the implications of these multiple comic types as the foundational elements upon which the novel's humor is based. Each is essential to *Don Quixote* and demands critical attention since, as the Peruvian novelist and humorist

Alfredo Bryce-Echenique recently said, absolutely all theories of humor are correct, but none is totally complete.[8] In the second part of this essay I also explore and give fuller meaning to humor's organic and inextricable relationship to violence in the novel, a relationship which has perplexed many readers and critics.

To address the first comic current in the novel, we should consider the term "humor," still one of the most elusive and unstable used in literary analysis. Its linguistic roots lie in the classical medical doctrine known as humoral theory which was first expounded in the fifth century BC by Hippocrates, the Greek physician and ethicist known as the Father of Medicine, and in the second century AD by the Greek physician and philosopher, Galen. Reasserted in Cervantes' time, this doctrine stressed the importance of the four bodily humors – phlegm, blood, bile, and black bile – as the sources of life. It was believed that a correct proportion between the four humors produced robust physical and mental health, while an imbalance was believed to cause illness. In his best-selling treatise on pedagogical psychology, *Examen de ingenios para las ciencias* (*Examination of Men's Wits for the Purpose of Science*, 1575), the Spanish physician Juan Huarte de San Juan insisted that each individual's physical and psychological profile is determined by his or her relative proportion, or temper, of humors. By natural extension, during the late sixteenth century the term humor was used throughout Europe to mean mental disposition or temperament. Huarte asserted that because an equal balance of the humors is impossible owing to the rigors of climate, customs and life-style, all people are to some extent "distempered," or mentally imbalanced. Thus he established a causal progression between humor, individual idiosyncrasy, and madness. Because of humoral differences – temperament – all human beings display their own particular brand of folly. At the same time the *word* humor is irrevocably linked to the *idea* of folly, madness, and extravagant behavior. "To have a humor" or to be "humorous" assumed the meaning of "to be mad."

Huarte was a source of inspiration for many Golden Age writers in Spain, including Cervantes, and the presence of a nucleus of his theory is undeniable, at least in *Don Quixote* and "El licenciado Vidriera" ("The Glass Graduate"). Both novels are clinical studies of madmen who function, unwittingly, as a source of amusement for others. While the Glass Graduate's madness is caused by the ingestion of a poisoned quince, Don Quixote's lunacy is literary in essence and stems from his intemperate reading of romances of chivalry. As readers know, he passed countless sleepless nights devouring book after book until his brain finally dried up and his peculiar, selective madness set in.[9] Don Quixote's particular derangement is an uncontrollable imagination, which nevertheless leaves his understanding and memory unimpaired. Because of this the knight can hold forth intelligently on any topic which does not concern chivalry. In this way the novel exemplifies how humor is linked to extravagant behavior in the mind of Cervantes and his contemporaries, both in Spain and abroad.

For readers other than Cervantes' contemporaries, Don Quixote's madness is highly problematic and many (including Vladimir Nabokov) either find it difficult to laugh at this highly idiosyncratic madman, or do not find his antics funny at all. However, it should be remembered that madness or folly was traditionally associated with the risible throughout the Middle Ages and the Renaissance. "Natural" fools (the mentally defective) were not institutionalized but integrated into medieval communities and supported by them as dependents, and were a ready source of amusement for societies less sensitive to the handicapped. The fifteenth century also witnessed the rise and rapid development of the "artificial" fool. Whether simple public entertainers or highly esteemed court jesters, these "buffoons" or "fools" assumed the guise of the mentally imbalanced to make a living of ridiculing and criticizing with the impunity traditionally granted to the mentally deficient.[10] Thus folly, whether real or feigned, was a highly visible presence in Renaissance society.

The literary tradition of madness gained tremendous popularity in the fifteenth and sixteenth centuries, especially after the publication in 1511 of *Praise of Folly* by the Dutch humanist and theologian Erasmus of Rotterdam. *Folly* in fact legitimizes madness by teaching that to be foolish is to be human, but it is also to be Godlike since the ultimate folly is to lose oneself in God and to follow His teachings. Therefore human beings should not be condemned, Erasmus suggests, but should be understood and accepted in all their folly; in other words, one should be tolerant of human idiosyncrasy. Erasmus's lessons are imparted largely through the supreme manipulation of irony and paradox. *Folly*'s protagonist, Stultitia, ironically presents both sides of a series of questions to show that for any given truth, the opposite may be equally true, thus pointing out the necessity of considering all sides to any question and the subjectivity of truth statements. These are lessons that Cervantes learned well, as his text confirms in the most paradigmatic way through the contrasting and shifting perspectives held on reality by Don Quixote and Sancho Panza. One of the most iconographic examples of such perspectivism in *Don Quixote* is the heated debate regarding the "true" nature of the barber's basin/Mambrino's helmet, which is finally resolved in chapter 45 of Part I. The identity of the basin or helmet is determined by each observer's unique perspective, which in turn is a product of that person's condition and, in this case, their relationship with Don Quixote.

For this reason Don Quixote's neighbors and companions at the inn declare the disputed object to be Mambrino's helmet. Their "reading" of the object's ambiguous essence is determined by their desire to encourage Don Quixote in his folly, keep the joke going, amuse all the onlookers, and tease the poor barber who has effectively lost his shaving basin. But of course, the joke is lost on those who do not know Don Quixote since, as the narrator says, "those who knew Don Quixote's madness found all this excruciatingly funny, but those who didn't thought it the stupidest thing they'd ever seen" (I, 45). Thus Sancho's humorous linguistic invention of *baciyelmo* (basin-helmet) is a stroke of comic genius that resolves ambiguities by combining both perspectives in one.

The growing awareness of the ambiguous nature of the world and of mankind, as allegorized by Erasmus and acknowledged by Kundera in the quotation that opens this essay, is further exemplified in episodes such as Don Quixote's attacks on giants and armies (windmills and flocks of sheep). It is also best expressed from the ironical distance established earlier by *Praise of Folly*. Irony and paradox enable us to perceive the absurdities of life at the appropriate emotional distance, and the resulting self-conscious expression of mankind's folly, underlain with an acknowledgment and acceptance of the same quality in oneself, is humor. The recognition of folly as underlying the human spirit facilitates a benevolent attitude toward it. While satirists refuse to forgive or to see in themselves the "vices" they castigate and instead remain at a critical distance, humorists use ironical distance to allow them to include themselves in the collective object of their humor. This is one of *Don Quixote*'s most important lessons to the reader: the recognition that all of us are to an extent quixotic or pancine. By laughing at Don Quixote and Sancho, we also recognize our own tendency to fix ourselves into rigid roles. Thus literary humorism is not simply madness, but a reaction to it. We smile at it, but our smile is indulgent since we recognize such lunacy within ourselves.

Don Quixote is not the only madman in the novel; for a variety of reasons many other characters engage in what can only be described as temporary, often voluntary, insanity. Sancho Panza, for one, becomes effectively crazed with the idea of becoming governor of an island. Several other characters act madder than the madman, whether to trick Don Quixote out of his delusions and bring him home (the priest and barber in drag), to avenge their defeat at his hands (Sansón Carrasco), to use him as courtly entertainment (the Duke and Duchess), or to vent their own lovesickness (Cardenio). Thus when Carrasco, disguised as the Knight of the Mirrors, is ignominiously vanquished in mortal combat by Don Quixote, Tomé Cecial, Carrasco's squire of the prodigious fake nose, raises the notion of the relativity of madness by remarking to his master, "Don Quixote's crazy, and we're both right in the head, but he comes out all in one piece, and smiling, and you, your grace, are beaten to a pulp and not smiling a bit. I think we have to stop and ask ourselves: who's crazier – the lunatic who can't help himself, or the one who's crazy of his own free will?" (II, 15). Thus madness, whether feigned or real, literary or voluntary, is the source of a great deal of *Don Quixote's* humor.

But Cervantes' genius lies precisely in the ambiguities and profundity of his exploration of the literary relationship between humor (madness), comedy, and seriousness of purpose and meaning. This is the type of ambiguity and complexity that Avellaneda, author of the apocryphal continuation of *Don Quixote*, opposed. In his false *Quixote* he created a madman with none of the subtleties of the original's character. This has been noted by Albert Sicroff, who maintains that Avellaneda interpreted *Don Quixote* as a purely comic work and that his apocryphal continuation of the novel attempted to reduce the Cervantine original to the ridiculous history of a madman.[11] Sicroff concludes that neither in its individual episodes nor in its totality does Avellaneda's work approximate the problematic complexity of Cervantes' novel ("En torno al *Quijote*," p. 365).

However, the differences between Cervantes' and Avellaneda's conceptions of comedy have been studied in more detail by James Iffland in his recent book, *De fiestas y aguafiestas*.[12] Iffland affirms that Avellaneda did interpret Cervantes' novel as a comedy, thus he begins his apocryphal second volume as follows: "Since almost the entire history of Don Quixote de la Mancha is a comedy, it cannot nor should not go without a prologue" (quoted in *De fiestas*, p. 571; my translation). The point is Avellaneda's use of the word *comedia*. Iffland shows how he is using it in its acceptance not only of humor, but also of the classical theatrical genre of comedy and its strictures. Avellaneda was opposed to the type of hybridization found in *Don Quixote*, whose humor is multidirectional and profoundly liberating as compared to his own unidirectional, narrow, and corrective conception of comedy (*De fiestas*, p. 574). Avellaneda's preoccupation with generic purity leads him to create a totally mad Don Quixote who ends up in an insane asylum, and a Sancho Panza who is a total buffoon. His emphasis on decorum in creating a strictly and purely comic work (without the intellectual and philosophical subleties of the original) comes from his aesthetic preoccupations, with their profoundly sociopolitical roots. Avellaneda's ideological positioning approximates the aristocratic perspective, which was concerned with counteracting the alarming symptoms of social destabilization caused by the incipient bourgeoisie, of which Cervantes was a member (*De fiestas*, pp. 580–81). Thus in the final analysis, Avellaneda serves to reveal the aesthetically *and* socially subversive nature of Cervantes' utilization of madness in the novel.

We should also keep in mind in our considerations of the link between madness and humor that Don Quixote's is a purely literary madness, not without its precursors in Alonso Quijano's own mind. Don Quixote seeks to imitate and emulate both Orlando Furioso and Amadís of Gaul in their erotic madness, most significantly when in Sierra Morena he imitates Amadís's penitence (as Beltenebros) in the Peña Pobre (I, 25). The paradox, of course, is that Don Quixote's mad actions, which include turning grotesque somersaults half-naked, are totally gratuitous. But this does not matter to him, for the fact that he acts without reason (and reasoning) is further proof of his dedication not only to his beloved Dulcinea, but also to his literary models. What is essential is that he emulate the knight upon whom he bases his chivalric and poetic strategies. For this reason, Don Quixote's poetic madness, as funny as it may be, ultimately illustrates the enchantment of the written word, the power of literature and its capacity to move us. As Allen Thiher has said, "*Don Quixote* shows that the power of madness is that it can replace rationality, or our worldview based on interpretive constraints and critical distance, with a circle of self-sustaining fictions that can be as powerfully self-justifying as any linguistic construct."[13] These self-sustaining fictions that Don Quixote creates in order to be Don Quixote are a result of the genius both of Alonso Quijano the mad reader, and of Cervantes the comedic writer.

For all the reasons discussed above, *Don Quixote* is a foundational fiction of the literature of madness – fool literature – that had been legitimized at the conceptual level in the sixteenth century by *Praise of Folly*. The basic allegory of folly which Don Quixote embodies is at the core of Cervantes' humor and his vital philosophy. The author teaches us the truth through laughter, a new laughter different from the comedy of previous literature. It is a laughter that ridicules but also understands our folly and our humanity. Cervantes' targets were both social and literary; *Don Quixote* is to a great extent a comment on the problematic nature of "reason" in an age of social unreason, one in which Spain's semitic and other minorities continued to be subjected to repressive ideological and physical control by the State. This, we should remember, is the case with the good Morisco Ricote, who was forced to leave his homeland when the Moriscos were expelled from Spain in 1609. His poignant words, "Wherever we are, we weep for the Spanish homeland where, after all, we were born and raised" (II, 54), are an eloquent and touching testament to the cruelty and social violence of the expulsion. Cervantes realized that simple comedy was no longer enough in an age of institutionalized madness, where knights errant and their idealized values were obsolete, and fools (such as the type of idle aristocrats personified by the Duke and Duchess) had taken their place.[14] Through the metaphor of madness Cervantes incorporates marginality, authenticity, and the transgression of conventions into life and literature. He is violating societal norms by suggesting that self-imposed madness is the only valid response to the institutionalized madness of society; at the same time his new "novel" transgresses current literary norms and maintains the immediacy of response we now associate with the humorous.[15]

A second festive current in *Don Quixote* is the broadly comic strain of mockery, laughter, and slapstick that has its roots in the popular tradition. In the twentieth century, the most influential study of popular, and especially carnivalesque, elements and imagery in literature was initiated by Mikhail Bakhtin in his seminal analysis of Rabelais in light of medieval popular folk culture, *Rabelais and His World*.[16] Bakhtin shows how Carnival was a time of freedom and laughter, a festive season of misrule and license when established order was reversed. It was a period of systematic inversions, parodies, and travesties. During Carnival the world is stood on its head in an explosion of ritual madness which is designed to serve as an escape valve in preserving people's sanity during the remainder of the regimented year. An integral part of Carnival is the concept of masquerade. Bakhtin identifies it as the most complex theme of folk culture, one related to metamorphoses, to the violation of natural boundaries, and to mockery. The ubiquitous presence of masquerades within the body of *Don Quixote* is one of its outstanding comic elements. Masquerade episodes such as Dorotea's creation of Princess Micomicona, Sansón Carrasco's performance as the Knight of the Mirrors and the Knight of the White Moon, Countess Trifaldi the Dueña Dolorida, and Sancho's government of the chimerical island Barataria can be viewed as reflections of this popular tradition.

A more specific, and transgressive, aspect of the carnivalesque masquerade echoed in *Don Quixote* is ludic transvestism. In this regard, Iffland has explored in detail the connections between the priest's and barber's transvestism and transformation into a supposed damsel in distress and squire, and the transgressions and symbolic inversions associated with Carnival. For example, as part of his female disguise, the priest decorates his forehead with a black garter and uses another strip of the same material to fashion a mask to cover his face and beard. As Iffland points out, such garters or bands are associated with the lower part of the female body (*De fiestas*, p. 92). At the same time, the barber fashions a long beard out of a donkey's tail. The tail of course covers the animal's anus, a place exalted during Carnival as part of the lower bodily stratum and as the organ of defecation, an act associated with expulsion and regeneration. These men's transvestism is, therefore, a mark of humiliation and ridicule equal only to the ridicule suffered by Don Quixote in part two of the novel when he arrives in Barcelona.

In his theoretical work on Rabelaisian humor, Bakhtin also remarks on *Don Quixote* to stress that the "fundamental strand of Cervantes' parodies is a 'coming down to earth,' a contact with the reproductive and generating power of the earth and of the body" (*Rabelais and His World*, p. 22). He contrasts Sancho and Don Quixote by means of the traditional materialist/idealist dichotomy, associating Sancho with the body, the materiality of human existence: "Sancho's materialism, his potbelly, appetite, his abundant defecation, are of the absolute lower level of grotesque realism on the gay bodily grave (belly, bowels, earth) which has been dug for Don Quixote's abstract and deadened idealism" (*Rabelais and His World*, p. 22). Although perhaps not all critics and readers would agree with Bakhtin's take on Don Quixote's idealism, his association of Sancho to the body and bodily functions is apt. For example, the misadventure or non-adventure of the fulling mills (1, 20) does function, as Bakhtin puts it, as the popular corrective of laughter to idealistic and spiritual pretense.

This head-on encounter of the body with the ideal occurs when Sancho, terror-stricken in the cold blackness of a wood echoing with dreadful banging sounds, secretly hobbles Rocinante in order to prevent his master from abandoning him in pursuit of an unknown adventure that will prove his valor. The squire is subsequently forced to answer the call of nature while glued to Don Quixote's side out of fear. The indiscreet noises, the smell, the reader's glimpse of Sancho's outsized buttocks are, as Bakhtin says, a bodily and popular (and hilarious) corrective to Don Quixote's misplaced idealism. Indeed, Don Quixote slams head first into Sancho's materialism and is forced to hold his nose to keep it out. A similar moment occurs when knight and squire imbibe the famous balsam of Fierabrás, a mythical concoction Don Quixote prepares to help them recover from the trouncing they suffer after their nocturnal encounter with Maritornes in Part 1. When the balsam's emetic properties backfire on Sancho, causing him uncontrollable diarrhea and vomiting, Don Quixote remarks to him, "I think, Sancho, that you've been so sorely afflicted because you've not been dubbed a knight, for it strikes me that this magic liquid ought not to be employed by those who are not knights" (1, 17). In other words, Sancho's is the material world of food, wine, and excrement, while Don Quixote's is the ethereal realm of the chivalric ideal. As Sancho quite graphically finds out, the two do not mix well, and the class implications should not be lost on the reader.

But of all the transformations and carnivalesque masquerades in the novel, the first, and perhaps most fundamental, is the authorship masquerade. Cide Hamete is a masked Cervantes, as, for example, are the "authors" of the poems that frame part one of the novel. These brief paratexts introduce, reflect, and summarize the inverted world of the novel. In the introductory poems knights, damsels, and squires of romances of chivalry (Amadís of Gaul, Oriana, Gandalín, Orlando Furioso) are revived and transformed into literati to praise the novel and its protagonists with an accumulation of silly absurdities and sly insults. In the poems that close Part I a group of wretched Argamasillian poetasters pose as knowledgeable academicians to do the same. In masquerading as these "authors" Cervantes is parodying and mocking writers' (especially his rival Lope de Vega's) custom of including exaggerated laudatory poems among the preliminaries of their published works. At the same time, the closing poetic sequence lampoons the institution of the literary academy in Golden Age Spain.[17]

Other comedic inversions and transformations abound in the novel, beginning with Alonso Quijano's initial transformation of himself into Don Quixote, Aldonza Lorenzo into Dulcinea del Toboso, Sancho Panza into a squire, and his old nag into Rocinante. In a series of paradigmatic episodes well known to all readers of the novel, the knight will subsequently transform prostitutes into fair ladies, inns into castles, innkeepers into chatelains, windmills and wineskins into giants, sheep into armies and puppets into real people. In the second part of the novel other characters (especially the Duke and Duchess) will stage the transformations based on their expectations of Don Quixote's actions after reading Part I.

One of the most memorable transformation episodes in the novel occurs during the furtive encounter between Don Quixote and Maritornes, the Asturian servant girl at Juan Palomeque's inn. The initial description of Maritornes clearly falls within the parameters of the risible as described by the only contemporary theorist of the comic whose work Cervantes would likely have known, Alonso López Pinciano. In his poetic treatise in dialogued epistle form, *Philosophía antigua poética* (1596), López Pinciano explains that the risible consists of ugliness and crudeness in both words and actions.[18] Echoing the Aristotelian definition of the ridiculous, the author affirms that it also lies in ugliness: "lo ridículo está en lo feo" (*Philosophía*, III, 32). Thus both to the contemporary reader and to readers today, Maritornes' initial description is hilarious precisely because of its ironic depiction of her dubious physical delights, which, the narrator reports, were enough to make anyone but a muledriver vomit:

> There was also an Asturian girl working in the inn, blessed with a broad face, flat head, stubby nose, one blind eye and the other not entirely functional. But still, her figure was so elegant that it compensated for her other deficiencies: she was about four and a half feet tall, from the top of her head to her feet, and her shoulders, which pretty distinctly weighed her down, made her stare into the ground more than she would have liked. (I, 16)

Later on, when Maritornes bumps into Don Quixote in the darkness while on the way to her assignation with the muledriver, he mentally transforms her into the type of beautiful princess about whom he had read in his chivalry books. The humor in the servant girl's metamorphosis lies in the incongruity between her overwhelming physical unattractiveness and Don Quixote's idealized and illusory mental portrait of her. Cervantes' rendering is an expertly constructed, perfectly balanced juxtaposition of the real and the ideal, the grotesque and the lovely:

> Then he felt her chemise and, though it was burlap, to him it seemed the finest and most delicate silk. She wore glass beads on her wrists, but they made him see visions of precious oriental pearls. Her hair, though it was more like a horse's mane, to him was strands of the most magnificent Arabian gold, so radiant that they darkened the sun itself. And though her breath surely smelled of garlic and stale salad, he thought her mouth gave off a delicate, gracious fragrance. (I, 16)

The humor in this instance is both ludic and ironic, and clearly within the realm of parody and burlesque. Don Quixote's cliché-ridden imaginary vision (the silk chemise, oriental pearls, strands of golden hair, sweet breath) becomes – for him – a heightened sensorial experience within the silence and darkness of the enchanted castle. For the reader, who is presented with the contrasting "truth," it is a sensorial experience of another kind. The subsequent comedy of errors when the indignant muledriver attacks Don Quixote and collapses his bed reaches a comic climax with the arrival of the innkeeper. Imagining the source of the quarrel, he enters the room shouting "Where are you, you whore? This is your work, dammit!" Thus the parody is complete; the chatelain's beautiful, virginal, and pure daughter of the chivalric imaginary is transformed back into a coarse peasant girl of doubtful virtue. The sublime language of romance is interrupted and subverted by a word from the lowest register, the vulgar and picaresque-sounding "whore" (*puta*). However, precisely because she is "real" and familiar within the context of the novel, Maritornes retains her appeal as a simple young innocent who is merely trying to earn a living, and the reader sympathizes with her.

The previous passage also functions as one brief example of the endless play of language in *Don Quixote*, in this case the ludic juxtaposition of the extremes of linguistic register. Don Quixote's discourse also occasionally parodies the type of archaic language common in chivalric romances, to great comic effect. Of course, this absurd speech creates incongruities and misunderstandings, as when he addresses the prostitutes at the first inn: "Flee not, noble damsels, nor anticipate the slightest inappropriate behavior. No!

The order of knighthood to which I profess allegiance neither troubles nor afflicts anyone, and certainly not such noble virgins as you, by your bearing, clearly show yourselves to be" (I, 2). Most listeners within the book are baffled and burst into laughter when Don Quixote lapses into language such as this, leaving the knight mortified. At the other end of the linguistic register from Don Quixote's stilted, imitative speech are Sancho's popular proverbs, rustic diction, malapropisms, and general linguistic nonsense, which Don Quixote insists on correcting throughout the course of the novel.

As a writer Cervantes resisted affectation and verbosity in writing, hence Don Quixote's advice to Sancho when he is about to embark on his governorship: "speak calmly – but not as if you're listening most attentively to your own words, for affectation is always bad" (II, 43). Immediately afterwards, however, the scrupulous knight advises his squire never to use the word "belch" (*regoldar*) but "eructate" (*eructar*), a word which Sancho does not understand of course. The lesson about the subjectivity of language could not be more serious, for behind the many humorous exchanges in the novel regarding appropriate and correct speech is an engagement with cultural debates initiated in the Renaissance. Given that period's elevation of the vernacular as the language of culture, speaking eloquently and correctly had become an indispensable element of appropriate conduct (see, for example, Castiglione's *The Courtier*). Thus all Don Quixote's advice to Sancho (cut your fingernails, don't eat garlic or onions, dress neatly, and drink in moderation) can be seen from the perspective of the growing concern over manners and urbanity in early modern Spain. This push toward courtly conduct was naturally accompanied by a movement toward cultured speech, which in turn met with resistance from the lower classes.[19] These are the cultural tensions implicit in Don Quixote's and Sancho's arguments regarding correct speech. As a result, throughout the novel Cervantes blends registers, dialects, idiolects, archaic speech and epic speech, gravity, levity, puns, jokes, proverbs, and comical prevarications, in a *tour de force* of linguistic acrobatics. As we have seen, *Don Quixote*'s humorous heteroglossia not only illuminates cultural debates of the period, but serves as a rich mine of linguistic humor.

Intimately related to these linguistic aspects of the text is yet another comic mode which must be considered in analyzing humor in *Don Quixote*: parody. Although a comprehensive study of parody in *Don Quixote* is yet to be done, a very brief selection of books from the numerous works that treat the subject to varying degrees includes a diversity of approaches, ranging from the philosophical to the stylistic and studies of sources.[20] What unifies these treatments is the authors' recognition of the fact that *Don Quixote* is without question a parody, although not a conventional one. As P. E. Russell has said, "Any serious study of Cervantes's book... must start from the fact that it was conceived by its author as an extended parody of romances of chivalry."[21]

In his recent study of parody, Simon Dentith affirms that the novel establishes itself in the beginning of the seventeenth century by its deployment of parody to devalue alternate genres (specifically romance) and their ways of depicting the world (*Parody*, p. 55). He asserts that the novel is a secular genre, "inhabiting the world as it is and not as it might be, and consistently debunking the claims of romance by making them bump up against the harder, but also more ordinary, facts of existence" (*Parody*, p. 55). Obviously, the entire *Quixote* could be analyzed from the perspective of its parodic function within the history of the novel. Parody in *Don Quixote* is not simply a technique but the backbone of all the adventures in the novel, and is its *raison d'être*. As the final "author" of the novel, Cide Hamete's pen, says at the very end, "all I ever wanted was to make men loathe the concocted, wild-eyes stories told as tales of chivalry, nor can there be the slightest doubt that this truthful history of my Don Quixote has already begun to pull those books to the ground, just as surely as it will bring down every last one of them" (II, 74). Thus in the case of *Don Quixote*, parody is transforming literary history from within. As Margaret Rose has said, "*Don Quixote* encodes the world of the romance through the enthusiasms and imitative heroic actions of its hero, and does so from within the text-world of Cervantes's novel where reality is set up as an antidote to the hero's illusions" (*Parody: Ancient, Modern, and Post-Modern*, p. 41). As we have seen in the episode with Maritornes, Don Quixote transmutes her in his mind following the conventions and language of chivalric romances. Through this process Cervantes the writer parodies those same conventions and language from within by making fun of Don Quixote the reader of romance.

Another comic current underlying *Don Quixote* is that of subtle illusions or personal invective. The novel contains thinly veiled and highly ironic allusions to the works and private life of Cervantes' arch-rival Lope de Vega, Spain's most successful playwright at the time. For example, the poems that frame part one of *Don Quixote* contain many allusions to issues that Cervantes would often criticize.[22] First was Lope's supposed vulgarization and commercialization of poetry; Cervantes felt he wrote plays of no artistic merit that pandered to the masses instead of using his popularity to elevate standards in the Spanish *comedia*. This aspect of literary criticism is most apparent at the end of Part I where the priest and canon speak at length about the theatre. Cervantes includes the following severely critical allusion to Lope: "because if drama, as Cicero says, must be the mirror of human existence, founded in the way people actually act and look, what we're seeing today are reflections of poppycock, examples of stupidity, and images of lewdness" (I, 48). It is clear that Cervantes is referring to Lope, since he practically names him further on in the same chapter by mentioning "one of the finest talents in this kingdom."

Another object of Cervantes' ironical criticism was Lope's penchant for arrogant display. For example, in the Ormsby translation of *Don Quixote* Urganda the Unknown's preliminary verses contain the following exhortation: "Put no vain emblems on thy shield / Or pompous coats-of-arms display."[23] The lines are a repudiation of the spurious Carpio (Lope's) family shield with its nineteen towers and pompous motto "the coat of arms is Bernardo's, the misfortunes mine" which Lope displayed on several of his works. In the prologue to Part I, Cervantes also alludes to Lope's (and others') penchant for including numerous encomiastic sonnets among the preliminaries to their published books when he says: "And there aren't any sonnets at the beginning of my book – at least, not sonnets by noblemen, dukes, counts, bishops, society ladies or celebrated poets." In Lope's case, the sonnets were often written by just such personalities as Cervantes describes, or he would write them himself and baptize them with another's name. This was the case with his *El peregrino en su patria* (*Pilgrim in his Homeland*, 1604), which contains an encomiastic sonnet "written" by Lope's illiterate lover Micaela de Luján. Thus the mention of the *dama* or "lady" poet is a not-so-oblique allusion to Lope's sexual improprieties, especially his long-standing and adulterous affair with Luján, which was still going on when Cervantes was writing his novel. These and numerous other personal allusions locate *Don Quixote* clearly within the close literary community of turn-of-the-century Madrid, a place were literary and personal relations were interwoven to such a degree as to render the two inseparable. Literature was the medium through which friendships and rivalries were nourished and wars were waged, through either subtle allusions or the most bitter personal invective. It was a form of social violence based on the envy and partisanship that is part of the human condition, a means of public humiliation for the victim and cause for laughter for everybody else.

As we have been examining in the previous pages, to concede that humor is heterogeneous in human nature and in its literary representation is not discovering critical gunpowder. However, one discovery that merits amplification is the fact that much of *Don Quixote*'s humor is often paradoxically linked to violence. This is perhaps yet another means of expressing the dialogic nature of human communication. In fact, the cruelty and violence of the novel have been pointed out by several critics. The earliest among these were contemporary readers of Part I of the novel, since the Bachelor Sansón Carrasco informs Don Quixote and Sancho Panza early in Part II that "Some who have read the book say they wish the author had quietly forgotten a few of the endless beatings Señor Don Quixote receives, in various encounters" (II, 3). Leading among late twentieth-century critics of the novel's brutality is Vladimir Nabokov. His Harvard *Lectures on "Don Quixote"* reveal his evident distaste for the novel, which he declares to be neither humane nor funny and instead "a veritable encyclopedia of cruelty."[24] Nabokov is accurate in noting the cruelty of many episodes of the novel, and more than one twenty-first-century reader would agree, although not necessarily for the same reasons. However, humor and cruelty (a branch of violence) are, in fact, inextricably linked in the novel and the relationship between them illuminates contemporary conceptions of the risible. This aspect of *Don Quixote* can certainly be examined in terms of the dynamics of the reading process and sociohistorical readerly expectations, as revised versions of reception aesthetics posit lately. Indeed, what Nabokov does not acknowledge is the simple fact that humor ages rapidly, that it is perishable (to use Daniel Eisenberg's phrase), and that our contemporary sense of humor has changed.[25] As a consequence we are now reluctant to laugh at the less fortunate, the mad, and those who suffer practical jokes, beatings, and humiliation at the hands of others. It is not an issue of considering Nabokov a grumpy throwback to the hypocritical American fifties which he himself criticized, but rather one of historicizing the realities of a period that was not as liberal or tolerant as the twenty-first century.

Issues of gender, race, and the societal transgressions that exacerbate them come to the fore in contemporary literary criticism, and scholars have generally opted to theorize violence through explanations of the erotics of domination, the violence of pity, and above all by the binary opposition between aggressor and victim. However, despite his universal message, Cervantes was a man of his times and could not be expected to circumscribe his worldview (as ahead of its time as it was) to the sentimental satisfaction of his contemporary critics or today's interpreters. Nor could he reduce it to what he might have thought they wanted to hear, thereby yielding to a false form of civility and authority. Perhaps our twenty-first-century understanding of the term incorporates too much under the name of violence, including an excessively negative moral loading which it did not have in this particular novel. These considerations are by no means a justification of violence but, as we will see, a bridging of aesthetics and subjective experience.

Already in the first chapters of Part I of the novel several episodes are paradigmatic of this seemingly oxymoronic interlacing of the cruelly violent and the comical: Don Quixote and Sancho are beaten by the muledrivers in punishment for Rocinante's sexual advances upon their mares and the knight is subsequently humiliated by having to mount Dapple (1, 15); they are both pummeled in eerie silence by Maritornes' suitor (1, 16); Sancho is ignominiously tossed in a blanket at Juan Palomeque's inn (1, 17); and they are both stoned and beaten by the ungrateful galley slaves they have liberated (1, 22). The violence continues throughout Part 1 until in the final chapter it reaches a true lowpoint when Don Quixote has a sordid and vulgar bare-fisted fight on top of the dinner table with the goatherd Eugenio, to the delight of his companions: "Both clerical gentlemen were bursting with laughter, the policemen were jumping up and down with delight, urging first this one and then that one of the combatants on, exactly like the people at a dogfight" (1, 52). As undignified and distasteful as this scene is to many readers today, it obviously was the type of farcical representation that would elicit laughter at the time. It is very similar, in fact, to the comic interludes (*entremeses*) performed between the acts of Spanish Golden Age plays. These brief farces staged the explosion of disordered instinct and typically ended in rowdy fight scenes. Proof that such violent episodes were read and experienced as comical in the early modern period is the fact that the other characters in the novel thoroughly enjoy the show, just as audiences today enjoy the ludicrous barroom brawls so dear to traditional Hollywood cinema. We can enjoy and laugh at it because we know it is not "real," therefore thinking that violence is merely a "representation" devoid of any permanent effect after the show is over.

These episodes of beatings, stonings, and floggings are omnipresent throughout the novel, but the question remains: are they funny? As we have seen, they obviously were to Cervantes' contemporaries, including the other characters in the novel and the readers of Part 1 who play tricks on Don Quixote and Sancho in Part 11. Most of these violent incidents follow a pattern which involves a display of humorous hubris by Don Quixote, or an argument which escalates into violence and culminates in the knight's defeat and humiliation. This pattern initiates early in the narrative when in chapter 3 of Part 1 Don Quixote attempts to watch over his armor before being dubbed. The would-be knight's wrath is aroused when the unsuspecting mule drivers try to remove his armor from the trough in order to water their teams. His subsequent rash and violent attack on them is rewarded by the first stoning he will suffer in the novel. At this point, however, he is not yet humiliated since the mule drivers desist from retaliating out of fear of the madman's violence and because, as the innkeeper advises them, a madman will not be held accountable even if he killed them all. This is a dialectic that can be understood today: where does one draw the line that allows a non-event to escalate into violence or that turns blame toward a victim, the law notwithstanding? We should also consider that, of all the characters in the novel,

Don Quixote himself is probably the most violent. Throughout Part I he is given to vehement outbursts, and attacks without warning whoever happens to unintentionally slight his Dulcinea.

A similar episode is the one involving the Toledan merchants in I, 4, in which the freshly dubbed knight receives his first true thrashing. Here Don Quixote arrogantly demands that the travelers confess that Dulcinea del Toboso is the most beautiful damsel in the world. When they answer that they would certainly do so if he were to produce her or show them a portrait of her, Don Quixote becomes enraged, levels his lance and charges the merchants. The knight's subsequent fall and beating by the mule drivers bluntly address how violence only begets violence. Nonetheless, the visual and verbal humor in all these episodes stems from their parody of chivalric battles and rivalries. For this reason several motifs unify the episodes and bind them to the romances they parody: copious bloodletting, pride and humiliation, bravery and cowardice.

Part II of the novel would seem to be less inherently violent in that there are fewer episodes in which Don Quixote is physically trounced, yet they are also more humiliating and the psychological wounds inflicted are deeper, thus ascertaining the thoroughness of the author's views on comic violence. In this regard, the mocking, mortifying tricks Don Quixote and Sancho suffer during the course of the novel, especially in the hoaxes in the ducal palace, involve both deception and humiliation. Thus it is to be expected that the knight and squire emerge not only physically, but also psychologically and emotionally scarred from their experiences in the palace. If Don Quixote is scratched and terrorized by cats (II, 46), Sancho is starved, trampled, and ultimately disillusioned in Barataria (II, 44–53). And if one can also see violence as equally psychological and physical, one can come to a fuller realization of Cervantes' purpose in having his readers negotiate between humor and violence, as well as between the two parts of his novel.

In Part II humor and violence are especially conjoined through the notion of *burla*, meaning trick or mockery.[26] Close has pointed out that Cervantes subjects the traditional ploys and predicaments of *burlas* to a process of systematic refinement, and "imbues the hoax with a sportingly playful, even altruistic, spirit instead of a malicious one" (*Cervantes and the Comic Mind*, p. 330). Close feels that since the heroes are unaware of their status as figures of fun, they lack a sense of crushing mortification and that the *burlas* organized by the Duke's servants reveal the positive artistic values of wit and inventiveness that Cervantes associates with his novel. Cervantes essentially does this, Close says, "in order to celebrate the popular triumph of *Don Quixote*, Part I and of its two heroes" (p. 330). However, in spite of the fact that the hoaxes are ingenious and funny, often they are perceived as no less hurtful and, contrary to what Close avows, as intensely mortifying. This is why readers of the novel often learn to loathe the Duke and Duchess and commiserate with Don Quixote's numerous humiliations at their hands. Ultimately it is a question of the degree to which readers identify with the heroes, how they "complete" the novel with their expectations, which are both dynamic and ideologically varied as well as as dependent on various historical subjectivities. For this reason, while some will agree with Close's interpretation of these tricks as altruistic and non-malicious, other readers will not. After all, a knowledge of the book's initial reception will not prevent contemporary readers from finding a totally different meaning in it. This notion has been made evident most imaginatively by Jorge Luis Borges in his short story "Pierre Menard, Author of the 'Quixote.'"[27] Pierre Menard is a minor French symbolist poet who sets out to "write" *Don Quixote*, and produces chapters which on the surface are linguistically identical to Cervantes' novel, yet infinitely different. Menard's *Quixote* is "original" because the creative act is in the reading, not the writing of literature. Borges's message (an example of reception theory ahead of its time) is that because readers and the conditions under which they read are and will be dynamic, any book ultimately becomes a palimpsest for prior and subsequent readings. Following Borges's logic, the reader is the real producer of meaning in the literary text and the ultimate conclusion that can be drawn from "Pierre Menard, Author of the 'Quixote'" is that to read, reread, and translate (in the most ample sense) are all part of literary production.

To return to our text, the Duke and Duchess are prime exemplars of an idle nobility who use Don Quixote and Sancho as courtly entertainment, thus violating the knight's nobility of spirit. Their tricks are theatrical, high farce, and depend on an audience to be successful. Their primary purpose is not to harm Don Quixote and Sancho, but to use them for leisure-time amusement. All the hoaxes that take place in their home are extremely stylized, refined, involved, and witty. It is only on a few occasions that they complicate violence by acquiring a patina of maliciousness. This happens, for example, when Altisidora and the Duchess burst in upon Don Quixote and Doña Rodríguez after they overhear her divulge the ugly secrets about Altisidora's bad breath and the Duchess's suppurating ulcers (II, 48). The aggrieved women spank Rodríguez furiously with a slipper and pinch Don Quixote out of spite and a desire for revenge. The resentment issuing from the double humiliation of being rejected by Don Quixote and unmasked by Rodríguez are Altisidora's motivations for the insulting and vengeful song with which she sees off Don Quixote when he abandons the ducal house (II, 57).

Nonetheless, all the tricks and hoaxes are a celebration and affirmation of the success of Part 1 and readers' engagement with it, which has been the position assumed by Cervantine criticism that is less concerned with the novel's relation to various types of societal politics. Close thus determines, "So, the *burlas* of *Don Quixote* are filled with a merrily ludic, theatrically creative, and celebratory spirit; they preserve the outward form of traditional hoaxes but transform the semantic content" (*Cervantes and the Comic Mind*, p. 330). The ludic spirit to which Close refers can more easily be seen in another episode in the novel that is a complex ruse based on Sancho Panza's character and actions in Part I. As the narrator tells us at the beginning of chapter 34 of Part II, because the Duke and Duchess take such infinite delight in their guests, and are such careful readers of Part I of the novel, they and their servants continue to devise jokes in the manner and guise of chivalric adventures. Thus, banking on the squire's simplicity and naiveté, they concoct a hoax which issues from Sancho's invention of Dulcinea's enchantment in Part I. It begins when Merlin the Magician interrupts a boar hunt to announce that Dulcinea will be disenchanted only when Sancho has given himself 3,300 lashes on his bare backside.

In relation to this, in Cervantes' time everyday violence was abundant and constant, as Augustin Redondo has observed, and its context has left ample evidence in both parts of *Don Quixote*.[28] For instance, early in Part I the young boy Andrés is tied to a tree and whipped by his master Juan Haldudo for supposedly stealing sheep (I, 4). Andrés's beating and the painful (for Sancho) process by which Dulcinea is to be disenchanted are, in fact, closely linked to common practices in early modern Spain. Whipping, or *vapulamiento*, was both a conventional method of public corporal punishment administered either by civil or by inquisitorial authorities, as well as a Counter-Reformation act of penitence. Crimes of delinquency carried a specific number of lashes (usually fifty, one hundred, or two hundred) which in the case of adults were administered to the back and shoulders, and to children on the naked buttocks. Redondo analyzes such customs as a "pedagogy of fear" that was intended to reduce crime and consolidate royal authority under the Austrias. In the Christian sphere, on the other hand, scourging oneself was related to the Christian desire for penitence and Counter-Reformation religiosity; it was an accepted practice intended to discipline and mortify the flesh and purify the spirit (Redondo, *Otra manera*, p. 175). It is within this spirit that Merlin emerges from the forest in chapter 35, preceded by the parodic procession of Penitents of Light. These were the penitents who carried lighted torches in religious processions, as opposed to the Penitents of Blood who carried whips and scourged themselves. Sancho's prescribed *vapulamiento* with its exaggerated number of lashes transforms him into an unwilling Penitent of Blood and calls into question contemporary obsessions with the external trappings of Counter-Reformation religiosity and their implicit and explicit violence. As Redondo points out, Sancho becomes a synthesis of all the penitents who participated in such early modern religious processions, and the equivocal disenchantment scheme is a subversive, carnivalesque criticism of common and often hypocritical religious practices (*Otra manera*, p. 182). Also, the fact that Sancho is to whip himself on the buttocks instead of the shoulders infantalizes him since his penance clearly harks back to the early modern punishment meted out to delinquent children. Thus when Sancho protests, "Dulcinea" (one of the Duke's pages) denounces him as a coward, saying that every child learning his catechism receives as many lashes as he has been assigned. This is all part of the burlesque fun and serves to bring Sancho's ample hindquarters into view once again. The squire's final solution – to secretly whip trees so that Don Quixote will think he is completing the task and that Dulcinea will soon be disenchanted – reveals not only his picaresque ingenuity, but can also been viewed as another ironic statement about ostentatious Counter-Reformist religious practices.

In the *burlas*, as mentioned before, we see the madman put to use as entertainment, a notion that was naturalized in early modern Spain by the custom of court fools. While in the Duke and Duchess's country home, Don Quixote and Sancho function as the type of jester or fool who enjoyed a certain tenuous intimacy with the nobility by providing amusement in aristocratic households. The obvious difference is that Sancho and especially Don Quixote are generally unaware that they are being made into fools. In addition, the violence perpetrated against Sancho in Barataria is class specific, an example of aristocratic harassment of the peasantry. George Mariscal has pointed out that the acts perpetrated in the ducal house suppress Don Quixote's and Sancho Panza's capacity for growth and development; this is a type of violence exerted upon the novel by itself since its protagonists are straitjacketed.[29] Mariscal is basically correct, since most of the episodes of Part II prevent Don Quixote and Sancho from evolving as public beings in the same way that they do in private. Many of the people they meet have read Part I of the novel and want to have fun at the pair's expense, creating situations in which they must "perform" as the Don Quixote and Sancho Panza of Part I. It is ultimately a kind of essentialist or ontological violence perpetrated on the characters from within the novel since the protagonists are effectively locked into the roles they fulfilled in Part I by the characters they meet in Part II.

Beyond Mariscal's view, there is a need to identify violence with the maintenance of a pattern of dominance, and not merely as the breakdown of social order, for history and literature continually prove that it is possible to escape and overcome certain types of violence, as novelistic genres have tended to do at least since *La Celestina*. That might be the lesson and subtext behind such episodes of physical violence and humiliations, which are omnipresent throughout the novel. It would seem that in the commingling of Renaissance bodily humors that determined humans' disposition, bile would win out. Whether the reader experiences those events as funny or not ultimately depends on one's individual sense of humor, but the fact remains that they can be reconciled with our modern sense of violence and humor. Cruel and brutal they may be, but once again they are also comical when seen as part of the tradition of Carnival and other popular early modern traditions and festivities. Carnival, it is worth reiterating, was a festive season of laughter, travesties, practical jokes, humiliations, profanations, comic crownings and uncrownings. It was a time in which social and institutional violence was overcome by a ritualized, channeled violence that was accepted by all participants, if only for a few days' escape from social realities and determinations. In this manner Don Quixote is originally knighted by the innkeeper in a burlesque ceremony which acquires mythical tones and, naturally, a superficial quasi-legality which, as it turns out, actually serves to abuse the knight.

Stephen Gilman has asserted that "the actions and reactions of his two supremely naïve protagonists are used in order to illuminate ironically a society, swollen with self-importance, that refused to make a place for him [Cervantes] despite his past heroism" (*The Novel According to Cervantes*, p. 44), and in that world violence is used to preserve the law and propagate the actions inherent to that force. Gilman further affirms that

> Experience was for him a dimension of existence that was at once virtually unexplored and pathetically vulnerable. Appealing, comic, and forlorn, it was the conscious precipitate of violent interruption, the rueful result of trying to live meaningfully and not conventionally in a century and a society that revered conventionality and were prone to cut short deviant behavior with a rock, a club, or a torch. The *Quixote* itself is nothing less than an ironical two-volume interruption of the heroic version of national history that Spaniards were persistently engaged in telling themselves.
>
> (*The Novel According to Cervantes*, pp. 57–58)

Such an interpretation would seem to deny the purely comic aspects of violence in favor of the view of *Don Quixote* as a novel involved in a discourse of ironic, perhaps violent, opposition with the repressive sociohistoric conditions of Spain after the Council of Trent. However, both (and many other) interpretations can coexist and be "true." If violence and humor are part of that history of Golden Age Spain, they are also part of the desire for novelistic conclusions. This last idea is developed by René Girard in the last chapter of his *Deceit, Desire, and the Novel*, whose recurrence to the genius of Cervantes and his novel need not be reviewed.[30] In an overview of his theories Girard reminds us that "The self-justification the novelist had intended in his distinction between good and evil will not stand self-examination. The novelist comes to realize that he has been the puppet of his own devil. He and his enemy are truly indistinguishable."[31] Violence and humor will also not stand self-examination, and it has always been and will be up to the readers, critical or otherwise, to reevaluate their proper role. Gilman is thus justified in warning against the dangers of attributing to Cervantes' inventiveness criteria that are alien to it, and if "Cervantes, having read and disliked *Guzmán de Alfarache* as much as Fielding disliked *Pamela*, set out to write a work of fiction that not only would restore humanity to our laughter but also would present life with the profundity and multiplicity admired therein by Dostoevsky" (*The Novel According to Cervantes*, p. 88), violence is part of the imperviousness to verisimilitude that makes *Don Quixote*'s permanent potentiality the very definition of modernity. Since Cervantes' work is a symbiosis of life and literature, a relation one cannot emphasize enough, his work also exceeds humorous and violent motives yet abounds in their grave implications.

NOTES

1 Harold Bloom, *The Western Canon: The Books and School of the Ages* (New York: Riverhead Books, 1994) and *How to Read and Why* (New York: Scribner, 2000).

2 All quotations, unless otherwise indicated, are from Miguel de Cervantes, *Don Quijote*, trans. Burton Raffel (New York: W. W. Norton & Company, 1995), with part and chapter indicated in parenthesis.

3 Miguel de Cervantes Saavedra, *Don Quijote de la Mancha*, trans. Charles Jarvis, introduction by Milan Kundera (Oxford: Oxford University Press, 1999). I have used the Jarvis translation in this instance since it more closely approximates the original.

4 Miguel de Cervantes, *Viaje del Parnaso: Poesías completas, I*, ed. Vicente Gaos (Madrid: Castalia, 1973), p. 103, ch. 4, vv. 22–24. My translation.

5 Stephen Gilman, *The Novel According to Cervantes* (Berkeley: University of California Press, 1989), p. 74.

6 *Don Quijote de la Mancha*, Introduction, trans. Linda Asher, p. viii.

7 See, for example, P. E. Russell, "*Don Quijote* as a Funny Book," *Modern Language Review* 64 (1969): 312–26; Daniel Eisenberg, *A Study of "Don Quixote"* (Newark, DE: Juan de la Cuesta, 1987); Adrienne L. Martín, *Cervantes and the Burlesque Sonnet* (Berkeley: University of California Press, 1991); Laura J. Gorfkle, *Discovering the Comic in "Don Quixote"* (Chapel Hill: North Carolina

Studies in the Romance Languages and Literatures, 1993); Augustin Redondo, *Otra manera de leer el "Quijote"* (Madrid: Castalia, 1997); James Iffland, *De fiestas y aguafiestas: risa, locura e ideología en Cervantes y Avellaneda (*Madrid/ Frankfurt: Universidad de Navarra/Vervuert, 1999); and Anthony Close's work that culminates in *Cervantes and the Comic Mind of his Age* (Oxford: Oxford University Press, 2000).

8 Bryce contrasts the humor of Quevedo and Cervantes in "Del humor quevedesco a la ironía cervantina," *Estudios Públicos* [Chile] 77 (Summer 2000): 373–88.

9 Renaissance humoral theory and its interpretation by Cervantes, especially with respect to the causes of "dryness," is discussed in Daniel L. Heiple, "Renaissance Medical Psychology in 'Don Quijote,'" *Ideologies & Literature* 2.9 (1979): 65–72.

10 Regarding the fool in European history, see Enid Welsford, *The Fool: His Social and Literary History* ([1935]; Garden City, NY: Anchor Books, 1961).

11 Albert A. Sicroff, "En torno al *Quijote* como 'obra cómica,'" *Actas del II Coloquio Internacional de la Asociación de Cervantistas* (Barcelona: Anthropos, 1991), pp. 353–66. Sicroff also explores the serious and unorthodox implications of the comic episodes in *Don Quixote*, such as the relative nature of faith, belief, reality, and truth.

12 Iffland's is the best study of Avellaneda since Stephen Gilman's *Cervantes y Avellaneda: estudio de una imitación* (Mexico City: El Colegio de México, 1951). He points out that because of his insistence on Don Quixote's comic aspects, Avellaneda seems to be one of the first adherents to the "funny book" school of Cervantine criticism. *De fiestas y aguafiestas*, p. 572.

13 Allen Thiher, *Revels in Madness: Insanity in Medicine and Literature* (Ann Arbor: The University of Michigan Press, 1999), p. 92.

14 In this regard, see my discussion of the class tensions and social criticism underlying the burlesque letters in chapters 36–52 of Part II in "Public Indiscretion and Courtly Diversion: the Burlesque Letters in *Don Quijote II*," *Cervantes* 11.2 (1991): 87–101.

15 For an updating of madness in literature subsequent to *Don Quixote*, see Shoshana Felman, *Writing and Madness (Literature/Philosophy/Psychoanalysis)*, trans. Martha Noel Evans et al. (Ithaca: Cornell University Press, 1985).

16 Mikhail Bakhtin, *Rabelais and His World*, trans. Hélène Iswolsky (Bloomington: Indiana University Press, 1984). See Redondo, *Otra manera de leer el "Quijote"* and Iffland, *De fiestas y aguafiestas*, for adaptations of Bakhtin's work on Carnival to Cervantes.

17 For a complete analysis of the burlesque sonnets that frame Part I of *Don Quijote*, see Martín, *Cervantes and the Burlesque Sonnet*, pp. 126–171.

18 Alonso López Pinciano, *Philosophía antigua poética*, ed. Alfredo Carballo Picazo, 3 vols. (Madrid: Biblioteca de Antiguos Libros Hispánicos, 1953), vol. III, p. 33. Close discusses López Pinciano's and other contemporary theories of the comic in *Cervantes and the Comic Mind*, pp. 249–76.

19 On this subject see Amado Alonso's "Las prevaricaciones idiomáticas de Sancho," *Nueva Revista de Filología Hispánica* 2 (1948): 1–20.

20 See José Ortega y Gasset, *Meditaciones del "Quijote"*, reprinted in vol. 1 of his *Obras completas* (Madrid: Revista de Occidente, 1946); Edwin Williamson, *The*

Half-Way House of Fiction: "Don Quixote" and Arthurian Romance (Oxford: Clarendon Press, 1984); E. C. Riley, *Don Quixote* (London: Allen & Unwin, 1986); Luis A. Murillo, *A Critical Guide to "Don Quijote"* (New York: Peter Lang, 1988); and Eduardo Urbina, *El sin par Sancho Panza: parodia y creación* (Barcelona: Anthropos, 1991). Recent critical works on parody are Linda Hutcheon, *A Theory of Parody* (New York and London: Methuen, 1984); Margaret A. Rose, *Parody: Ancient, Modern, and Post-Modern* (Cambridge and New York: Cambridge University Press, 1993); and Simon Dentith, *Parody* (London and New York: Routledge, 2000).

21 Quoted in Eduardo Urbina, "Sobre la parodia y el *Quijote*," *Actas del II Coloquio Internacional de la Asociación de Cervantistas* (Barcelona: Anthropos, 1991), p. 395.

22 The personal allusions contained in the poems that frame Part 1 of the novel are analyzed in Martín, *Cervantes and the Burlesque Sonnet*, pp. 156–66.

23 Miguel de Cervantes, *Don Quixote*, ed. Joseph R. Jones and Kenneth Douglas (New York: W. W. Norton & Co., 1981), p. 15.

24 Vladimir Nabokov, *Lectures on Don Quixote*, ed. Fredson Bowers, Introduction by Guy Davenport (New York: Harcourt Brace Jovanovich, 1983), p. 52. See Francisco Márquez Villanueva's ironic retelling of the circumstances surrounding Nabokov's appointment to Harvard and his reluctance to teach *Don Quixote* in "La lección del disparatario nabokoviano (Clare Quilty-Avellaneda)," in Antonio Bernat Vistarini and José María Casasayas, eds., *Desviaciones lúdicas en la crítica cervantina* (Salamanca/Palma de Mallorca: Ediciones Universidad de Salamanca/Universitat de les Illes Balears, 2000), pp. 337–55.

25 Eisenberg, *A Study of "Don Quijote"*, p. 111.

26 The nature, production and lexicon of the *burla* in Cervantes' Spain is studied in great detail in Monique Joly, *La bourle et son interprétation: Recherches sur le passage de la facétie au roman (Espagne, XVIe–XVIIe siècles)* (Toulouse: France–Ibérie Recherche, 1982). Joly expounds on the specific importance of *burlas* in *Don Quijote* in the sub-section "Bourle et folie" of chapter 2 of her *Etudes sur "Don Quichotte"* (Paris: Publications de la Sorbonne, 1996), pp. 113–61.

27 Originally published in the collection *Ficciones* (Buenos Aires: Emecé Editores, 1956).

28 See the section "De vapulamientos y azotes en el *Quijote*," in chapter 1 of his *Otra manera de leer el "Quijote"*, pp. 171–87.

29 George Mariscal, "The Other Quixote," in Nancy Armstrong and Leonard Tennenhouse, eds., *The Violence of Representation: Literature and the History of Violence* (London and New York: Routledge, 1989), pp. 98–116.

30 René Girard, *Deceit, Desire, and the Novel: Self and Other in Literary Structure*, trans. Yvonne Freccero (1961; Baltimore and London: The Johns Hopkins University Press, 1988).

31 James Williams, "The Anthropology of the Cross: A Conversation with René Girard," in James G. Williams, ed., *The Girard Reader* (New York: The Crossroad Publishing Company, 1996), p. 284. For a post-Girardian vision of the greater implications of desire's presence in Cervantes' novel, see Anthony J. Cascardi, "The Archaeology of Desire in *Don Quixote*," in Ruth Anthony El Saffar and Diana de Armas Wilson, eds., *Quixotic Desire: Psychoanalytic Perspectives on Cervantes* (Ithaca: Cornell University Press, 1993), pp. 37–58.

FURTHER READING

Close, Anthony. *Cervantes and the Comic Mind of his Age*. Oxford: Oxford University Press, 2000.

The Romantic Approach to "Don Quixote." Cambridge: Cambridge University Press, 1977.

Eisenberg, Daniel. *A Study of "Don Quixote."* Newark, DE: Juan de la Cuesta, 1987.

Gorfkle, Laura J. *Discovering the Comic in "Don Quixote".* Chapel Hill: North Carolina Studies in the Romance Languages and Literatures, 1993.

Iffland, James. *De fiestas y aguafiestas: risa, locura e ideología en Cervantes y Avellaneda*. Madrid/Frankfurt: Universidad de Navarra/Vervuert, 1999.

Martín, Adrienne L. *Cervantes and the Burlesque Sonnet*. Berkeley: University of California Press, 1991.

Redondo, Augustin. *Otra manera de leer "El Quijote."* Madrid: Castalia, 1997.

Russell, P. E. *Cervantes*. Oxford and New York: Oxford University Press, 1985.

"Don Quixote as a Funny Book." *Modern Language Review* 64 (1969): 312–26.

9

ANNE J. CRUZ

Psyche and gender in Cervantes

The title of this essay brings together two controversial yet crucial areas of study within Cervantes scholarship. The concepts of psyche and gender, as I apply them to Cervantes' works, encompass the literary representations of psychological complexes – such as the unconscious and the manifestation and repression of desire – and of the sex/gender system. Their dynamics permeate not only the author's fiction, but many of the assumptions underlying its major critical approaches. No reader of Cervantes can fail to observe his abundant examples of literal and literary madness, of visual and verbal illusions, and of fragmented and fractured selves. The multiple ambiguities in his fiction, as well as the appearance of numerous "deviant" women and their relations with equally anomalous male partners, open the literature to an increasing range of psychoanalytical and gender-inflected analyses. My purpose in this chapter, therefore, is to trace the emergence of psychology and gender as vital categories of analysis, to identify their critical function in Cervantes studies, and to investigate the intricate relations between them.

Since psychology and its applied methodology of psychoanalysis intend an investigation of the mind's unconscious workings, psychoanalytical readings attempt to understand the verisimilar mental processes in fictional characters that sustain our interest and lead us to empathize with literary protagonists. Cervantes' first Freudian critic was Freud himself, whose early discovery of *Don Quixote*, which he read in the original Spanish during his student years in Vienna, first whetted his curiosity about the knight's "reason of unreason." As numerous critics have suggested, the roles of analyst and analysand in Freud's "talking cure" – that is, the part of the psychiatrist who listens and that of the patient who narrates her life – may well have been inspired by Cervantes' talking dogs Cipión and Berganza in "El coloquio de los perros" ("The Colloquy of the Dogs").[1] The intended and unintended connections between the author and his works are also open to interpretation through psychoanalytical theories. Certainly, it is the reader's ideology or belief system that presupposes whether the author's intentions may be detected in his writing. Most readers, however, still adhere strongly to their belief in the author's power to create and command his characters. For the reader, this is not solely a matter of assuming that the characters "speak" for Cervantes, but of granting the author full control over his works, even when his multiple narrators displace his authorial voice. Yet, while Cervantes' distance from his characters may block any direct cognizance of his thought, this detachment does not inhibit an approach that attributes to the characters the acting out of their unconscious desires independently from either the author or his fictional narrators.

In Cervantes' works, madness is often employed to characterize the unconscious. Don Quixote's invention of an archaic chivalric world populated by giants and enchanters and his pursuit of an nonexistent lover make him Cervantes' most famous "mad" character, but the knight is not the only protagonist driven by impulses he scarcely understands. Tomás Rodaja in the exemplary novel "El licenciado Vidriera" ("The Glass Graduate"), Cardenio in *Don Quixote*, and Anselmo in the novel-within-the-novel "El curioso impertinente" ("The Tale of Foolish Curiosity") all go strangely mad due to their eroticized longings. Other characters, whose passions similarly confound their sense of reality, are regarded as examples of excess. In "The Colloquy of the Dogs," a soldier's dream induced by venereal disease conjures up talking dogs and their witch mothers; in "El celoso extremeño" ("The Jealous Man from Extremadura"), an avaricious old man's obsession with honor proves the undoing of his loveless marriage to his beguiled child-bride. The characters' desire for what they cannot have – and for what they cannot express – manifests itself in behavior that requires the reader to probe below the narrative's surface to fill in its gaps, that is, to discover other meanings than what is overtly stated in or represented by the text.

It was not until the twentieth century that readers acquired the theoretical language needed to categorize individual behavior through psychoanalytical notions. Critical interest in the psychological force of Cervantes' texts came about at the time when Freud's terms of the unconscious, the Oedipal complex, dream interpretation, and the divided self entered the cultural vernacular. To be sure, the Romantics had already anticipated the movement by diagnosing Don Quixote's malady as the corollary to his monomaniacal ego and then by proceeding to assess his actions accordingly. If the "enlightened" eighteenth-century reader found mainly satire in Cervantes' most famous novel, the nineteenth-century Romantic elevated the figure of the Don to that of an idealist whose serious message eclipsed his madness. Whereas neoclassicism saw in Don Quixote the perennially laughable figure of the fool, Romanticism applauded his heroic absurdity in order to rebuke modernity's pervasive cynicism.

In contrast, the early twentieth century interpreted Cervantes' fiction as transparently representative of its geographical place and historical time. Following Renaissance humanist thought, modern readers sought to unravel the biographical and historical aspects of Cervantine fiction. They argued that a text's meaning issues forth from the author's particular point of view, expressed in his language and style, as well as from its cultural context. Indeed, the novelist Miguel de Unamuno declared Cervantes the "instrument" by which seventeenth-century Spain and its people gave "birth" to Don Quixote. This positivist view of literature was followed after World War I by Spanish critic Américo Castro's highly influential *El pensamiento de Cervantes* (1925).[2] His method owed much to stylistics or the analysis of poetic language as an autonomous expressive system. The study thus lent consistency, for the first time, to the author's entire literary production. Castro expanded and reedited his study in 1972, but even his earlier version clearly showed his interest in the character's interior development and psychological motivation. Castro's view of Cervantes' fiction is that of a world based not on any kind of reality or objectivity, but on appearances and life circumstances.

Relying on Romantic notions of the protagonist's virtuous demeanor, Salvador de Madariaga's *Guía del lector del Quixote* (1926), translated ten years later as *An Introductory Essay in Psychology*, similarly attributed the behavior of the characters in *Don Quixote* to their different personalities, perceptively noting the psychological effect each character has on one another.[3] In the same way that Don Quixote "quixotifies" Sancho through his example, Sancho "sanchifies" his master. Yet not until the decade of the 1980s – almost a century after Freud – would the psychoanalytical approach make significant inroads in Cervantes studies. *Cervantistas* continued to be swayed by Castro's early writings, with the result that the more speculative kinds of literary criticism, which owed a heavy debt to Freudian and Jungian psychology, failed to dislodge the main trends exemplified by stylistics. Cherishing their rationalist roots, most Spanish émigrés in the wake of the Spanish Civil War repeatedly espoused humanist approaches that aspired to seek the truth as told by the author. Literary critics who remained in Spain through the Franco regime likewise opted for philological or formalist analyses of Cervantes' fiction. Despite Castro's influence, these formal approaches distanced the literature from European interpretations such as Leo Spitzer's perspectivist approach, whose analogy of optical terminology proscribes any "right" view, underscoring Cervantes's relativism.[4]

Criticism outside Spain was predisposed early on toward psychoanalysis. Its influence was felt in perspectivist critiques and in existentialist analyses, which developed from the philosophical movement that proposed to account for the social alienation exacerbated by World War II. Both methods of analysis emphasized irony, duality, dissimulation, and ambiguity, as much in the author as in his fiction. While these approaches were not explicitly labeled psychoanalytical, they supported the belief that positivist and rationalist readings of literary texts could no longer accommodate either a narrative of progressive, "true" history or its fictional facsimile. That neither history nor literature is ever completely objective or truthful is, of course, one of the lessons that Cervantes aims to teach in *Don Quixote*; by repeatedly confusing literary exploits with historical deeds, the knight succeeds in calling attention to their inherent instability. Paradoxically, Don Quixote's insatiable reading implanted so much "impossible nonsense" in his mind that to him, "no history of the world was better substantiated" than through the fictive novels of chivalry (I, I).[5]

In 1971, the American critic Arthur Efron postulated Don Quixote's invention of an unattainable Dulcinea as a means for Cervantes to critique social conformism.[6] For Efron, Dulcinea's purpose in the narrative was meant to symbolize Spanish culture's repressed sexuality, a reading other critics labeled "idiosyncratic" for not following conventional views. Efron's interpretation, however, implied that the *narrative* had a psyche that needed deciphering in order to understand its message. That same year, Margaret Church, another American critic, suggested that *Don Quixote*'s structure was organized by key points that paralleled the protagonist's psychological state.[7] Her approach superimposed the development of the character's psyche onto the narrative. She explained that the novel outlines a pattern of involvement and one of retreat: while Part I deals with Don Quixote's relation to others and to society, Part II concerns the knight's self-discovery. This interpretation concurred with the general move toward structuralism, a critical program that emphasized the organic relations within literary works but suspended their chronological, historical, and extratextual connections. Church's study was important, moreover, in that it foreshadowed the analogy that critics would make between the fragmented character Don Quixote and his author. She maintained that the "inner" Cervantes projects his beliefs and speaks through his numerous "alter egos."

Sustained by a long rationalist tradition, Cervantes studies in the United States nevertheless had yet to fully accept psychoanalysis as a critical method. In contrast, Cervantes studies in France were influenced by existentialist writers such as Jean-Paul Sartre and Albert Camus, whose interest in the psychological motivations of their fictional characters pervaded their works. Existentialism's denial of objectivity elicited new readings that focused on the characters' subjectivism. French critic René Girard drew a triangular relationship between Don Quixote and his squire dependent on the mediation of desire.[8] According to Girard, Don Quixote's fascination with chivalric novels inspires him to imitate their heroes, creating an external mediation whereby their desires become Don Quixote's, and his desires those of Sancho Panza. In the United States, Cesáreo Bandera extended Girard's thesis to Cervantes, whom the critic perceived as caught within the structures of desire – the chivalric genre – that he wished to ridicule.[9] The philosophical shift from existentialism to structuralism, impelled in part by Cold War totalitarianism, strongly affected French *cervantistas*. Maurice Molho, in his 1976 study of *Don Quixote* and the comic interlude "El retablo de las maravillas" (*"The Miracle Show"*) spoke of a "crypto-psychology" in the hidden recesses of Cervantes' works, apparently beyond the author's conscious realm of knowledge.[10] Yet despite attempts to disregard the author by granting primacy to his writing, Cervantes continued to prove too overpowering an authorial figure. Molho ended by praising the author's choice of popular and folkloric motifs, attributing the selection to his psychological intuition.

Four years after Molho's study, Louis Combet broke interpretive ground by establishing what he called "a new enterprise for Cervantology."[11] Defining the erotic as the psyche's structuring principle throughout Cervantine fiction, Combet took other critics to task for not attempting, since Castro, an overview of *all* of Cervantes' fiction as a literary system. For Combet, Cervantes' fiction centers above all on stories of love; the characters' desire, however, is constantly deferred, as we see in so many unrealized relations. No matter how frequently Cervantes is displaced by his own narrators, the French critic contends that the continuous deferral of desire evinces the horror that the erotic induces in Cervantes (*Cervantès*, 34). Nonetheless, psychostructuralist accounts of the novel such as those by Church and Combet resist any attempt to uncover the author's intention or otherwise "discover" him within his fictional texts. Combet affirms that it is impossible to speculate on the degree to which Cervantes expresses his ideas or his thoughts through any of his protagonists (*Cervantès*, 12). He and Church are instead willing to investigate only the narrative's structural coherence.

For those critics who prefer to psychoanalyze the protagonists, the 1575 treatise on human behavior *Examen de ingenios* (*Examination of Men's Wits*) by Cervantes' contemporary Juan Huarte de San Juan provides an early modern corollary to modern psychological formulations. Its pseudo-medical analysis of human aptitudes and skills in proportion to the four bodily humors, together with its distinctions of nationality, food, climate, and astrological signs, surely colored Cervantes' description of his characters. The knight's melancholy nature, his frequently intemperate actions and his yellow-tinged complexion, for example, all result from an excess of bile.

According to Church, Huarte's notions explain Cervantes' "genius" in "his treatment and understanding of the inner man behind the mask" (p. xix). This is also one of the premises posited by Carroll Johnson, one of the earliest openly Freudian critics of *Don Quixote*.[12] Johnson opted to focus on the protagonist's psyche rather than on his role in the narrative's plot. His position was far more controversial in that it attributed Don Quixote's psychotic reactions not to his readings of the ubiquitous novels of chivalry but to the middle-age crisis brought about by his unspoken sexual desire for his young niece. Johnson has been reproached for proposing a psychological case history that contradicts the knight's statements, which acknowledge his desire for a "real" village girl who is then transformed by him into the illusory Dulcinea. Critics claim that Johnson's thesis conflicts with Don Quixote's apparent fixation on the village maid Aldonza, whose modest and shy demeanor, he tells Sancho, had first sparked his interest. Sancho attempts to correct his master's opinion by pointing out the girl's coarse, mannish behavior: "She can fling a crowbar as well as the strongest lad in all the town...And the best part is that she is not a bit prudish...she jokes with everybody and has a grin and a wisecrack for everything" (1, 25). With a wicked wink at Sancho (and at the reader), Don Quixote quickly counters by comparing his situation with that of a rich noblewoman who chooses for her lover a none-too-bright but strapping young man. By utilizing this surprisingly lucid and provocative analogy, the knight makes clear that, whatever he really wants with Aldonza or Dulcinea, neither their behavior nor indeed their actual existence makes any difference (1, 25). The retort is significant, as it confirms that something else is at play in the episode besides the literal truth. Similarly, Johnson's conviction in Don Quixote's unconscious motivation for fleeing his feminized household cannot be disputed solely by an appeal to the novel's factual statements. Don Quixote's behavior follows his own elusive logic, as the knight's state of mind oscillates ceaselessly between reason and madness.

At times, in an attempt to understand the author, *cervantistas* like Church extend their analysis of the fictional protagonist's psyche to that of Cervantes. This interpretive shift is abetted by the likeness often drawn between him and his literary creation. In the preface to Part II, the novel's official censor may just as well be describing Don Quixote when he affirms that Cervantes "was old, a soldier, a gentleman, and poor" (II, 412). Some critics align the fictive knight's adventures with his author's experiences, claiming that it is Cervantes and not Don Quixote whose psyche is split into idealist and realist categories, a diagnosis that then justifies what seems to be the author's inexplicable ambivalence. Given Cervantes' pride in his own military exploits, the novel's equivocal portrayal of the flummoxed knight has been attributed to the author's vacillation in making a laughing-stock of the hero, even one so dejected as Don Quixote. Readers have noticed the dilemma when considering the knight's misfired intentions, which nevertheless spring from a strong sense of patriotism acknowledged in the novel: "He fancied it was right and requisite, no less for his own greater renown than in the service of his country, that he should make a knight-errant of himself, roaming the world in full armor and on horseback in quest of adventures" (I, I). Cervantes' patriotic pride is again echoed with no hint of irony in the comment made by the captain in the "Captive's Tale." He boasts of his participation at Lepanto, the same battle where his author lost the use of his hand: "I may say, in short, that I took part in that glorious expedition [the battle of Lepanto], promoted by this time to be a captain of infantry, to which honorable charge my good luck rather than my merits raised me. And that day – so fortunate for Christendom, because then all the nations of the earth were disabused of their error in imagining the Turks to be invincible on sea" (I, 39).

Efforts to clarify and comprehend Cervantes' ambiguities by ascribing to the author's psyche the fragmentation evinced in his work makes psychological sense when we consider early modern Europe's profound radicalism. Cervantes wrote the novel at the time when scientific discoveries were shattering traditional belief systems. His shifts and displacements in narrative perspective bespeak the splits caused by the impact of new rational thought. Frequently subverting his own authorial role, Cervantes asserts he is not his novel's father, but its stepfather. The fictional translator of Cide Hamete Benengeli's fictional history anticipates the impossibility of disentangling truth from fiction and madness from reason when he states "I see no way of accepting [the Cave of Montesinos episode] as true, as it so much exceeds all reasonable bounds. It is impossible for me to believe that Don Quixote could lie, since he is the most truthful gentleman and the noblest knight of his time" (I, 24). In a narrative twist reminiscent of Freud's dreamwork, the episode in the Cave of Montesinos becomes a figment imagined by Cervantes that occurs within the *knight*'s mind. Moreover, it is not the author, but the presumably unreliable Moorish translator of a presumably mendacious Arab historian, who expressly exonerates the protagonist from any accusation that he has fabricated a falsehood.

As the unbounded limits of Cervantes' fiction finally compelled critics to undertake psychoanalytical studies, their belatedness in Spain and the United States caused diverse psychoanalytical approaches to emerge and circulate simultaneously rather than to proceed consecutively from one method to the next. Hence, Freudian readings frequently intersect with Jungian criticism and with recent Lacanian and other post-Freudian methods of analysis. The psychological concepts by these different critical positions all derive from each method's salient vocabularies. Freudian psychoanalysis emphasizes how the unconscious, in particular its repression of sexuality, becomes actualized in text and protagonist. Although founded on Freudian concepts, the analytical system devised by French psychoanalyst Jacques Lacan stresses desire and lack as expressed through language, replacing the patriarchal system based on biological paternity with a symbolic realm controlled by what Lacan calls the Law of the Father. Readings influenced by Carl Gustav Jung, the Swiss founder of analytical psychology, feature archetypal symbolism and the collective unconscious to underscore the psychological effects of the literary text on the reader. Although splintered into several methodologies at times in contention with one another, psychoanalytical criticism has tended to focus on two main subjects of analysis: the psychology of the characters and the psychology of the narratives themselves. Both these methods, either explicitly or implicitly, extend beyond literature to involve not only the author's, but the reader's psyche as well.

The proposal that characters in novels can be considered clinical "cases" continues to fuel debates among readers, who argue whether or not fictional beings, like their real human counterparts, are accessible through psychoanalysis. In these "cases," fictional characters are presumed to manifest and reflect the same psychological characteristics of their authors and their readers. The hermeneutic advantage to this approach is that it recognizes the protagonists' capacity to transform themselves psychologically throughout the novel, unlike one-dimensional allegorical figures. From the perspective of literary history, the major significance in the protagonist's transformation is that its imitation of reality privileges the novel as a uniquely modern genre. *Don Quixote*'s attack on the novels of chivalry works successfully as satire precisely because Don Quixote's metamorphoses, from Alonso Quexana to Alonso Quijano "el Bueno," are convincingly depicted as credible psychological behavior. Lacanian critic Henry Sullivan has recently ascribed Don Quixote's final transformation to his Purgatorial experiences throughout Part II.[13] Sullivan charts the knight's changes – from his early Oedipal crisis to his disenchantment and release from dementia – to conclude that Don Quixote simultaneously saves his soul and heals his psyche. To prove that this redemptive reading makes as much historical as psychological sense, Sullivan first presents ecclesiastical documentation on the doctrine of Purgatory. Drawing on the Lacanian notion that humanity is entrapped by language, he defends the psychoanalysis of fictional characters and real persons alike, since both express themselves and are expressed through language. Both fictional characters and historical beings constitute cultural symbols that in turn may only be decoded by means of other cultural symbols.

The psychoanalytical strategies utilized by Sullivan and Johnson depend on an analogy between the psyches of fictional characters who narrate their lives to the reader and of "real-life" persons who are capable of confessing their thoughts directly to an analyst. Like the analyst, readers may perceive the fictional characters' psychological make-up through their words and actions in the narrative. For Johnson, psychoanalysis allows the reader to understand what, on the surface, may appear senseless in the text: "the apparently nonsensical becomes verisimilar within the context of psychoanalytical theory, and a minor episode can provide major insights into a character's personality."[14] Hence, his critical focus proposes to formulate both a comprehensible narrative structure and a psychologically coherent, intelligible protagonist. Although Johnson attempts to fill the gaps in the narrative, by seeking to prove the coherence of the plot and the characters, he remains allied with the humanist tradition that seeks consistency and continuity within the narrative. The compulsion by many critics, including Johnson, to search for unity in the text leads them to ascribe to the author an intentionality that paradoxically often challenges their psychoanalytical perspective. These critics attribute the narrative structure and the workings of the protagonist's psyche to a textual design that they then accredit to the author's intentions.

In contrast, readers who assume a critical stance based on postmodernism – a philosophical and artistic program that defines our current historical period by its indeterminacies, ambiguities, ruptures, and displacements – acknowledge literature's equally disruptive and ambiguous condition. The preeminence assigned these features over the narrative unity sought by traditional critics who hold to literature's essential truthfulness results from postmodernism's intensely disillusioned sense of the world as irredeemably chaotic. As part of that world, Cervantes' twentieth-century readers faced two world wars and the worsening threats of nuclear warfare, ecological destruction, cultural conflict, and global economic instability. By reconfiguring the Baroque period into an analogue of their darker sensibilities, postmodernists reject the conventional critical perception of Cervantine ambiguities as merely narrative games that always manage to transcend historical uncertainties. Some, such as the Argentine critic Félix Martínez Bonati, have attempted to resolve the differences between idealist and postmodern readings. Martínez Bonati finds in the narrative a neutralized skepticism that is "played out in the redemptive space of the archetypal fantasy of optimism." For him, therefore, the novel's moments of sadness and hopelessness are always converted into "happy melancholy."[15] Most idealist readings, however, elevate all events into transcendental moments wherein rational and moral truths win over unreason, as in Don Quixote's transformation at the end into

Alonso Quijano "el Bueno." Instead, postmodernists view this change as an ultimately ironic questioning of reason, reached only by Don Quixote's death and ignored by all around him. In such an interpretation, the textual ambivalences and ambiguities stand for multivalent arbitrary signs that gesture toward an unrepresentable, because meaningless, future.

The lingering conservative bent of many *cervantistas,* manifested mainly in Spain but also among traditional readers in the United States and Latin America, has favored the humanist notions of authorial control, textual unity, and literary origins. The many declarations affirming Cervantes' assured purposes when writing fiction illustrate that the concept of authorial presence still gives comfort to many of his readers. Nonetheless, the disruptive spaces uncovered by postmodernism confirm that the reader's comprehension has more often than not been aided by the incursion of diverse psychoanalytical commentaries. The gaps in Cervantes' stories are pointed out in Mary Gossy's aptly-titled study, *The Untold Story.*[16] Her Lacanian reading of the exemplary novels "El casamiento engañoso" ("The Deceitful Marriage") and "El coloquio de los perros" shows how the first novel frames and unfolds into the other through the deviant women in the text, the prostitute doña Estefanía and the witch Cañizares. In both novels, evil is associated with female sexuality; the dishonest ensign, in turn tricked into a deceitful marriage by the prostitute, is left syphilitic and fleeced of his belongings. Yet he cannot refrain from evoking her, as doña Estefanía's disappearance leaves the tale untold and its exemplarity undecided: "[E]ven without looking for her, she's always in my mind, and wherever I am my disgrace goes with me."[17] But if doña Estefanía's absence forecloses the novel's ending, the ensign's ambiguous dream, caused by contagion with the diseased prostitute, begets its sequel, which gives the witch Cañizares center stage. Although the ensign narrates only what he remembers and can logically explain, he portends the novel's evil secret: "There are things I could tell you which surpass all imagination, for they go beyond the bounds of nature" ("Deceitful Marriage" 190). In contrast, by revealing the name of the dogs' mother, the witch appears to disclose the mysterious source of the dogs' power to speak. Following the Lacanian notion of the mirror stage, whereby the child disengages from the pre-Oedipal or maternal imaginary to enter the symbolic order – the patriarchal realm of language – Gossy attributes the dogs' powers of speech to their separation from their mother. She thus remits the undisclosed origins of the story to the maternal womb. The witch's bodily gap becomes the novel's central mystery, one the reader endeavors futilely to fill through the desire to know. Like its frame novel "The Deceitful Marriage," however, "The Colloquy of the Dogs" nonetheless remains inconclusive and its female characters outside the patriarchal norm.

Gossy's Lacanian analysis anticipated the marked increase in the 1990s in the number of psychoanalytical studies of Cervantes' fiction. The collection of essays edited by Ruth El Saffar and Diana de Armas Wilson in 1993 first attempted to give a full dimension to these perspectives.[18] The fifteen essays comprise a broad sampling of Freudian, anti-Freudian, and post-Freudian theories, from Freud's Oedipal complex to Julia Kristeva's notion of the abject, from the Lacanian mirror stage to the maternal in Abraham and Torok. The spectrum of approaches reflects the belated acceptance of psychoanalytical methods by *cervantistas*, as numerous essays in the collection allude to other compatible categories of analysis. One essay merges psychoanalytical theory with materialist analysis to critique the recurrent appearance of money in Don Quixote's dreams.[19] Another essay heralds the applications of queer theory to Hispanic studies, as its novel interpretation of the "Captive's Tale" underscores the impulse of homosexual desire.[20] The collection's psychoanalytical readings disclose the unexpressed desires of the characters, their author, and his texts, but they also reveal the critics' literary, philosophical, and political concerns. Edited by two feminist *cervantistas*, the essays do not fail to uncover and give voice to the *female* psyche silenced in the narratives. As with Gossy's feminist application of psychoanalytical theories, psychoanalytical approaches coalesce with and demonstrate their reliance on contemporary feminist theories.

The anthology edited by El Saffar and Wilson demonstrates just how successfully psychoanalytical studies make the text "speak more than it knows." The essays also exemplify the continued difficulties experienced by readers when approaching literature from this perspective. Most critics persist in relinquishing to Cervantes, as a writer completely aware of his powers, the authority to psychoanalyze his characters and impose order on his text. Even those who bracket Cervantes' authorship in order to investigate his work as an expression of early modern culture through its conflicting modes of desire, still grant him an all-knowing awareness that leaves the author in control, if not of his own, then of his characters' desires. However, despite their frequent reversion to authorial intention, psychoanalytical critiques enrich our comprehension of Cervantes' fiction by giving voice to what is left unsaid in the texts. Their significance is noteworthy when we consider that fiction enacts, above all, the circulation of desire. Fictional narratives can have no definitive interpretation because desire itself has no point of origin or end. The Cervantine text's (post) modernity is assured in its recognition that desire is always unfulfillable and that narration is unending. By underscoring Don Quixote's desire for death, which can only be accommodated by his *ceasing* to desire – that is, by his death – psychoanalytical approaches confirm the implausibility either of the completely autonomous self or of an originary narrative.

Because desire is that which can never be apprehended by the subject, it contains the capacity to impersonate whatever – or perhaps more accurately, *who*ever – eludes the subject's grasp. Fiction becomes an exemplary network of intersecting narratives that encircle this shadowy "other" as the object of desire. Since the "other" is constructed by and against a masculinized subjectivity, its form more often than not assumes a feminine shape. This shape need not be cast into that of a biological woman, although as we shall see, in many instances it embodies the female element. In that the mechanisms of psychoanalysis allow – indeed, require – the silenced to speak, and as the silenced in patriarchal societies include women and the "other," pychoanalytical criticism gives recurrent impetus to feminist and gender studies. As I discuss more fully later, the outcome has not occurred without a struggle, especially in Cervantes studies. Gender-inflected psychoanalytical modes of analysis call into question readers' presuppositions about Cervantes' thoughts on women, women's role in fiction, and the general representation of gender relations in early modern Spain. They also examine the reader's own views on gender roles. It is no coincidence that *women* critics first felt the need to speak out, to address what simply had not been addressed before or what previously had been addressed in far too simple or dismissive a manner.

Ruth El Saffar's study *Beyond Fiction: The Recovery of the Feminine in the Novels of Cervantes*, published in 1984, anticipated her and Wilson's anthology by combining Freudian and Jungian psychoanalytical concepts with feminist analysis, an alliance that productively traced the psychic development of Cervantes' fictional characters, whether gendered male or female. Her observation that "the story of unfulfilled desire is the very substance of fiction" confirmed the mediation of psyche in the development of narrative.[21] El Saffar identified the characters' conflicts of unfulfilled love and failed expectations with Cervantes' search for an escape from the erotic entanglement of desire. She conceived this escape as a progressive goal set by Cervantes from his first to his last writings. According to El Saffar, in his earliest published work, the pastoral novel *Galatea*, the author struggles to release the protagonists from the genre's conventional structures as an attempt to resolve the problems brought about by triangular desire. In *Don Quixote*, Cervantes moves from the tangled plots of love triangles to advance instead a series of women of all types who exist independently from erotic conflict. In his final work *Persiles y Sigismunda* (*Persiles and Sigismunda*), the author introduces a mother figure as the instigator of the young couple's journey toward truth, allegorizing through her presence the possibility of fulfillment.

Holding to her belief in the author's control of his text, El Saffar's early study perceived Cervantes' effort to resolve the problems of desire in fiction as a reflection of his need to reconcile his own lack. She extended the contests that she saw in the narratives – the oppositions between fiction and history, the temporal and the eternal, and the literary and the real – to what she took as the discontented author's hostility toward escapist literature. The book's title *Beyond Fiction* thus infers the author's trajectory as an extension of his protagonist's. Through his struggles, depicted in fictional terms, Cervantes increasingly reaches self-discovery, undergoing a personal and professional transformation inscribed in the move from the novel *Don Quixote* to the romance *Persiles and Sigismunda*. El Saffar's study asserts that Cervantes meant to pursue truth through his fiction and unite "the highest and the lowest aspects of the self." Recalling the Romantics, it remains grounded in a pre-postmodern idealism. According to El Saffar, the women protagonists introduce the concept of the "fourth term." They function as conciliatory female figures whose harmonious number reinstates balance and resolution to the triangular structure of desire. What distinguishes her interpretation from others that also enmesh the protagonist with his author is its specifically feminist approach to Cervantes' female characters. For El Saffar, the "undesired, undesirable female" stands literally for the unconscious.

El Saffar affirms that the category of the feminine need not be limited to women, as it also embraces the images of night, moon, cave, sea, and death. These elements mysteriously keep Don Quixote from attaining his conscious desire to succeed as a heroic figure. They serve to chart the world of the author's unconscious as much as that of his major works. The fourfold structure that organizes the pastoral novel *Galatea*, for example – sets of four characters and four interpolated tales, associated with the seasons and the elements – challenges the very genre that, El Saffar tells us, Cervantes *thought* he was imitating (*Beyond Fiction* 19). The significance of El Saffar's study lies in its recognition of how the feminine shares an undivided, unconscious aspect of Don Quixote's psyche. Her Jungian analysis traces Part II's emphasis on strong, active women in seeming opposition to the knight. The turn of events, however, evokes the return of consciousness in Don Quixote with the "emergence of the feminine as an independent force" (*Beyond Fiction* 125). In contradistinction to the conventional object constructed by male desire, Don Quixote's object of desire becomes an increasingly independent, *uni*deal woman whose transformation ends by liberating him as well.

Beyond Fiction was the first study by an American Hispanist to speak out clearly on the feminine presence in Cervantes' writings. Although El Saffar's

concerns reached beyond conventional critiques that ignored women altogether, her analysis intended to seek a reconciliation of gender opposites.
Unlike later feminist critics whose revisionary analyses focus on the oppo-
sitional sexual categories structured by patriarchal norms, El Saffar did not
analyze the gender ideology of either the author or his fiction in order to
denounce and destabilize its politics. Rather, she questioned the tacit belief
promulgated by male critics that the masculine always represents the norm
for Cervantes. At the time, only two explicitly feminist analyses, both written
by professors of English, demonstrated an engagement with contemporary
Anglo-American and French feminist theories.[22] Despite the growth of psychoanalytical readings since the 1970s, and despite the points of contact
and relatedness of these two methodologies, feminist criticism has taken a
decidedly longer time to develop in Cervantes studies.[23] Although several
books on Cervantes' women characters were published as early as 1916,
the overwhelming majority maintained the representation of his female protagonists as liberal, heroic spirits akin to their creator.[24] By doing so, these
studies presented the women characters as merely standing for and proclaiming the author's philosophy, rather than asserting their own agency. None of
the studies may be properly classified as feminist, since they appeared years
before feminism was effectively incorporated into modern literary criticism.

Allied to the women's movement of the 1960s, feminism as a concerted
interpretive category remained constrained in American Cervantes studies
by the protracted dominance of male Hispanists, whose focus of analysis
favored a traditionally male-authored canon with its representation of masculine concerns. Thus, while feminist studies in other literary fields emerged
in tandem with the development of feminist politics, the pressure from conservative *cervantistas* ensured the continuance of what they deemed acceptable approaches to literature. The myriad women characters who parade
through Cervantes' fiction amid richly ironic circumstances, however, have
increasingly generated a decidedly gender-based critical perspective, mainly
among – but not limited to – women readers. This perspective has in
turn encouraged a view toward Cervantes' engagement with the "Other,"
the cultural minorities and foreigners who, like women, were considered
less than equal to Spanish men of Old Christian background. Diana de
Armas Wilson's *Allegories of Love: Cervantes's "Persiles and Sigismunda"*,
and Barbara Fuchs's essay on the exemplary novel "Las dos doncellas"
("The Two Damsels") remark on the gender transgressions in Cervantes that
challenge generic conventions, transgressions that also stand for his critique
of Spain's imperial pursuits.[25]

The current explosion of gender studies in Cervantes is no doubt indebted
to the large numbers of women faculty and students who have entered

American universities since the 1980s. In 1989, the *Journal of Hispanic Philology* published a collection of ground-breaking feminist essays on various Spanish male and female writers. Guest edited by Alison Weber, the essays took seriously the urgency of portraying Cervantes' women characters as subjects and active *survivors*, rather than mere passive victims. Marcia Welles thus revises the mitigating criticism that dulls the violence of the rape scene in the exemplary novel "La fuerza de la sangre."[26] She commends Cervantes' reliance on female agency to arrive at plot resolution through the bonding between women and the final love between husband and wife. In the same issue, Diana de Armas Wilson salutes, by way of Cervantes' tribute to the "equal rights" version of Genesis, the "new science" of feminist rereadings, an exercise she further elaborates in her book-length study of the *Persiles*. Wilson's explicitly feminist critique, published shortly after her essay, utilizes contemporary French theories and Freudian analysis to contest neo-Aristotelian readings of Cervantes' "Christian" romance. Cervantes himself, she argues, defied chivalric fictions about women, love, and marriage in his quest for civil relations – in both the legal and the social meanings of the term – between opposites. Wilson transforms the romance's sociogeographical locus of the Barbaric Isle into a spatial allegory for gender, ethnic, and linguistic difference oppressed by the phallocentrism of patriarchal Western culture (*Allegories*, 129). She shows how Cervantes exploits the figure of the androgyne, the trope of sexual parity, in order to displace hierarchy through a nondominant sexual difference (*Allegories*, 79).

Wilson's assessment of the *Persiles*' discourse, while mobilizing postmodern expectations, refrains from deconstructing the work in its entirety. Her study concurs with El Saffar's Jungian analysis in that she also attributes to Cervantes authorial control over the text, stating that he is "experimenting with new structures of desire [and] laboring to generate a nonlinear, nontriangular, nonsacrificial paradigm of a plot" (*Allegories*, 222). Other feminist analyses also assign this same control to the author; the questions posed implicitly or explicitly in recent criticism, in fact, have to do with whether Cervantes assumes what we might call a proto-feminist stance in his depictions of women characters. The matter forms part of the doubts surrounding the author's intentionality, since it is again the ambiguous nature of Cervantes' fiction that disallows a distinct and clear response. The ways in which Cervantes delineates gender difference correspond more closely to how the reader identifies with these differences than to what the author may or may not have wished to assert. Feminist criticism, therefore, while no more "truthful" in its diverse conclusions than other, more conventional readings, is no less illuminating for its revelation of the concerns that its practitioners bring to the interpretive task.

More often than not, Cervantes places his women characters in trying circumstances as part of a larger narrative framework in which numerous social problems may be questioned and scrutinized. Nevertheless, the female protagonists cannot be dismissed as mere pretexts for analyzing social issues; their sheer number – and the marked differences among them – cannot help calling attention to their individual concerns as women. Cervantes' foray into the pastoral convention through *La Galatea* reformulates tradition by populating the idealized landscape with desiring women.[27] Furthermore, the women bond with each other by sharing their desires through storytelling, in the process constructing their selves through language. The female protagonists befriend and accept one another, illustrating varying patterns of behavior that contrast with the repetitive actions of the male shepherds in traditional pastoral literature. The female community bespeaks a democratized space that allows each the potential for agency and self-sufficiency. Yet not all of Cervantes' depictions of women are as positive as the shepherdesses that appear in *La Galatea*. The boisterous female protagonists of his one-act *Entremeses* (*Interludes*) are kept in check by their conformity to social standards. The same is true of the majority of women in *Don Quixote*: Maritornes, despite her sexual aggressivity, remains limited always by her low social position. Although Teresa Panza exchanges gifts with the Duchess, she reveals her commonsensical peasant mentality in her annoyance at Sancho's impractical dreams, while the Duchess enjoys the privileges of her noble birth. Deprived of the kind of female community created in *La Galatea*, the play-acting shepherdess Marcela wanders alone into the woods after rejecting her many enamored suitors, never to be heard from again. Only Dorotea, whom Edward Dudley has labeled the heroine of "a new language and a new narrative," creates and recreates her own persona by breaching socially acceptable female conduct.[28] Despite her inventiveness, however, she ends by reverting to the same social and narrative constraints imposed on the others.[29]

Unfolding over the length of Part II, Dorotea's character offers surprisingly modern insight into the female psyche, yet it also attests to Cervantes' desire to script a singularly new fictional narrative by proffering both the delimitations imposed on and the choices open to real women in early modern Spain. Dorotea breaks with contemporary normative precepts as she freely expresses her sensuality yet still prevails as a highly desirable marriage partner to a nobleman. She achieves an authenticity that at once challenges and submits to social control. Her final speech to Fernando as she argues her case begins by stressing her humble station, but soon transforms into a rhetorical display of impeccable logic. Her discourse singles out her agency by pronouncing a speech act that efficaciously binds the couple in marriage.

Even though marriage to her seducer may not constitute a liberating act for today's feminist readers, it restores Dorotea's honor while elevating her to a higher social class and ensuring her seducer's redemption.

Though admitting to the complexity of Cervantes' female protagonists, feminist critics at times have been less generous in granting them even partial freedom to pursue their desire. Theresa Ann Sears, for example, utilizes stereotypes lifted from American popular culture to describe the kinds of women whom she sees passing through Cervantes' fiction.[30] The "Sweet Blonde Babe" appears most often and embodies the archetypal object of desire until, with age and through conventional marriage, she becomes a "Saintly Mother," while the "Wild Child" has a more forceful character and a less resolved fate. The categories, although imprecise, clue the reader to Sears's contention that these female characters are deluded in their freedom and constrained by their choices. Assuming what she believes are Cervantes' intentions, Sears asserts that his more ambiguously complex women, in particular the *Persiles*' Feliciana de la Voz, epitomize the author's uneasy relations with the feminine. Like psychoanalytical critics who ascribe the fictional characters' psychological problems to their author, some critics attribute the fictional complications of gender to Cervantes' personal aversion to treating the erotic. At least one writer proffers the view that Cervantes was troubled by the overt expression of sexuality – especially that of his female relatives – which he then sublimated in his fiction. The American biographer William Byron depicts Cervantes' mother and other women in his family as imbued with the same strongly aggressive, "virile" qualities of some of his female characters.[31] Following the idealized behavior of his diffident shepherdess Marcela, Cervantes distances himself from sexual desire through its transformation "into a transmuted sensuality of art and a safely dispersed love of humanity" (*Cervantes*, 56).

The Spanish translation of Rosa Rossi's psychoanalytical study came out in 1988, the same year that Byron published his biography.[32] For the Italian feminist, the writer's personal difficulties and extended suffering, so similar to those experienced by women in patriarchal cultures, not only compelled the author to respond like a woman, they actually turned him *into* one. Rossi's extreme opinion was based on Cervantes' extended captivity in Algiers, which according to the critic undoubtedly recast both his religious orthodoxy and his sexual orientation, a change that resulted in a fragmented, "divergent" Cervantes (*Escuchar a Cervantes*, 26). However, readers need not transform the author into an "other" Cervantes or into his own literary characters – whether that of Don Quixote or of his female protagonists – to understand how psyche and gender act to probe and tease out narrative meaning. At the crux of these categories is the need to determine the narrative's literary function in light of its sense to the reader – that is to say, how fiction makes sense and the kind of sense it makes. What becomes increasingly evident is that, like other critical approaches, the categories of psyche and gender in Cervantine fiction challenge the belief that literary values derive solely from the author or from the immediate historical context. Psychoanalytical criticism identifies the author with his literary creation, but it also investigates the characters' motivations in isolation, as psychological case studies. Similarly, gender analysis serves both to compare literary female protagonists to their historical homologues and to elucidate contemporary social problems. These double perspectives not only identify Cervantes as witness to his own historical moment, they uncover and convey the concerns of each community that continues to read and revel in his writings.

NOTES

1 Freud's biographer Peter Gay notes that in his youth he and a close friend formed a "Spanish Academy," writing under the names of the two dogs. See *Freud: A Life for Our Time* (New York; London: W. W. Norton, 1998), p. 22. See also León Grinberg and Juan Francisco Rodríguez, "Cervantes as Cultural Ancestor of Freud," in Ruth Anthony El Saffar and Diana de Armas Wilson, eds., *Quixotic Desire: Psychoanalytic Perspectives on Cervantes* (Ithaca and London: Cornell University Press, 1993), pp. 23–33.

2 Américo Castro, *El pensamiento de Cervantes* (Madrid: Casa Editorial Hernando, 1925); reed. Julio Rodríguez-Puértolas (Barcelona: Noguer, 1972).

3 Salvador de Madariaga, *Guía del lector del "Quijote"* (Madrid: Espasa-Calpe, 1926); *"Don Quixote": An Introductory Essay in Psychology* (Oxford: Clarendon, 1935).

4 Leo Spitzer, "Linguistic Perspectivism in *Don Quixote*," in *Linguistics and Literary History* (Princeton, NJ: Princeton University Press, 1948), pp. 41–85.

5 Miguel de Cervantes, *Don Quixote*, ed. Joseph R. Jones and Kenneth Douglas, trans. Richard Ormsby (New York: W. W. Norton, 1981). All quotations are from this translation.

6 Arthur Efron, *Don Quixote and the Dulcineated World* (Austin: University of Texas Press, 1971).

7 Margaret Church, *Don Quixote: Knight of La Mancha* (New York: New York University Press, 1971).

8 René Girard, *Mensonge romantique et vérité romanesque* (Paris: B. Grasset, 1961); trans. Yvonne Freccero as *Deceit, Desire, and the Novel: Self and Other in Literary Structure* (Baltimore: Johns Hopkins University Press, 1965).

9 Cesáreo Bandera, *Mímesis conflictiva: Ficción literaria y violencia en Cervantes y Calderón* (Madrid: Gredos, 1975).

10 Maurice Molho, *Cervantes: Raíces folklóricas* (Madrid: Gredos, 1976).

11 Louis Combet, *Cervantès ou les incertitudes du désir: Une approche psychostructurale de l'œuvre de Cervantès* (Lyon: Presses Universitaires de Lyon, 1980), p. 15.

12 Carroll B. Johnson, *Madness and Lust: A Psychoanalytical Approach to Don Quixote* (Berkeley: University of California Press, 1983).

13 Henry Sullivan, *Grotesque Purgatory: A Study of Don Quixote's Part II* (University Park: Pennsylvania State University Press, 1996).

14 Carroll B. Johnson, "Psychoanalysis and *Don Quixote,*" in Richard Bjornson, ed., *Approaches to Teaching Cervantes' "Don Quixote"* (New York: The Modern Language Association of America, 1984), p. 106.

15 Félix Martínez Bonati, *Don Quixote and the Poetics of the Novel*, trans. Dian Fox (Ithaca; London: Cornell University Press, 1992), p. 150.

16 Mary S. Gossy, *The Untold Story: Women and Theory in Golden Age Texts* (Ann Arbor: University of Michigan Press, 1989).

17 Miguel de Cervantes, *The Deceitful Marriage: Exemplary Stories*, trans. C. A. Jones (New York: Penguin, 1984), p. 189.

18 Ruth Anthony El Saffar and Diana de Armas Wilson, eds., *Quixotic Desire: Psychoanalytic Perspectives on Cervantes* (Ithaca: Cornell University Press, 1993).

19 Diana de Armas Wilson, "Cervantes and the Night Visitors: Dream Work in the Cave of Montesinos," in El Saffar and Wilson, eds., pp. 59–80.

20 Paul Julian Smith, "'The Captive's Tale': Race, Text, Gender," in El Saffar and Wilson, eds., pp. 227–35.

21 Ruth El Saffar, *Beyond Fiction: The Recovery of the Feminine in the Novels of Cervantes* (Berkeley: University of California Press, 1984), p. 6.

22 Adrienne Munich, "Notorious Signs, Feminist Criticism and Literary Tradition," in Gayle Greene and Coppèlia Kahn, eds., *Making a Difference: Feminist Literary Criticism* (London: Routledge, 1985), pp. 238–59; and Diana de Armas Wilson, "Cervantes's *Labors of Persiles*: Working (in) the In-between," in Patricia Parker and David Quint, eds., *Literary Theory/Renaissance Texts* (Baltimore: The Johns Hopkins University Press, 1986), pp. 150–81.

23 Anne J. Cruz, "Cervantes and His Feminist Alliances," in Anne J. Cruz and Carroll B. Johnson, eds., *Cervantes and His Postmodern Constituencies*, Hispanic Issues, vol. XVII (New York: Garland Publishing, 1999), pp. 134–50.

24 See, among others, José Sánchez Rosas, *Las mujeres de Cervantes* (Barcelona: Montaner y Simón, 1915); Sadie A. Trachman, *Cervantes's Women of Literary Tradition* (New York, 1932); and Martha K. Trinker, *Las mujeres en el Don Quijote de Cervantes comparadas con las mujeres en los dramas de Shakespeare* (Mexico City, 1938); Concha Espina, "Mujeres del Quijote," *Obras completas de Concha Espina* (Madrid: FAX, 1944).

25 See Diana de Armas Wilson, *Allegories of Love: Cervantes's "Persiles and Sigismunda"* (Princeton: Princeton University Press, 1991); and Barbara Fuchs, "Empire Unmanned: Gender Trouble and Genoese Gold in Cervantes's 'The Two Damsels,'" *PMLA* 116 (March 2001): 285–99.

26 Marcia Welles, "Violence Disguised: Representations of Rape in Cervantes' 'La fuerza de la sangre,'" Alison Weber, guest ed., *Journal of Hispanic Philology* 13 (1989): 240–52.

27 Rosilie Hernández-Pecoraro, "Cervantes's *La Galatea*: Feminine Spaces, Subjects, and Communities." *Pacific Coast Philology* 33 (1998): 15–30.

28 Edward Dudley, *The Endless Text: "Don Quixote" and the Hermeneutics of Romance* (Albany: State University of New York Press, 1997), p. 268.

29 Anne J. Cruz, "Redressing Dorotea," in Francisco LaRubia-Prado, ed, *Cervantes for the 21st Century/Cervantes para el siglo 21: Studies in Honor of Edward Dudley* (Newark, DE: Juan de la Cuesta, 2000), pp. 11–32.

30 Theresa Ann Sears, "Sacrificial Lambs and Domestic Goddesses, or, Did Cervantes Write Chick Lit? (Being a Meditation on Women and Free Will)." *Cervantes* 20 (Spring 2000): 47–68.

31 William Byron, *Cervantes: A Biography* (New York: Paragon, 1988).

32 Rosa Rossi, *Escuchar a Cervantes: Un ensayo biográfico* (Valladolid: Ámbito, 1988).

FURTHER READING

Bleznick, Donald W. "An Archetypal Approach to *Don Quixote*." In Richard Bjornson ed., *Approaches to Teaching Cervantes' Don Quixote*. (New York: The Modern Language Association of America, 1984. Pp. 96–103.

Cascardi, Anthony J. "The Archaeology of Desire in *Don Quixote*." In Ruth Anthony El Saffar and Diana de Armas Wilson, eds., *Quixotic Desire: Psychoanalytic Perspectives on Cervantes*. Ithaca and London: Cornell University Press, 1993. Pp. 37–58.

Cruz, Anne J., and Carroll B. Johnson, eds. *Cervantes and His Postmodern Constituencies*. Hispanic Issues, vol. XVII. New York: Garland Publishing, 1999.

Garcés, María Antonia. "Zoraida's Veil: The Other Scene of 'The Captive's Tale.'" *Revista de Estudios Hispánicos* 23 (1989): 65–98.

Higuera, Henry. *Eros and Empire: Politics and Christianity in Don Quixote*. Lanham, MD and London: Rowman & Littlefield, 1995.

La Rubia-Prado, Francisco. *Cervantes for the 21st Century/Cervantes para el siglo XXI: Studies in Honor of Edward Dudley*. Newark, DE: Juan de la Cuesta, 2000.

Wilson, Diana de Armas. *Cervantes, the Novel, and the New World*. Oxford: Clarendon Press, 2001.

10

DIANA DE ARMAS WILSON

Cervantes and the New World

Cervantes launched his writing career in 1585 with the publication of *La Galatea*, an unfinished, and today unreadable, bucolic fantasy. Some twenty years later he would reassess this first fiction, during the scrutiny of Don Quixote's library, as inconclusive: "it proposes something, and concludes nothing" (I, 6).[1] One thing this early work did propose was the importance of transatlantic poetry. *La Galatea* includes, among other classical furniture, a Muse who catalogues an impressive number of Spanish poets installed in "the faraway Indies."[2] Why this strange encounter between classical Arcadia and early modern America? The publishing date of Cervantes' first book coincided with what Fernand Braudel describes as a new "physics of Spanish policy": "For in the 1580s the might of Spain turned towards the Atlantic. It was out there, whether conscious or not of the dangers involved, that the empire of Philip II had to concentrate its forces and fight for its threatened existence. A powerful swing of the pendulum carried it towards its transatlantic destiny."[3] Evidently Cervantes wanted to be carried there too. This essay, which discusses his lifelong preoccupation with the Indies, is divided into three parts. We begin with a biographical section, largely focused on Cervantes' efforts to emigrate to the New World. This is followed by a survey of various kinds of American images found in his work, including their links to the Chronicles of the Indies. The essay closes with a look at two interlocking New World themes: Don Quixote as a "conquistador" and the conquistadores as "quixotic."

Searching for *mercedes*

Cervantes' return to Spain in 1580 as a maimed veteran of Lepanto and an ex-captive of Algiers was scarcely triumphal. After a harrowing ransom expedited by the Redemptionist friar Juan Gil for 500 gold escudos, and a defensive inquest that included a dozen witnesses to his life and habits as a captive in Barbary, Cervantes returned to freedom in Spain as a traumatized

206

and debt-ridden subject.[4] Although not yet suffering the plight of those "old and maimed soldiers" whose cause Don Quixote would later embrace – Cervantes was only thirty-three when he was ransomed – those "slaves to hunger," as the not-so-mad knight calls them (II, 24), would remain an enduring cautionary image for his creator.

One way to avoid hunger in Golden Age Spain, if not always a reliable one, was to emigrate to the New World. During the lean years of the early 1580s, as Cervantes increasingly recognized the bleak state of his postwar career prospects, he began vigorous preparations to secure a post in the Indies. A letter in his own hand, dated 17 February 1582, was unearthed in 1954 from the royal archives at Simancas. Alluding to some earlier negotiations, the letter was addressed to Antonio de Eraso, a member of the Council of the Indies who appears to have backed Cervantes' application for a post in the New World. The letter laments that His Majesty is, in fact, *not* going to fill the post.[5] Although Cervantes' marriage in 1584 to Catalina de Salazar, an *hidalga* from Esquivias, tied him to the family circle of the Quesadas, an American kinship by now well documented,[6] he was still unable to secure any kind of job in the Indies. He settles down for a few years with his new wife in Esquivias, a restless conjugal situation given his frequent trips to Madrid, Toledo, and even Seville. In 1587, he requests a post as a commissary officer under Diego de Valdivia, a deputy headquartered in Seville, and a new stage of life begins for Cervantes. He is commissioned to wander from one village to another across Andalucía, forcing grudging villagers to yield up their assigned quotas of olive oil, wheat, and fodder – provisions largely targeted for King Philip's "Invincible Armada."

A few years after the destruction of the Armada in 1588, a disastrous event for the nation, Cervantes tries yet again to emigrate to America. In a petition to the Council of the Indies on 21 May 1590, he begs to be considered for one of four managerial posts being advertised as vacant. His letter names them all: comptroller of the New Kingdom of Granada (present-day Colombia), governor of the province of Soconusco in Guatemala, accountant of the galleys at Cartagena, or magistrate of the city of La Paz (in present-day Bolivia). This second and final petition is rejected on 6 June 1590, when the Council of the Indies curtly denies Cervantes his emigration papers. A functionary named Dr. Núñez Morquecho brusquely scribbles at the foot of the petition the utopian response that this job search should be closer to home: "Let him search around here for some favor."[7] Formulated in the language of lords to vassals, this official bureaucratic rejoinder exemplifies a discourse that Cervantes would later mock. Don Quixote's mad investment in the feudoaristocratic institution of *mercedes* (favors), elegantly argued by Carroll B. Johnson, instances this kind of mockery: during his labor-wage negotiations with Sancho, who understandably wants to become a salaried employee, Don Quixote can only envision him as a vassal requiring *mercedes*.[8] Denied the one *merced* that Cervantes himself applied for – a post in the faraway Indies – he would not only parody the pre-formed feudal language of lords to vassals, but also satirize the economic order propped up by this kind of chivalric discourse.

By 1592, after a brief stint in a jail in Castro del Río for a shortfall in his tax moneys, Cervantes must have understood that all colonial prospects were closed to him. His books, not his person, would cross the Atlantic to settle and, indeed, flourish in the Spanish Indies. The Cuban writer Alejo Carpentier describes a grain of rice, displayed in a provincial museum in Venezuela, on which several paragraphs of *Don Quixote* have been copied.[9] Inverting this minimalist image, I would argue that *Don Quixote* itself contain many "grains of rice" on which the Indies are inscribed, and that Cervantes' last novel, the posthumous *Persiles and Sigismunda* (1617), contains even more. Spain's New World enterprise, in short, informed Cervantes' personal history as well as his imaginative writing. Twice frustrated in his desire for a transatlantic destiny, he would sometimes enact and often allegorize the matter of America in his writings. His fictions are haunted, intermittently but insistently, by vivid images of the New World.

Perhaps the most cited of these is the passage that opens "El celoso extremeño" ("The Jealous Man from Extremadura"), a novella whose protagonist is an *indiano* – a type who has returned from the Indies a rich man. As Covarrubias explains in his 1611 Castilian dictionary, "these men ordinarily return wealthy."[10] In his catalogue of various types of emigrants to the Indies, Cervantes pictures the New World as the

> refuge and haven for all the desperate men of Spain, the sanctuary of the bankrupt, the safeguard of murderers, an asylum for those gamblers whom professional cardplayers call *ciertos*, the promised land for ladies of easy virtue, a lure and disillusionment for many, and a satisying solution for few.[11]

Cervantes reiterates the idea of America as a "refuge" in "La española inglesa" ("The English Spanish Lady"), where the parents of the titular protagonist determine, at a low point in their fortunes, to emigrate to the Indies – "a common refuge of the impoverished nobility."[12] Apart from the fanciful addendum of "nagging wives," the historian Braudel provides some concrete profiles of the "hungry crowd of emigrants to America" during the sixteenth century:

> impoverished gentlemen hoping to restore their family fortunes, soldiers seeking adventure, young men of no property hoping to make good, and along with

them the dregs of Spanish society, branded thieves, bandits, tramps all hoping to find some lucrative activity overseas, debtors fleeing pressing creditors and husbands fleeing nagging wives.[13]

Cervantes does not depict the New World as merely a refuge, however – whether for the dregs of Spanish society or for its impoverished nobles. He also portrays the Indies as a land of opportunity for the professional classes: the Viedma brothers in *Don Quixote*'s interpolated "Captive's Tale" are a good instance of these flourishing colonials (I, 39–41). But Cervantes' final sketch of the New World – a posthumous and ironic image of his own imperial nation – is that of a tribe of cannibals living on a "Barbaric Island" and plotting world conquest. Age and illness may have prompted these later, and darker, New World mindscapes. In his "Parable of Cervantes and the *Quixote*," Jorge Luis Borges portrays the aged Cervantes as ultimately vanquished by his nation. "Fed up with his homeland of Spain, an aged soldier of the king sought solace in the vast geographies of Ariosto."[14] The literary appeal of Ariosto's oriental deserts and lunar valleys, for both Cervantes and Don Quixote, is undeniable. But I would add to these imaginary homelands some other, less literary but equally vast, geographies. For at the end of his life Cervantes was also writing westward, to the Indies – to the place where chivalry rode again, perhaps for the last time.

The discourses of America

Scattered across Cervantes' writings – his novels, novellas, plays, and poetry – are a number of isolated references to transatlantic geographical names, not only to the great land masses of America, the Indies, or the New World but also to such exotic particular sites as Arauco (present-day Chile), the Bermudas, Cartagena de Indias, Florida, Mexico, New Spain, Guanuco (in Peru), Peru itself, and Potosí (in modern-day Bolivia). Although many of these references appear in Cervantes' minor works, the Americana found in his major novels – *Don Quixote* (1605, 1615) and the *Persiles* (1617) – open up new areas for exploration. The references in *Don Quixote* to persons or places in, or affiliated with, the Indies are neither frequent nor strident. But the range of these references – from the topical to the ornamental to the rhetorical – is impressive. Of the dozen or so passages in this novel that gesture directly to the New World, one of them portrays the ungainly global reach of contemporary drama. Defending the Unities against Lope de Vega's new art of making *comedias*, the Canon of Toledo complains about a play whose first three acts were set in Europe, Asia, and Africa: "and if it had four acts, the fourth would end up in America" (I, 48). Other passages in

Don Quixote quarry America for new similes, as when Sancho compares the Enchanted Dulcinea's masculine riding skills to that of a Mexican horseman (II, 10). Several passages in this novel exploit "Potosí" – the American silver mine in present-day Bolivia – a regular destination for Clavileño, for example, the enchanted wooden horse that Don Quixote and Sancho use for their sham ascent into the stellatum (II, 40). Another passage hints at the normative aversion of Old Christian Spanish peasants to the otherness of New World peoples, including those of the ruling class: Sancho would just as soon become a "cacique" (Indian chief), he insists, as disenchant Dulcinea by flagellating his buttocks (II, 35).

A more rhetorical nod to the Indies occurs in Don Quixote's fevered homage to "the most courteous Cortés" ("el cortesísimo Cortés") (II, 8). Searching for a modern example through which to personify Fame, Don Quixote asks Sancho to consider who "scuttled the ships and left the valiant Spaniards high and dry in the New World under the command of the most courteous Cortés?" (II, 8). Cervantes' use here of a *ploce* – a particular species of the rhetorical figure *antanaclasis* or extended pun designating an individual and the general qualities that person is thought to possess – recalls the arcane rhetoric of the professional humanists. Don Quixote links Cortés's proverbial courtliness here to his famous deeds, specifically to the legendary burning of the ships that prevented the Spanish soldiers from returning to Cuba, leaving them with few options save to march on to Tenochtitlán (II, 8).

Although the propriety of Cervantes' use of the superlative "cortesísimo" ("most courteous") has been justly questioned by critics since Clemencín, we should recall that Cortés was also celebrated for his "cortesías" in various other Golden Age texts.[15] Considering that these "courtesies" were so transparently opportunistic and so resolutely mercenary, Don Quixote's instance of "word folding" here would seem decidedly ironic. Cervantes must surely have been aware of Cortés's infamous role in the court of Charles V, of the vision of universal monarchy that the conquistador shared with other members of the imperial entourage. Indeed, the central question that Cervantes poses in the Barbaric Isle narrative that opens the *Persiles* – a question also invoked in many virulent sixteenth-century European debates – is "What constitutes a barbarian?" Cervantes' text enacts an unambiguous answer to this question. Barbarians are men who, like Cortés, harbor aspirations of universal empire, men who consume other men's hearts in their aim to become "lords of all the world."[16] This would incriminate not only conquistadores like Cortés, but also the countless peninsular Spaniards who until 1588, the year of the Armada, subscribed to messianic and global visions of empire.[17]

Unlike Don Quixote, who is content to celebrate Cortés for his risk-taking, the narrator of "El licenciado Vidriera" ("The Glass Graduate") praises "the great Hernando Cortés" for the aesthetic results of the conquest.[18] In a cartographical balancing act, the unbalanced narrator of this text, who often merges with its mad and fragile protagonist, depicts Cortés as having conquered Mexico so that Venice would have a comparably splendid city to match it: "the European one, wonder of the Old World, the American one, astonishment of the New World" (p. 30). This desire to match Old and New World cities may puzzle readers who remember that Cortés not only conquered but also leveled Mexico City. We are left to decode this strange panegyric for ourselves. The simultaneous aggrandizing and trivializing of Cortés's fame also extends to Columbus in this text: had the Admiral not been born, the narrator of "El licenciado Vidriera" concludes, no city in the world would have been comparable to Venice (p. 30).

Columbus is, in fact, the object of one of the most rhetorical treatments of the New World in Cervantes. In the dedication to Part II of *Don Quixote*, Cervantes taps into the devious trope of allegory for a sly imitation of Columbus. The passage in question fictionalizes the arrival of a letter from "the great emperor of China," who begs Cervantes in Chinese ("en lengua chinesca") for a copy of *Don Quixote* to use as a Spanish language textbook. Wishing to learn more about Castilian letters, this fictional Chinese emperor even offers to found a college with Cervantes himself as its rector. All of this gestures to Columbus's fantasy, recorded at various points in his *Diario*, that some generic Great Khan might wish to learn more about the Spanish Crown. Alluding to the embassy sent by the Great Khan to Pope Eugenius, asking for wise men to instruct him in the faith of Christ, Columbus had even offered himself up as an instructor.[19]

Readers may wonder, in addition, whether Cervantes did not also borrow, for the character of Don Quixote, some well documented traits of Columbus himself. Calling him "a kind of Quixote a few centuries behind his time," Tzvetan Todorov catalogues some of the Admiral's documented character traits: a credulous and overtaxed imagination; a great fondness for the ceremonies of naming; an alertness to the appearances of enchantment; an ideology based on prescience rather than experience; a tendency to adjust the data, as well as challenge the humanity, of informants bearing unwelcome intelligence; a penchant for imposing oaths on other people; and, finally, a kind of injudicious bookishness.[20] Every one of these behavioral tics finds a place in Don Quixote's characterization.

Not unlike *Don Quixote*, which opens in a nameless place in La Mancha, various murky allusions to the New World inaugurate the posthumous *Persiles and Sigismunda* (1617). As noted above, this novel opens on a

"Barbaric Isle" that gestures, through both language and imagery, to the Caribbean. In the first chapter, for example, Cervantes uses an American word – *bejucos* – for the vines tying up a raft rather implausibly used to sail in the North Sea.[21] Instead of a conventional Castilian signifier for these vines (e.g., *lianas*), Cervantes chooses a word of Caribbean origins: *bejucos* is a Taíno word, from a language that linguists have assigned to the Arawakan family and traced back to the middle of the Amazon Basin. Cervantes may have accessed this *indigenismo* through various popular historiographers of the Indies, Fernández de Oviedo or López de Gómara.

The term *bejucos* also appears in Alonso de Ercilla's *La Araucana* (1569–89), a long narrative poem about Spain's conquest of Chile that Cervantes repeatedly quarries for his writings. He strategically places this colonial war epic in Don Quixote's library, where it is saved from the bonfire because of the excellence of its heroic verse (I, 6). Ercilla's violent portrait of the Chilean Indians plotting to conquer Spain and, after that, the whole world (VII, 16) foreshadows Cervantes' barbarians at the opening of the *Persiles*, who entertain the same ambitions.[22] The same Caribbean vines that Ercilla deploys in the construction of the Araucan arms are used in Cervantes to construct rafts that sail to and from a violent all-male island whose inhabitants trade in gold and pearls, fight with bows and arrows, and communicate either by signs or through a kidnapped female interpreter – all practices that strenuously reference the New World.

Cervantes' islanders, whom the text calls "barbarians" ("bárbaros"), also eat a suggestively American diet, including a wheat-free bread ("pan que no era de trigo"). Peter Martyr's *De Orbe Novo*, a text accessible to Cervantes, had informed Europe about a bread "made from the cooked flour cazabi, a bread better suited to human stomachs than wheat bread."[23] Aligning this New World bread with a suggestively American beverage, Cervantes constructs a tribe of barbarians who ritually drink the powdered ashes of male human hearts – a kind of cannibalism. This cannibal island may have motivated Samuel Taylor Coleridge to remark, in an 1818 lecture, that in Cervantes' "Persilis [sic] and Sigismunda, the English may find the germ of their Robinson Crusoe" – a wholly ignored but quite promising intertextuality.[24] Coleridge's remark, had it been pressed into service, would have challenged Ian Watt's notorious claim, in 1957, that the rise of the novel began with Defoe's *Crusoe* – a claim recanted by Watt a decade later but still malingering in many Anglo-American literary histories.[25] If we think in terms of coevolutionary rather than evolutionary histories of the novel, focusing less on historical origins than on geographical locations, we soon recognize that *both* the Spanish and English rises of the novel were linked to European voyages to America. It is important to reconsider not only Defoe's various unacknowledged debts to Cervantes, but also the debt of both writers to legends of Caribbean cannibals.

One could cite many more Cervantine quotations, allusions, and ventriloquisms that forge connections between the conquest and colonization of the New World and the rise of the novel in Spain. Although the historical movements that Columbus inaugurated in the Indies resonate throughout Cervantes' writings, what is needed at this point is a more *spatial* understanding of his achievement. Both of Cervantes' long novels, *Don Quixote* and the *Persiles*, were stimulated, far more than criticism has acknowledged, by the geographical excitement of a New World. In a recent book about mapping in early modern France, Tom Conley suggests that "even Cervantes's tales of a knight errant's misinformed adventures" were "born of a new cartographic impulse."[26] Stereotyped visions of Don Quixote as the provincial "Man of La Mancha" have tended to cloud this impulse.

The discovery of the Indies, which gave Spain a whole continent to conquer and Castilianize, reverberates through Cervantes' novels. In addition to the multiple targets of satire proffered for *Don Quixote* – pulp fictions, bad readers, the ideals of knighthood, utopian evasionism, or a penchant for living in the past – we might acknowledge the mid-twentieth-century claim, by the Peruvian scholar Raúl Porras Barrenechea, that *Don Quixote* is "a benevolent satire" of the conquistador of the Indies.[27] Although Cervantes' novel displays satires of perhaps all of the above, it is reductive to consider it essentially or generically a satire. John Jay Allen rightly explains that "*Don Quixote* abounds in subtle, perceptive, devastating satire, compounding ironies and deflating presumption and pretension, *but it is not a satire.*"[28] It does contain, however, the most subtle and perceptive satire of the institution of chivalry ever written – not only as represented in the literary genre that *Don Quixote* avowedly aims to destroy, the books of chivalry (*libros de caballerías*), but also as present in the real-world discourses connected with the conquest and colonization of the Hispanic Indies.

It is scarcely fortuitous that Cervantes' novels appear at the close of Spain's age of exploration, given that they arise – much as Bakhtin claims that pre-novelistic discourse arose in antiquity – from a multilingual imperial culture. Recalling how this kind of discourse developed on the peripheries of the Hellenistic world – "on the boundary line between cultures and languages" – Bakhtin claims that the novel began to constitute itself as a genre out of this new polyglot consciousness.[29] Cervantes' novels are pervaded by this kind of consciousness, emerging not only from the "Babel" of Algiers,[30] but also from the "bar-bar" of the Indies. Still episodic in *Don Quixote*, which represents some half-dozen languages (Spanish, Basque, Arabic, German, Italian, and the *lingua franca* of Barbary), this polyglot consciousness increases exponentially in the *Persiles*, whose characters speak in, and translate from, a dozen different tongues: Spanish and Portuguese, English, French, German, Italian, Norwegian, Polish, Valencian, a *lengua aljamiada* (texts written in Spanish but in Arabic characters), and a *lengua bárbara* (a "barbaric" language that requires an interpreter).

Beyond the languages spoken by his characters, however, Cervantes' use of American loan words from Caribbean, Mexican, or Peruvian languages (Taíno, Nahuatl, and Aymara) bears noting. This usage falls under the rubric of "hybridization," a process that Bakhtin describes as the mixing of at least two linguistic consciousnesses "within a single concrete utterance" (*The Dialogic Imagination*, p. 429). One may discuss the mixture of Castilian and native American languages in Cervantes' novels under the rubric of "hybridity" or, as is more commonly done in Latin America, as diglossia, transculturation, and heterogeneity. Many of the hybrid utterances in Cervantes' writings emerge from the great ensemble of lived and fictional practices that we now call Spanish colonialism, practices being consolidated precisely during his lifetime.

Spain's New World enterprise, as suggested above, informed both Cervantes' personal history and his writing projects. There is no doubt that he was familiar with some of the Chronicles of the Indies (*Crónicas de Indias*), a massive collection of texts of multiple genres covering America's exploration, conquest, and colonization. Cervantes had access to, and was clearly indebted to, many members of this huge textual family of Chronicles. It has become a distended family in recent years, embracing everything from memoranda and letters, to theological debates and papal bulls, to literary genres such as essays and epics. At present under intense investigation within colonial studies, these Chronicles anticipated, and in some cases coincided with, the emergence of the Cervantine novel. Over a dozen major contributors to the Chronicles of the Indies – from Amerigo Vespucci (c. 1507) to Inca Garcilaso (1609) – published accounts of the New World both before and during Cervantes' lifetime and, as recent inventories of peninsular libraries show us,[31] many of these accounts were available to him as a reader, some in multiple editions and continuations.

Histories of American missionary orders were also available to Cervantes, who used one to write *El rufián dichoso* (*The Fortunate Pimp*), a little-known religious play set largely in the New World. Based on Fray Agustín Dávila Padilla's 1596 history of the Dominican missionary order in Mexico, Cervantes' play dramatizes the life of Fray Cristóbal de la Cruz, who served as the provincial head of this order in Mexico before his death in 1565. The play's protagonist is a man without rank or wealth who begins life as a *pícaro* in Seville to end it as a leper and a saint in Mexico. In the play's second

jornada, he memorably combines both Florida and Bermuda in a single poetic utterance when he delivers a series of negative blessings to a transatlantic voyager: "May the hurricane not pursue you,/may you not suffer a
destructive landfall in Bermuda,/or in Florida,/killer of a thousand bodies"
(*Obras completas*, 1, p. 415).[32] The French Hispanist Jean Canavaggio has
no doubts that Cervantes consulted this text – "and abundantly."[33] Apart
from this missionary history, however, Cervantes may have also consulted
a contemporary chronicle for his knowledge of Florida. In March of 1605
in Lisbon, the Flemish printer Pedro Crasbeeck published a pirated edition
of *Don Quixote de la Mancha* simultaneously with the first edition of *La
Florida del Ynca*. It is possible that the latter text – Inca Garcilaso de la Vega's
vivid chronicle of the Spanish conquest of Florida – contributed to Cervantes'
negatively personified portrayal of that "homicidal" New World territory.

   Although a number of scholars had earlier catalogued Cervantes' references to America – to parrots and alligators, cannibals and tobacco – the
American connection has been seriously underestimated and, until recently,
undertheorized in Cervantine studies. There was no lack of inventories, in the
style of a 1915 essay titled: "Cervantes americanista: Lo que dijo de los hombres y cosas de América" (The Americanist Cervantes: What He Said about
the Men and Things of America).[34] The increasing availability of Spanish
colonial traditions of historiography, however, has been shedding new light
on what had seemed, for centuries, a shadowy partnership between early
modern Europe and America. J. H. Elliott's wise admonition that these two
continents "should not be subjected to a historiographical divorce"[35] began
to resonate in Cervantine circles in the 1970s. Since that decade, a series of
important critical studies has been connecting Cervantes' fictions with the
American imperial process of which they were manifestly a part. These studies – some of whose titles are appended to this essay as a "Guide to Further
Reading" – have moved our New World interpretations of Cervantes' writings well beyond the inventories of Americana that opened the century. On
the occasion of the Columbian Quincentenary in 1992, marking 500 years
since Columbus arrived in the New World, one reviewer even wondered
whether the existence of Don Quixote would have been possible "without
the Discovery."[36] To move from inventory to interpretation is to sort out the
variety of ways in which Cervantes' writings – ever alert to the compromised
nature of all historical accounts – absorb and reply to the historiography of
this so-called Discovery.

   One way *Don Quixote* does this is by parading the same kind of intentionality already found in many of the Chronicles of the Indies, which claim
to downgrade the same genre that *Don Quixote* aims to topple, the books of
chivalry that dried up its hero's brain. The habit of vilifying these chivalric

fictions began early in the sixteenth century with the Spanish humanists, who ritually censured them as a filthy and lying genre – every bit as toxic to readers as "scorpion oil" ("aceite de escorpiones").[37] A similar kind of censoriousness – this time fortified by bans – was carried across the Atlantic. Although fond of reading books of chivalry during his siestas, Charles V evidently did not consider them proper fare for his transatlantic subjects. On April 4, 1531, his queen, acting as sovereign in his absence, published a royal decree prohibiting exports of these books to the New World: reading them, the decree stated, was "bad practice for the Indians and something with which it is not well for them to be concerned." Further instructions from the Queen to the Viceroy of Mexico in 1536 suggest that the earlier ban needed to be fortified. The ban was once again reissued seven years later, in 1543, this time by Prince Philip, who forbade all entry into the Indies of "profane and imaginative" books "such as those about Amadís and others of this type of lying histories."[38] These bans on the books of chivalry disclose the kind of paternalistic control that imperial Spain tried, not very successfully, to exercise in the colonies.

Whether influenced by the ban or by the censoriousness of the humanists, many of the Chronicles make a point of divorcing their work from the books of chivalry, a response playfully iterated in Don Quixote. In his Historia general y natural de las Indias (1535), for example, Gonzalo Fernández de Oviedo, Spain's official chronicler of the Indies, is most explicit in his censure of the genre: "I do not recount the nonsense of the books of Amadís or those that depend on them."[39] Given the earlier publication of his own chivalric novel Don Claribalte (1519), a book that earned him the status of America's first novelist, Oviedo was well acquainted with that kind of "nonsense." A similar notion of the books of chivalry as harmful fables that need to be separated from historical truth moves Pedro de Castañeda de Nájera to advertise himself, in his chronicle of the Coronado expedition (1540–42), as a reliable author who does not write fables like those found in the books of chivalry.[40] Bernal Díaz del Castillo similarly trashes the chivalric genre in chapter 151 of his "true history" of the conquest of New Spain (Historia verdadera de la conquista de la Nueva España) (c. 1568; pub. 1632). Having movingly described the conquistadors' initial sighting of today's Mexico City through the filter of the books of chivalry – "it seemed like an enchanted vision from the tale of Amadís" – he later refuses to give details about the daily carnage of many Mexicans, because readers would consider his account untruthful: "it would resemble the books of Amadís or chivalry."[41] As late as the 1590s – when Cervantes is probably hatching Don Quixote, Part I – the New World Jesuit historian José de Acosta still worries that peninsular readers might confound his Historia natural y moral de las

Indias with the lying books of chivalry. Acosta feels obliged to remind his readers that the world of the American Indians does not in the least resemble "the fabulous stories cooked up in the books of chivalry."[42]

The above protestations, iterated by Cervantes' own fictional recoil from the genre, document only one way in which the books of chivalry were affiliated with the New World. Another link was through nomenclature. In at least two cases, toponyms taken directly out of the books of chivalry were given to American territories: "Patagonia" from a tribe of savage monsters in *Primaleón*, and "California" from a kingdom of Amazons in *Las sergas de Esplandián*, the fifth book of the *Amadís* cycle. Of the many books instrumental in crazing Cervantes' hero, this last was the first to be consigned to the bonfire during the inquisition of Don Quixote's library (1, 6). Published before 1510 by Garci Rodríguez de Montalvo, the *Sergas* introduced Europe to a tribe of Amazons living on a fictional island called California. California makes its inaugural appearance as a toponym in Montalvo's address to the reader – which included the reader Cervantes: "You should know that on the right hand of the Indies there was an island, named California ... " (Leonard, *Books of the Brave* [rev. edn.], 539). The case of the Amazons provided, for Irving A. Leonard, a compelling demonstration of the links between the Books of Chivalry and the conquistadors.[43] The books of chivalry, we should stress, were linked to but not precipitated by the matter of America, as were a number of other genres or subgenres. The utopias, the colonial war epic, and American ethnohistory, for example, were all generic products of the encounter with the New World, and Cervantes incorporated all three kinds of writing into his novels.[44]

Apart from the above iterations and incorporations, another way that Cervantes replies to the New World encounter is by slyly aligning Don Quixote with the conquistador mentality. The mad knight has been increasingly assimilated, in our postcolonial era, to the historical figures of the conquistadores. Where one critic sees Cervantes' hero as "a comic incarnation" of "the conquistador mentality of Golden Age Spain," another regards him as an "aspiring" and even "divinely inspired" conqueror, a figure who embodies "what is great and what is insane about Spanish imperialism." This last critic, Henry Higuera, actually considers Don Quixote as "the greatest novelistic portrait ever penned of an important kind of would-be conqueror."[45] Such recent New World axes of identity for Cervantes' hero are an intrepid development from older constructions, which saw Don Quixote as everything from an amusing lunatic to a tragic Christ figure, but avoided looking too closely at his more imperial antics. By confining Don Quixote's identification to the heroes of the books of chivalry, by seeing him play the role – both by the book and to the hilt – of an abject Amadís or a furious Orlando – readers could avoid focusing on the mad knight's confessed desire to be a conquering hero. At the very start of his career, for example, Don Quixote imagines himself "already crowned through the valor of his arm, at the very least, of the empire of Trebizond" (I, I). Soon after this gratifying self-image, Don Quixote poses a rhetorical question of manifest triumphalist weight: "What greater contentment or pleasure can there be in the world than winning a battle and triumphing over one's enemy?" (I, 18). Although Don Quixote's chosen vocation is unimpeachable – to rescue damsels, succor widows and orphans, and give aid to the needy – it is not altogether disinterested. Or as he himself puts it, a knight errant is always "on the very verge of becoming the most powerful lord in the world" (II, 39). This world includes the Indies, which Don Quixote describes, while giving Sancho an early lesson on the arts of governance, as "the newly conquered kingdoms and provinces" (I, 15).

In his antic madness, Don Quixote plays at being not only a knight errant but also a conquistador. Let us consider, to take only one example of this New World behavior, his wish to dole out an island to Sancho. The gift of a governorship (courtesy of the Duke, who has read about Don Quixote's long-standing promise to Sancho) serves, needless to say, as a literary parody of the books of chivalry, in which knights occasionally dispense islands as gifts to their squires. But the island also serves as social satire of the territorial gifts often promised, and sometimes delivered, by many of the conquistadors to their "vassals." One thinks of Columbus's notorious gift of the island of La Bella Saonese to Michele da Cuneo, for example, a gift which Cuneo himself discusses in a letter, written to Jeronimo Annari in 1495:

> In deference to me the Admiral named it the Bella Saonese and gave it to me as a gift. And under the accustomed modes and forms, I took possession of it just as the Admiral did with the other islands in the name of his Majesty the King. That is, according to the document of a notary public concerning the island, I tore up some grass, cut down some trees, planted the cross, erected a scaffold, and in the name of God I baptized the island the Bella Saonese.[46]

The island that Columbus gave to Cuneo with such aristocratic largesse was populated with 30,000 souls and is today called Saona or, by the indigenes, Adamaney. In the mode of Columbus, in short, Don Quixote yearns to dole out islands. The same qualities that make him into a latter-day "conquistador" will in time, and through the pressure of critical readings, make the conquistadores "quixotic."

The quixotic conquistadores

The relations between the conquistadores and Don Quixote are triangulated, obsessive, and preposterous. As this last adjective suggests, Don Quixote's adopted surname would, in time, turn into an adjective for New World conquerors, who are ritually described as "quixotic." Because of its long and international history, the term "quixotic" remains hard to define: "admirably idealistic," "romantically exalted," "wildly delirious," or "hopelessly hallucinated" are some of the definitions generally proffered. One Hispanist justly pins the term "quixotic" on Shakespeare's Coriolanus, who also sets out, like Don Quixote, to seek "a world elsewhere."[47] The term took a curious lexical swerve during the first half of the eighteenth century, acquiring some of its more demeaning aspects. When *Don Quixote* began to be admired for its satire and its irony, when it began to be understood as a burlesque epic and a parody, even a caricature, of the chivalric hero – then terms like "quixotic" entered the lexicon with a depreciatory meaning.[48]

The term itself is closely tied to Don Quixote's status as a sterile imitator. Decades before any postcolonial notions of mimicry were circulating, René Girard proposed this imitative quality from a metaphysical perspective. In his classic study of the history of imitative desire in novels beginning with Cervantes, Girard proposed a novel portrait of Don Quixote as an ontologically sick man, a figure whose governing desire is to be somebody else.[49] This reading prepared the ground for postcolonial interpretations of Don Quixote as a mimic man, a character whose strategic vocation is to mime another. As in the Girardian scheme but with more bellicose subjects, a form of triangulation operates among the fictional heroes of the books of chivalry, the real-life conquistadores who imitate them, and Don Quixote who imitates both. Two discursive domains are operative here: chivalry, the feudal institution whose available and automatic language Don Quixote aims to revive, and imperialism, the more contemporaneous, and more American, institution to which his exploits often allude.

Although the intersection between feudalism and imperialism has become more visible in the present climate, Cervantes' responses to chivalric practices in the Hispanic colonies demands closer critical attention. William H. Prescott – the nineteenth-century, Harvard-educated, Protestant historian who wrote about the conquests of both Mexico and Peru – had a name for these practices: "ocean chivalry."[50] Prescott brought to bear a kind of influence on American historical scholarship of Spain that has indirect bearings on Cervantes. Richard L. Kagan's remarkable exposé of "Prescott's paradigm" explains, among other things, the inability of Americans "to associate Spain with anything except the pathetic figure of Don Quixote tilting at windmills."[51] Beyond inaugurating much stereotyped writing of Spanish history in the United States, however, Prescott also forges some preposterous links between Don Quixote and the conquistadores. It is instructive to look at the relations between these figures from the ecstatic American perspective of Prescott, who avails himself of the one in order to describe the other: "What wonder, then, if the Spaniard of that day, feeding his imagination with dreams of enchantment at home, and with its realities abroad, should have displayed a Quixotic enthusiasm, – a romantic exaltation of character, not to be comprehended by the colder spirits of other lands!" (*History*, II, 59). Elsewhere, and in the same exalted language, Prescott celebrates the "bold spirit" of the Spanish conquistador, who, "not content with the dangers that lay in his path, seemed to court them from the mere Quixotic love of adventure" (II, 45). In yet another effusion, one that sheds light on these "quixotic" qualities, Prescott compares the chivalry of "romantic Spain" with the spirit of enterprise of "our own Puritan fathers," who,

> with the true Anglo-Saxon spirit, left their pleasant homes across the waters, and pitched their tents in the howling wilderness, that they might enjoy the sweets of civil and religious freedom. But the Spaniard came over to the New World in the true spirit of a knight-errant, courting adventure, however perilous, wooing danger, as it would seem, for its own sake. With sword and lance, he was ever ready to do battle for the Faith; and, as he raised his old war-cry of "St. Jago," he fancied himself fighting under the banner of the military apostle, and felt his single arm a match for more than a hundred infidels! It was the expiring age of chivalry; and Spain, romantic Spain, was the land where its light lingered longest above the horizon.   (*History*, III, 60–61)

Although Prescott's breathless interpretations make it clear that chivalry was alive and well in sixteenth-century America, they disguise the economic realities of conquest and colonization to represent the New World enterprise, instead, as a kind of glorious chivalric fiction.

Of central interest here, however, is that these Prescottian "cavaliers" in the New World manage to display "quixotic" qualities long before Don Quixote himself does. Cervantes' hero lends his adopted surname, in brief, to behaviors anticipating him by over a century. Although Prescott's formulation was preposterous – in the rhetorical scheme of *prae-postere* or putting the cart before the horse – it was not outrageous: the notion of the conquistadores as "quixotic" figures is not uncommon. One mid-twentieth-century critic sees the conquistadores as participants in the "delirious dream of Don Quixote," and even celebrates one of them, Francisco de Pizarro, for the "quixotic words" that he vented on the Isla del Gallo, several years prior to his conquest of Peru.[52] A more recent critic continues the preposterous trend, celebrating Columbus for the "quixotic enterprise" that would inspire Cervantes.[53] As the first of the countless conquistadores whose "quixotic" words and deeds were located in events prior to Cervantes' age, Columbus instances how the later text of *Don Quixote* has altered our readings of the earlier historiography of the Indies. The New World, in short, had been manifestly hospitable to "quixotic" careers long before Don Quixote was born.

The medieval and feudal institution of chivalry that Don Quixote so manically embraced, in sum, was still an empowered discourse during Spain's age of conquest and colonization. Not only did many of the discourses of chivalry remain intact until well into the sixteenth century, but some of them gained strength through a transatlantic crossing. The same books of chivalry that inspired the conquistadors and alarmed their chroniclers would supply Cervantes with his avowed motive for writing *Don Quixote*: he would, as the Prologue puts it, "dismantle the authority" of the entire genre. The emergence of the Cervantine novel – a transnational, crosscultural, and multilingual achievement that made chivalry risible – was intricately linked to the New World colonial adventure. The matter of America must be factored into the rise of the Cervantine novel.

Cervantes himself factors it into the adventure of the Enchanted Boat in *Don Quixote* (II, 29), an episode whose source may lie in *Palmerín de Ingalaterra*, one of the books of chivalry spared the bonfire of the hero's library (I, 6). In Cervantes' industrialized version of the Enchanted Boat adventure, which depicts a voyage down Spain's River Ebro, Don Quixote lectures Sancho about astrolabes and equatorial lines, poles and polar circles, zodiacs and ecliptics, solstices, equinoxes, and geographical bearings. Fully expecting to emerge into the broad Atlantic, the hero plunges instead into the Ebro, his oarless boat saved from a maritime disaster by a group of alert millworkers. This pivotal episode ends on an early note of despair for Don Quixote: "I can do no more," he cries out.

The Enchanted Boat episode may be read as an allegory of, among other things, Cervantes' foiled transatlantic desires. No boat, enchanted or otherwise, was available to help him emigrate to the Indies. His great novels had to go in his place. Within a year of its publication in 1605, as Irving Leonard documents, nine copies of the edition princeps of *Don Quixote* had journeyed – across the Atlantic and the Panama jungles, down the Pacific, and up the terrifying precipices and craggy ravines of the Andes – all the way to Cuzco.[54] Cervantes' last novel, the posthumous *Persiles*, also managed the transatlantic crossing a few years after his death in 1616, and it became a popular book in the seventeenth-century Hispanic colonies. The rest is history – American history.

NOTES

1 Miguel de Cervantes, *Don Quixote de la Mancha*, edition directed by Francisco Rico, with the collaboration of Joaquín Forradellas et al., 2 vols. (Barcelona:

Instituto Cervantes, 1998). All translations of *Don Quixote* – and of all other Spanish texts cited in this essay – are mine. I have occasionally consulted Burton Raffel's translation of *Don Quixote* in *The History of that Ingenious Gentleman Don Quixote de la Mancha*, Norton Critical Edition, ed. Diana de Armas Wilson (New York: W. W. Norton, 1999). All references to *Don Quixote* will be given by part and chapter number, so as to orient readers to their favorite edition of the text.

2 Miguel de Cervantes Saavedra, *La Galatea*, ed. Juan Bautista Avalle-Arce, 2 vols. (Madrid: Espasa-Calpe, 1968), vol. II, p. 189.

3 Fernand Braudel, *The Mediterranean and the Mediterranean World in the Age of Philip II*, trans. Siân Reynolds, 2 vols. (London: Collins, 1972), vol. I, p. 19.

4 For details on this inquest, known as the *Información de Argel*, and for an extended analysis of the effects of captivity on Cervantes' fiction, see María Antonia Garcés, *Cervantes and Algiers: A Captive's Tale* (Nashville: Vanderbilt University Press, 2002).

5 For more on this letter, see Jean Canavaggio, *Cervantes*, trans. J. R. Jones (New York: W. W. Norton 1990), pp. 102 and 157.

6 See Germán Arciniegas, "El hijo de don Quesada," *Senderos, Publicación Semestral de la Biblioteca Nacional de Colombia* 933 (1998): 1246–51.

7 For the whole text of Cervantes' 1590 application, see Pedro Torres Lanzas, *Transcripción de Información de Miguel de Cervantes de lo que ha servido a S. M. y de lo que ha hecho estando captivo en Argel... (Documentos)* (Madrid: Ediciones El Árbol, 1981), pp. 11–13.

8 See Carroll B. Johnson, "The Drama of Sancho's Salary," in *Cervantes and the Material World* (Urbana: University of Illinois Press, 2000), pp. 15–36.

9 Alejo Carpentier, *The Lost Steps*, trans. Harriet de Onís (New York: Bard/Avon, 1979), p. 66.

10 Sebastián de Covarrubias Orozco, *Tesoro de la lengua castellana o española*, ed. Felipe C. R. Maldonado (Madrid: Editorial Castalia, 1994), p. 665.

11 Miguel de Cervantes, "El celoso extremeño," in *Novelas ejemplares*, ed. Francisco Rodríguez Marín (Madrid: Espasa-Calpe, 1975), vol. II, pp. 88–89.

12 Miguel de Cervantes Saavedra, "The English Spanish Girl / La española inglesa," in *Exemplary Novels II / Novelas ejemplares*, gen. ed. B. W. Ife, trans. R. M. Price (Warminster: Aris & Phillips Ltd., 1992), pp. 20–21.

13 Braudel, *The Mediterranean*, vol. II, p. 740.

14 Jorge Luis Borges, "Parábola de Cervantes y de Quixote," in *El hacedor* (Buenos Aires: Emecé, 1960), p. 38.

15 *El ingenioso hidalgo don Quixote de la Mancha*, Nueva Edición Crítica, ed. Francisco Rodríguez Marín (Madrid: Atlas, 1948), vol. IV, pp. 184–85n.

16 Anthony Pagden's comparative study of three European empires is titled *Lords of All the World: Ideologies of Empire in Spain, Britain, and France, 1492–1830* (New Haven: Yale University Press, 1995).

17 On Spain's "global vision of empire," see J. H. Elliott, *Old World and the New: 1492–1650* (Cambridge: Cambridge University Press, 1970), pp. 84–87.

18 Miguel de Cervantes, "El licenciado Vidriera," in *Novelas ejemplares*, ed. Marín, vol. II, p. 30.

19 See *The Four Voyages of Columbus*, trans. and ed. Cecil Jane, 2 vols. (New York: Dover Publications, 1988), vol. II, pp. 104–05.

20 See Tzvetan Todorov, *The Conquest of America*, trans. Richard Howard (New York: Harper, 1987), pp. 3–50.

21 Miguel de Cervantes, *Los trabajos de Persiles y Sigismunda*, ed. Carlos Romero Muñoz (Madrid: Cátedra, 1997), vol. i, p. i. All citations are from this edition of the *Persiles* and will be parenthetically documented in my text by book and chapter number. All translations are my own.

22 Alonso de Ercilla y Zúñiga, *La Araucana*, ed. Marcos A. Morínigo and Isaías Lerner, 2 vols. (Madrid: Clásicos Castalia), vol. i, 19.

23 Peter Martyr, *De Orbe Novo: The Eight Decades of Peter Martyr D'Anghera* [1494–1526], trans. Francis Augustus MacNutt, 2 vols. (New York: G. P. Putnam's Sons., 1912), vol. i, p. 2.

24 Samuel Taylor Coleridge, "Lecture viii: Don Quixote, Cervantes," in *Coleridge's Miscellaneous Criticism*, ed. Thomas Middleton Raysor (London: Constable & Co., 1936), p. 110.

25 Ian Watt, *The Rise of the Novel* (Berkeley: University of California Press, 1957).

26 Tom Conley, *The Self-Made Map: Cartographic Writing in Early Modern France* (Minneapolis: University of Minnesota Press, 1996), p. 2.

27 Raúl Porras Barrenechea, *El Inca Garcilaso en Montilla (1561–1614)* (Lima: Editorial San Marcos, 1955), p. 238.

28 John J. Allen, "The Transformation of Satire in Don Quixote: 'Dine with Us as an Equal' in Juvenal and Cervantes," in Ellen Anderson and Amy Williamsen, eds., *Ingeniosa Invención: Essays on Golden Age Spanish Literature for Geoffrey L. Stagg in Honor of His Eighty-fifth Birthday* (Newark, DE: Juan de la Cuesta Press, 1999), pp. 6–7; italics added.

29 M. M. Bakhtin, *The Dialogic Imagination: Four Essays*, ed. Michael Holquist, trans. Caryl Emerson and Michael Holquist (Austin: University of Texas Press, 1981), p. 50.

30 See Ottmar Hegyi, "Algerian Babel Reflected in *Persiles*," in Anderson and Williamsen, eds., *Ingeniosa Invención*, pp. 225–39.

31 See Trevor J. Dadson, *Libros, lectores y lecturas: estudios sobre bibliotecas particulares españolas del Siglo de Oro* (Madrid: Arco/Libros, [c. 1998]).

32 See Cervantes' *El rufián dichoso*, in *Obras completas*, ed. Angel Valbuena Prat, 2 vols. (Mexico: Aguilar, 1991), vol. i, p. 415.

33 Jean Canavaggio, *Cervantès dramaturge: un théâtre à naître* (Paris: Presses Universitaires de France, 1977), p. 46.

34 José Toribio Medina, "Cervantes americanista: Lo que dijo de los hombres y cosas de América," in *Estudios cervantinos* (Santiago de Chile: Fondo Histórico y Bibliográfico José Toribio Medina, 1958).

35 J. H. Elliott, *The Old World and the New: 1492–1650* (Cambridge: Cambridge University Press, 1970), p. 7.

36 Pedro Acosta, review of *El Quixote y el Almirante* by Roa Bastos, *El Tiempo*, July 4, 1993, "Lecturas dominicales," p. 15.

37 See Barry Ife's remarks on these peninsular responses in *Reading and Fiction in Golden-Age Spain: A Platonist Critique and Some Picaresque Replies* (Cambridge: Cambridge University Press, 1985).

38 Irving Leonard, *Books of the Brave* [1949], with a new introduction by Rolena Adorno (Berkeley and Los Angeles: University of California Press, 1992), p. 81.

39 Gonzalo Fernández de Oviedo, *Historia general y natural de las Indias* (1535), ed. José Amador de los Ríos, 4 vols. (Madrid: Real Academia de la Historia, 1851–55), vol. I, p. 179.

40 Pedro de Castañeda de Nájera, "Castañeda's History of the Expedition," in George P. Hammond and Agapito Rey, eds., *Narratives of the Coronado Expedition, 1540–1542*, Coronado Cuarto Centennial Publications, 1540–1949, vol. II (Albuquerque: University of New Mexico Press, 1940), p. 276.

41 Bernal Díaz del Castillo, *Historia verdadera de la conquista de la Nueva España*, ed. Joaquín Ramírez Cabañas, 12th edn. (Mexico City: Porrúa, 1980), pp. 159 and 346.

42 Joseph de [José de] Acosta, *Historia natural y moral de las Indias* [1590], ed. Edmundo O'Gorman (México: Fondo de Cultura Económica, 1962), p. 278.

43 Leonard, *Books of the Brave*, p. ix of Adorno's introduction.

44 My book *Cervantes, the Novel, and the New World* (Oxford: Oxford University Press, 2000), elaborates on these generic incorporations.

45 These critics are, respectively, John Skinner, "Don Quixote in 18th-Century England: A Study in Reader Response," *Cervantes* 7.1 (1987): 54, and Henry Higuera, *Eros and Empire: Politics and Christianity in "Don Quixote"* (Lanham, MD: Rowman & Littlefield, 1995), pp. 1–2 and 185.

46 Miguel de Cuneo, *Cartas de particulares a Colón y Relaciones coetáneas*, ed. Juan Gil and Consuelo Varela (Madrid: Alianza Editorial, 1984), p. 256.

47 Eduardo Gónzalez, *The Monstered Self: Narratives of Death and Performance in Latin American Fiction* (Durham, NC: Duke University Press, 1992), p. xvi.

48 See Edward C. Riley, *Introducción al Quijote* (Barcelona: Editorial Crítica, 1990), p. 226.

49 René Girard, *Deceit, Desire, and the Novel: Self and Other in Literary Structure*, trans. Yvonne Freccero (Baltimore: Johns Hopkins Press, 1965), p. 98.

50 William Prescott, *History of the Conquest of Mexico*, ed. John Foster Kirk, 3 vols. (Philadelphia: Lippincott, 1873), vol. I, p. 217.

51 Richard L. Kagan, "Prescott's Paradigm: American Historical Scholarship and the Decline of Spain," *American Historical Review* 101.2 (1996): 444.

52 Valentín de Pedro, *America en las letras españolas del Siglo de Oro* (Buenos Aires: Editorial Sudamericana, 1954), pp. 78–80.

53 Fernando Arrabal, *Un esclavo llamado Cervantes* (Madrid: Espasa Calpa, 1996), p. 153.

54 Leonard, *Books of the Brave*, pp. 270–89.

FURTHER READING

Correa-Díaz, Luis. "El Quixote Indiano / Caribeño: Novela de caballería y crónica de Indias." *Anales cervantinos* 34 (1998): 85–123.

Fernández, James D. "The Bonds of Patrimony: Cervantes and the New World." *PMLA* 109.5 (1994): 969–81.

Gaylord, Mary M. "The True History of Early Modern Writing in Spanish: Some American Reflections." *Modern Language Quarterly* 57.2 (1996): 213–35.

Greene, Roland Arthur. *Unrequited Conquests: Love and Empire in the Colonial Americas*. Chicago: University of Chicago Press, 1999.

Ife, Barry W. "The Literary Impact of the New World: Columbus to Carrizales." *Journal of the Institute of Romance Studies* 3 (1994): 65–85.

Kagan, Richard L. and Geoffrey Parker, eds. *Spain, Europe and the Atlantic World: Essays in Honour of John H. Elliott.* Cambridge: Cambridge University Press, 1995.

Mayer, María E. "El detalle de una 'historia verdadera': Don Quijote y Bernal Díaz." *Cervantes* 14.2 (1994): 93–118.

Mignolo, Walter D. *The Darker Side of the Renaissance: Literacy, Territoriality, and Colonization.* Ann Arbor: University of Michigan Press, 1995.

Quint, David. *Epic and Empire: Politics and Generic Form from Virgil to Milton.* Princeton: Princeton University Press, 1993.

Reiss, Timothy J. "Caribbean Knights: Quixote, Galahad, and the Telling of History." *Studies in the Novel* 29.3 (1997): 297–322.

Valderrama, Pedro Gómez. "En un lugar de las Indias." *Senderos* 9.33 (1998): 1266–71.

ANTHONY J. CASCARDI

Appendix: electronic editions and scholarly resources

The state of the editions of Cervantes' works and of the critical apparatus for their study is rapidly changing under the influence of electronic means of archiving and disseminating information. The result is a staggering instability in the status of some scholarship. But changing modes of communication are nothing new to Cervantes. We should not forget that Cervantes himself wrote at a moment in history that was just beginning to feel the full impact of a related paradigm shift: that from orality to print. Contrast Don Quixote's visit to the printing press in Barcelona in *Don Quixote*, Part II, with the episode in *Don Quixote*, Part I, where some of the characters gather at Juan Palomeque's inn and listen to the "Tale of Foolish Curiosity" read aloud.[1] Cervantes' texts are now available in print, on CD-ROM, and on line. Print remains the dominant mode of publication among scholars, with work in English focused in the journal *Cervantes* (the Bulletin of the Cervantes Society of America), but there is increasing use of electronic media in research publication as well as for the dissemination of texts. Among the principal electronic resources are the following.

Electronic Texts Cervantes' complete works are currently available on CD-ROM in an edition published jointly by the Centro de Estudios Cervantinos and Ediciones Micronet (1997).[2] Also on CD-ROM is *Miguel de Cervantes. Selección de textos e introducciones*, ed. Roberto González Echevarría (Woodbridge, CT: Primary Source Media, 1998). On the internet[3] there are ever-changing links to

---

[1] The research of Margit Frenk provides the best resource for understanding the nature of these changes in early modern Spain. See *Entre la voz y el silencio: la lectura en tiempos de Cervantes* (Alcalá de Henares: Centro de Estudios Cervantinos, 1997).

[2] ISBN 84 87509 82 7.

[3] The publisher has endeavored to ensure that the URLs for external websites referred to in this Appendix are correct and active at the time of going to press. However, the publisher has no responsibility for the websites and can make no guarantee that a site will remain live or that the content is or will remain appropriate.

Cervantes' works in Spanish at http://cervantes.alcala.es/obras.htm and at http://www.ipfw.edu/cmı/jehle/web/cervante.htm. The *Quixote* is available on line at http://www.el-mundo.es/quijote/. As for English versions on line, the 1885 translation by John Ormsby is currently available at various sites, including http://csdl.tamu.edu/cervantes/spanish/ctxt/DonQ-JohnOrmsby/, http://www.port-aransas.k12.tx.us/SPAN/Quixote.html, and http://www.okanagan.net/okanagan/Quijote.

Scholarly reference sites and resources The *Don Quixote Dictionary* can be consulted at http://www.csdl.tamu.edu/cervantes/english/ctxt/dq_dictionary/ and the Cervantes International Bibliography at http://www.csdl.tamu.edu/cervantes/spanish/cbib/cibo/. These last-mentioned sites reflect the work of the project "Cervantes 2001" directed by Eduardo Urbina at Texts A&M University's Center for the Study of Digital Libraries, in collaboration with the Centro de Estudios Cervantinos at Alcalá de Henares: http://www.csdl.tamu.edu/cervantes/english/. This project embraces the Cervantes Digital Library, the International Cervantes Bibliography Online, and the Cervantes Digital Archive of Images, in addition to biographical information and relevant links.

Research and informational sites The Centro de Estudios Cervantinos maintains a website at http://cervantes.alcala.es/quijote/httoc.htm. The Centro Virtual Cervantes, Portal del Instituto Cervantes, Alcalá de Henares (http://cvc.cervantes.es/portada.htm) includes a useful section of "Reference Works" as well as a link to the Cervantes edition directed by Francisco Rico of the Instituto Cervantes. The site is gradually adding chapters to an on-line version of the *Quixote* at http://cvc.cervantes.es/obref/quijote/. "H-Cervantes: Life, Times and Work" is a useful English-language internet site maintained by D. Eisenberg, F. Jehle, and M. Wyszynski as part of the "H-Net, Humanities and Social Sciences On Line" network. It serves as a resource for scholars active in Cervantes studies and encourages exchange "on all aspects of the author, his works, his circle, his times, and scholarship on the era, and welcomes participation by scholars/specialists from all disciplines" (http://www2.h-net.msu.edu/ ~cervantes).

If recent experience is any guide, it seems safe to say that the field of online publication will change far more rapidly than print. A snapshot of the field in 1999–2000 nonetheless provides substantial guidance and detailed analyses of these and many other electronic resources: Eduardo Urbina, "Bibliografía analítica sobre ediciones, estudios críticos y otros materiales electrónicos sobre Cervantes y su obra," *Espéculo*, 13 (1999–2000).

INDEX

Abraham (Bible), 95–96
Abraham Adams (*The History and Adventures of Joseph Andrews*), 95
Abraham, Nicholas, 196
Achilles (*Iliad*), 38
Acis, 103
Acosta, José de, 216–17, 224 n. 42
Acosta, Pedro, 223 n. 36
Acquaviva, Cardinal Giulio, xii, 4, 32, 39
Acuña, Hernando de, 32
Adelaida (*The Idiot*), 89
Adorno, Rolena, 223 n. 38, 224 n. 43
Aeneas (*Aeneid*), 45, 51, 53, 121
Aeneid (Virgil), 37–38, 44–47, 51, 55 n. 11, 121
Aeschylus, 38
Aethiopica (Heliodorus), *see Historia Aethiopica*
Africa (Petrarch), 38
Agamemnon (*Iliad*), 95
Ajax (Sophocles), 71
Alba, Duke of, 22
Alcalá de Henares, xi, 4, 106, 113, 227
Alcázarquivir, 122
Aldana, Francisco de, 32
Aldonza (*The Divorce-Court Judge*), 152
Aldonza Lorenzo (*Don Quixote*), 170, 191; *see also* Dulcinea
Alemán, Mateo, xii
Alexander VI, Pope, 18
Algiers, xii, 5, 7, 30, 33, 62, 106, 138–41, 202, 206, 213
Allen, John Jay, xiv, 213, 223 n. 28

Alonso Quijano (*Don Quixote*), 29, 53, 60, 67, 72, 167, 170, 193, 195
Alonso, Amado, 183 n.19
Alter, Robert, 78, 98
Altisidora (*Don Quixote*), 178
Amadís (*Amadís of Gaul*), 43–44, 72, 89, 93, 167, 170, 216–17
Amadís of Gaul (Montalvo), 43, 58, 64, 72, 167, 217
Amadís of Greece, 72
Ambrosio (*The Comedy of Entertainment*), 146
Amezúa y Mayo, Agustin G. de, 126 n. 16
Anastasio (*The Labyrinth of Love*), 158 n. 16
Andalusia, xii, 113, 207
Anderson, Ellen, 223 n. 28 and n. 30
Andrés (*Don Quixote*), 86, 179
Angelica (*Mad Orlando*), 50, 71
Angelica (*Orlando in Love*), 44
Angelica (*The Abode of Jealousy*), 36, 143–44
Annari, Jeronimo, 218
Annotations to the Works of Garcilaso de la Vega (Herrera), 126 n. 7
Anselmo ("The Tale of Foolish Curiosity"), 187
Antonio (*The Comedy of Entertainment*), 146
Antonio (*The Trials of Persiles and Sigismunda*), 119
Apollo, 60
Apollo (*Voyage to Parnassus*), 50
Apollonius of Tyre, 58

228

CAMBRIDGE COMPANIONS TO LITERATURE

CAMBRIDGE COMPANIONS TO CULTURE

*The Cambridge Companion to Modern
German Culture*
edited by Eva Kolinsky and
Wilfried van der Will

*The Cambridge Companion to Modern
Russian Culture*
edited by Nicholas Rzhevsky

*The Cambridge Companion to Modern
Spanish Culture*
edited by David T. Gies

*The Cambridge Companion to Modern
Italian Culture*
edited by Zygmunt G. Barański and
Rebecca J. West